SAILORS TO THE END

Also by Gregory A. Freeman

Lay This Body Down:
The 1921 Murders of Eleven Plantation Slaves

SAILORS TO THE END

The Deadly Fire
on the USS Forrestal
and the Heroes Who Fought It

GREGORY A. FREEMAN

WILLIAM MORROW

An Imprint of HarperCollins *Publishers*

Grateful acknowledgment is made for permission to reprint lyrics from "Cast Your Fate to the Wind," by Vince Guaraldi, Carel Werber © 1947 (Renewed) Atzal Music, Inc. (BMI). All rights administered by Unichappell Music Inc. (BMI), all rights reserved, used by permission. Warner Bros Publications U.S. Inc., Miami, FL 33014.

HarperCollins books may be purchased for educational, business, or sales promotional use. For information please write: Special Markets Department, HarperCollins Publishers Inc., 10 East 53rd Street, New York, NY 10022.

FIRST EDITION

Designed by Bernard Klein

Printed on acid-free paper

Library of Congress Cataloging-in-Publication Data

Freeman, Gregory A.
    Sailors to the end : The deadly fire on the USS Forrestal and the heroes who fought it / Gregory A. Freeman.—1st ed.
        p.   cm.
    Includes bibliographical references and index.
    ISBN 0-06-621267-7
    1. Vietnamese Conflict, 1961—1975—Naval operations, American. 2. Forrestal (Aircraft carrier)
I. title

DS558.7 .F74 2002
959.704'348—dc21

                                                                                2001051386

02   03   04   05   06   RRD   10   9   8   7   6   5   4   3   2   1

This book is dedicated to the 134 men who died on the Forrestal *on July 29, 1967, and all the others on board that day who witnessed the tragedy of men dying young*

It is more useful to watch a man in times of peril, and in adversity to discern what kind of man he is; for then at last words of truth are drawn from the depths of his heart.

—Lucretius
99–55 B.C.

CONTENTS

Sailors to the End

Chapter *1*

Cast your fate
to the wind

July 1967

Bob Shelton was still troubled by the nightmare when he reached the
bridge of the aircraft carrier. He had hoped that getting out of his bunk
and making his way topside to watch the sun rise would help him shake
it off, but it was still with him—the puzzling images of fire and smoke on
the ship, and the vague sense of dread. He kept going over it in his
mind as he watched the horizon begin to glow golden, finally breaking
into brilliant sunlight while the USS *Forrestal* sailed in the waters off of
Vietnam.

For Shelton, sunrise on the carrier was one of the few reliable indicators that time had passed. Life aboard the carrier could be disorienting
and stressful as the young men worked long hours completely separated from the rest of the world. The *Forrestal* was an island where
nothing seemed just like home, not even the hours that made up a day.
Most of the crew worked belowdecks, the long workdays and irregular
sleep schedules melting together, with few clues from the outside world
that yesterday had ended and today had begun. But for those who

could see it, the sunrise was a reassuring reminder that there was life beyond the ship.

It hadn't taken Shelton long to realize that he didn't care much for life on board a carrier—even though he had always longed for a job in aviation, one that involved the planes that fascinated him so much. He wanted to be part of the fast-paced, glamorous world of navy flying even if he wasn't the one sitting in the cockpit. His deployment to the USS *Forrestal*, the world's biggest and most sophisticated warship, was a plum assignment by most standards and his actual workstation wasn't far from the flight-deck operations. But still, the novelty had worn off quickly and he had grown weary of standing in line for everything, whether it was a meal or a haircut. Like so many of the other thousands of young men on board, he was riding out his military service and looking forward to going home. Shelton had been in the navy for more than a year and still had a year left to serve on the *Forrestal*. The war in Vietnam was heating up, and the workload on the carrier had increased dramatically since the ship arrived in the Gulf of Tonkin a few days earlier and started launching air strikes against the mainland. He knew the next year on the *Forrestal* would be hard.

In the meantime, Shelton tried to take advantage of the little perks afforded him, and the sunrise was one of them. He reminded himself every day that many men belowdecks rarely got the chance to see daylight, much less something as beautiful as the day slowly breaking over the calm waters.

Shelton had access to this small joy because sheer luck and a few innate skills had resulted in his assignment to a group of sailors who worked on the bridge, standing within feet of the captain in the big control center that rose over the flight deck, the panoramic windows providing a bird's-eye view of everything happening on the flight deck and the world beyond. Shelton didn't work there every day, sometimes rotating through a few other assignments, but even if he wasn't working a shift on the bridge, no one minded if he hung around one of the nearby break areas for a cup of coffee and some conversation.

On this morning in late July 1967, Shelton was arriving even earlier than he had to. He wanted to take some time to relax before reporting to duty as quartermaster of the bridge, keeping detailed records of every order given and nearly everything that happened. It could be a demanding job if a lot was going on, so he liked to relax a bit first. And besides, he couldn't sleep after that nightmare.

Shelton was still a little shaken by it. The whole experience just seemed so unusual. Shelton wasn't the type to have nightmares; he couldn't even remember the last time he'd had one, and he rarely remembered any dreams when he woke up. He wasn't worried or upset about anything, so he was surprised by how much it had grabbed him. The experience was so bad that when he awoke, panicked and breathing like a racehorse, it took Shelton a minute to realize it was only a nightmare. The images were too vivid, the sense of horror too real. Shelton had sprung up and sat on the edge of his bunk, waiting for his heart to slow down, wiping the sweat from his face. He was glad to be awake. He was glad to see that everything was okay, and yet he couldn't get past the feeling that something wasn't.

Shelton had lain back in his bunk, wide awake and still energized from the nightmare. With the rustling and snoring of his crewmates in the background, Shelton's mind kept flashing with images from the nightmare. There were great bursts of light, loud noises, and fire. Nothing was clear, but he did see fire. More than anything else, though, there was a terrible sense of fear and dread.

Shelton realized he would never get back to sleep, and he wasn't sure he wanted to anyway. After lying in his bunk for a while, wide awake, he got up and dressed. He was assigned to work on the bridge that day, so he had to put on the crisp white uniform instead of the denim work clothes he might wear to other assignments. On the way out of his sleeping area, he passed by his buddy James Blaskis, who was sound asleep just a few bunks away from his. Shelton noticed that Blaskis had a new pinup of a girl taped to the bottom of the bunk above him, yet another added to the collection just a few inches from Blaskis's face. Shelton often wondered how many of those girls were from magazines and how many were girlfriends from back home, but Blaskis never seemed interested in talking about them. It was one of the things Shelton just accepted about Blaskis without question.

Shelton and Blaskis had become close friends soon after coming aboard the *Forrestal*, though it was unlikely that they would ever have met in the civilian world and there was even less chance they would have struck up a friendship. But the military has a way of throwing very different men together in close quarters, giving them no other choice than to be friends or be miserable. When Shelton and Blaskis first met on the *Forrestal*, the only things they had in common were their mutual awe of the massive ship, their assignment to the same division, and their shared duties.

Both of them were also a bit older than the typical crew member. Shelton was twenty-two years old and Blaskis was twenty-one. Once they were thrown together, they found their differences immediately. Shelton was from Longview, Texas, and Blaskis was from Akron, Ohio. Shelton didn't understand much about places where it snowed and nobody rode a horse, and Blaskis couldn't relate to people who drank iced tea so sweet it might as well be syrup. But soon they discovered that their personalities fit well together, sharing a sense of humor that nobody seemed to find as funny as they did. Shelton could see that Blaskis was a real character, a fun-loving type who made everyone comfortable around him. The two young men were soon laughing about their differences and finding more and more things that drew them together.

One of the young men's favorite pastimes was listening to music. After the ship sailed for Vietnam and out of civilian radio contact, they had to rely on their own recordings, and someone in Shelton's division had bought a reel-to-reel tape player when the ship stopped in Rio de Janeiro. The player had become a centerpiece for the crew's recreation. They would play the same music over and over again while they lounged around between work shifts or wrote letters home to their families. One song in particular had become Shelton's and Blaskis's favorite. "Cast Your Fate to the Wind," written by Carel Werber and Vince Guaraldi, was filled with a youthful optimism and willingness to see what the world would offer.

> *A month of nights, a year of days*
> *Octobers drifting into Mays*
> *I set my sail when the tide comes in*
> *I just cast my fate to the wind.*

They played the tape over and over, losing themselves in its dreamlike melody. The tune came to Shelton's mind as he stood there looking over the water, the sunrise and cool morning breeze helping to clear his head. A few cups of strong coffee also helped. The images from the nightmare were becoming fuzzier and he wasn't at all sure what had made it so scary. When it came time to start his shift, he stepped inside to the bridge and relieved the quartermaster who had worked the overnight shift. Shelton took his position behind the little desk where the logbook lay and prepared for a long day of taking careful notes, documenting any orders given and any activities on the bridge. As soon as he looked at the logbook, he saw that his buddy Blaskis had been there some time earlier.

"Bla is alive!" read a note in the margin. It was Blaskis's graffiti signature. Shelton saw it often.

The day was long, as usual, but fairly routine. The ship had just arrived in the Gulf of Tonkin a few days earlier to begin bombing targets in Southeast Asia, part of the escalating but still undeclared war against the communists trying to take over South Vietnam. Four hundred thousand ground troops were already fighting in the jungles, but the bombers from aircraft carriers stationed off the coast were playing a key role. They mostly targeted North Vietnamese supply lines, and in 1967 the bombing had moved closer to major cities like Hanoi and even to targets just shy of the Chinese border. The *Forrestal* launched bombing missions over Vietnam every day from a spot in the ocean called Yankee Station, several miles out but still close enough to see the coastline across the flat water.

That Thursday morning was uneventful, with the planes launching safely and then returning without harm. By late afternoon, Shelton was relieved from the bridge and he went belowdecks to perform a few small chores before dinner. After eating, he had a little free time to play cards and listen to music with his buddies. The day had turned out to be just another typical stretch of work, standing in line for meals, and a few moments with his friends. By the time he went to bed, Shelton had put the nightmare out of his mind. He fell asleep easily.

And then it happened again, but this time it was even worse.

Shelton was sound asleep when he suddenly shot up from his pillow with a stifled scream, sweat pouring off his face. There were explosions all around him, fire everywhere, and he was trapped. He was blinded by incredible flashes of light and the explosions were striking him as if he'd been kicked by a horse. Things were flying through the air, knocking people down and ripping bodies apart. He had little sense of what was happening, other than loud sounds and men screaming in pain and begging for help. He could see that they were still on the ship, that men were dying all around him, and he was going to die with them.

After he woke up, the details began to blur in his mind, but the nightmare was even more intense than the night before and it held him in its grip as he frantically looked around the dark compartment. He wanted to flee, but he didn't know what to do. Time stretched as he tried to separate the hell in his mind from what he saw around him. No fire in the compartment. No alarms. No explosions.

It was quiet on the ship.

Oh my God. That was worse than the last one.

Last night's had been bad, but Shelton was far more shaken by this nightmare. He couldn't get rid of the fear that it brought, even after he came to realize that he was safe in his bunk.

He was sweating and his chest was still heaving when he swung his legs out of the bunk and walked out of the compartment. There was no way in hell he was getting back to sleep. It was early, about 4:00 A.M., but Shelton had gotten all the rest he was going to get. As on the previous morning, he threw on his white uniform and headed up to the bridge. It was hours before he had to report to duty, but he couldn't have stayed in that bunk any longer.

Again, he had passed by his buddy Blaskis and watched him sleeping peacefully.

Chapter 2

THE SAFEST PLACE
TO BE

Bob Shelton and James Blaskis fit right in with the *Forrestal* crew, which was a mixture of young men who were inexperienced in nearly everything and old hands who had been riding the seas for many years. In some ways, they were a slice of America in 1967. The young far outnumbered the older men on the ship, and back home America was just getting used to having teenagers and young adults swarming the country in record numbers. Youthfulness has always been welcome in the military, however, because some jobs can be done only by someone who still thinks he will never die. The old hands on board knew better, because many of them had been through the kinds of experiences that will convince a young man of his mortality. On the *Forrestal*, these veteran sailors guided the youngsters through the daily hazards and lessons of life on an aircraft carrier, providing support that many of the boys would not understand or appreciate until they, too, were old enough to offer advice. It was a common scene to see an older sailor explaining the navy's ways to a lot of younger men who were eager to do the right thing, if only they knew how.

The navy has excelled at turning boys into men, and for many, it represented an opportunity for a career and travel that were otherwise out of reach. Times were difficult for young men in the States in 1967, with the looming possibility of a draft letter arriving in the mail. Even if they hadn't been drafted yet, any day they could be, so employers were reluctant to waste time hiring them.

If a young man did get drafted, he would most likely end up in the infantry and be sent to the jungles of Vietnam. Even though most American youths didn't know much about what was going on in Southeast Asia, they did know that a lot of boys already had been killed in the jungle wars. But if they volunteered instead of waiting to be drafted, they could select which branch of service they would serve in, and might even have some input into the sort of duty they were assigned. That is how a great many of the young men ended up on the *Forrestal*.

If you weren't a gung ho volunteer, eager to be in the thick of things, an aircraft carrier was the plum assignment. Vietnam had little navy to speak of, and carriers did all their work sitting out in the water, far away from any land-based threats. Being assigned to the *Forrestal,* one of the world's biggest and most powerful carriers, was a relief to many because they saw it as the safest place they could be. Safety is a relative matter, of course, and an aircraft carrier actually can be extremely dangerous. But for a young man going to Vietnam in 1967, there was little doubt that he would go home after a year or two on the *Forrestal*. They would ride out their tours of duty there and then return home to pick up the lives they left, satisfied that they had fulfilled their obligations.

Shelton and Blaskis joined the *Forrestal* about the same time as Ken Killmeyer, Robert Zwerlein, and Paul Friedman. When they first reported to the ship, they were all dumbstruck by its size. Especially for youngsters who grew up in small towns and had yet to see anything of the world, the ship looked like the biggest thing on earth. And they weren't too far from the truth.

When she was constructed, between 1951 and 1954, the *Forrestal* was the largest warship ever built. At 1,039 feet long, the carrier would reach the eightieth floor of the Empire State Building if stood on end. Even sitting in the water, she was as tall as a twenty-five-story building. The ship's tall masts, which are full of radar and other equipment, were designed to swing down and lie on the deck temporarily so the ship could pass under the Brooklyn Bridge.

The flight deck was 252 feet wide and as long as three and a half football fields, creating four acres of "sovereign U.S. territory," as the navy likes to brag. The ship displaced eighty thousand tons and was way too big to fit through the Panama Canal, making it necessary to go the long way around Cape Horn at the bottom of South America in order to get from her usual territory in the Atlantic to the Pacific.

The *Forrestal* was so powerful that she was considered to be the crown jewel in the navy's fleet, and she had to be named for a prominent leader from American history—the late James V. Forrestal, a former secretary of the navy and the first secretary of defense, acclaimed for building the modern navy. She was nicknamed "FID" for "First in Defense," a reference to both her namesake and her position as the country's big muscle that would be moved into position against an aggressor. Later, the navy added "Fidelity, Integrity, and Dignity" to the FID moniker.

Military ships tend to get a reputation as they age, and the *Forrestal* was known for always being on time, and also as the "ship with a heart" because of the charity work that her crew always did in the local communities they visited around the world. They would lend a hand with building a clinic or would donate books to a third-world library.

As the new men stood in long lines waiting to board the ship, her gray hulk was all they could see. It took up their entire field of vision. Once they boarded, the size of the ship was underscored by one of the first scenes they witnessed. As the newbies walked by with duffel bags slung over a shoulder and their jaws hanging open in awe, some of the crew already on board were playing football in one of the big open hangar decks. Not a scaled-down game on just a small piece of open deck; they were playing a full-sized football game, with plenty of room to spare.

The men arrived at the ship through slightly different paths, but many of them had similar motives. Shelton and nineteen-year-old Ken Killmeyer had both faced trouble getting work because of their draft status. In his hometown of Pittsburgh, Killmeyer had just graduated from high school and was still living with his parents while looking for work. The first question employers always asked was "What's your draft status?" And when Killmeyer told them he was 1A, meaning he was at the top of the list, employers rolled their eyes and sighed. The employers were as disappointed as Killmeyer that they couldn't hire the tall, lanky kid who obviously wanted to work. "You could be the best guy in the world, but you're only going to be around for a short while and then you're gone," they said.

After a lot of rejections, Killmeyer decided not to sit around and wait to be drafted. He talked it over with his dad, and they decided that the navy was a safe bet.

"Well, you're not going to be shot at. You'll survive it all, and you won't even be in the jungles," his dad told him one night. "You'll be coming home, Ken. We don't know that for sure if you get drafted."

Shelton had arrived at his decision in the same way, but he was out on his own and twenty-one years old by the time he started thinking about enlisting. Shelton had grown up in a little town called Kilgore, Texas, a flat piece of land with oil fields that employed nearly everyone there. He had worked in the oil fields himself as a teenager and then ambled around East Texas for a while before taking a job managing a gas station in Longview, Texas. It was a decent job, but he was smart enough to know there was no future in it. And when he tried to find a better job, he received the same response Killmeyer heard in Pittsburgh: "Thanks, but we're looking for men who have fulfilled their military obligation." Every time he heard that, it reminded him that he could be drafted and end up in the jungles of Vietnam.

So in August 1965, Shelton took a walk downtown to the air force recruiting office.

I might as well get this over with, he thought.

Shelton had been interested in flying since he was a child, so the air force seemed like a good choice. The recruiter was glad to have him and, after a pep talk about why he should join, sent Shelton home to get his birth certificate. Shelton came back an hour later, ready to sign up with the air force. But when he reached the recruiting office, it was closed. Shelton figured maybe the recruiter had just stepped out for a minute, so he waited outside the door. Before long, someone from the navy recruiting office next door stuck his head outside.

"Hey, it's hot out here. You might as well wait in here if you want."

Shelton took him up on the offer. It wasn't long before he had agreed to join the navy and pursue a career in aviation electronics. It wasn't the air force, but he'd be working in the exciting world of naval aviation on an aircraft carrier.

Killmeyer and Shelton first went through boot camp and studied different fields for a short while before being assigned to active duty. Killmeyer was excited about the prospect of serving in the navy and studied hard for various duties. But his first assignment to an active-duty post at a Philadelphia naval station was to keep the milk machines full in the mess hall. From morning to night, he was filling the machines with plain and chocolate milk. In between, he cleaned the floors.

When he was called to the *Forrestal* in March 1967, Killmeyer was eager to go. No matter what his job would be on board, surely it would be more exciting than filling milk machines.

When Shelton drove into the Norfolk, Virginia, naval base to board the ship, he didn't think much of the drab, utilitarian base. The *Forrestal,* on the other hand, was more impressive, a huge gray monster looming in front of him. He'd worked on marinas around the Texas coast, so he thought maybe he'd like being on a ship. He hadn't yet stood in too many lines.

When Paul Friedman graduated from high school in 1965, all of his buddies received a stern reminder that they might be drafted soon. They all had to strip down to their underwear and wait in line for preinduction physicals, the exams that would help classify them as good prospects or not so good prospects for an early draft. It was a clear warning that Friedman might not get to spend the next few years on the beach and working small jobs, as he had hoped. Like Killmeyer and Shelton, Friedman decided to join the navy as a matter of self-preservation, a way to control his destiny. He could have gone to college and deferred his draft for years, as many did, but Friedman just didn't see himself as college material. Joining the military was not a far-fetched idea for most young men anyway, because they had been raised in the John Wayne generation, an era in which military service generally was seen as honorable, though sometimes inconvenient. If they cared one whit about global politics, they probably believed that communism was a spreading scourge that must be stopped, and also probably believed in the domino theory as much as their parents did. In the early and mid-1960s, the antiwar movement had not yet seized the nation, and though being drafted and sent to Vietnam was scary, there was nothing strange about serving your country. Joining the military was a perfectly reasonable thing to consider, and if it gave you more control over your life, it could be the best option.

When a high school buddy returned from navy boot camp for a visit, Friedman grilled him about which assignments might be best. If Friedman volunteered, the navy would allow him to select his general track, but there would be no guarantees. Like a kid leafing through a toy catalog, Friedman looked through the navy manual to see which jobs he might like. Navy corpsman? No, they're the medics who go in with the marines. He might as well join the marines and go to the jungles. Weather forecasting? Hmmm, maybe. The school was in Lakehurst, New Jersey, so Friedman could spend time sending up weather balloons not too far from home. But then he saw navy aviation, which he knew meant carriers, and that was exciting to him. And besides, carriers never got to within one hundred miles of the real action.

Friedman was very reluctant to leave his home in Rockaway Beach, New York, a real beach community outside of New York City that provided this Jewish kid the opportunity to live the life of a surfer. He'd worked at the World's Fair that summer in New York City, but Friedman spent his days riding his surfboard along the waves and romancing beautiful girls on the beach. It was a sweet life for a good-looking eighteen-year-old. Like many young men in the mid-sixties, Friedman wasn't at all happy about being torn away from a good thing. The only consolation was that he was pretty sure he would return.

Down south in Atlanta, however, returning from the war didn't make Ed Roberts feel much better about going. Sure, he was glad to get in the navy and avoid the jungle fighting, but he just couldn't understand why the government wouldn't leave him and his friends alone. They had worked hard in the past years to make their rock-and-roll band a success, and they were finally getting somewhere. Then the draft notices started showing up.

Roberts grew up in Atlanta. He had started playing the drums when he was twelve years old, first in the school band, then in every other band he could join—the dance band, the all-district band, the all-city band. In 1964, the year he graduated from high school, he teamed up with some buddies and formed a band called the Fugitives, after the popular TV show. The Fugitives started out playing old standards they'd learned in school, like "Give My Regards to Broadway," but then the Beatles hit it big. They started learning all the Fab Four's songs and suddenly they were in demand for parties and were even booking commercial venues around Atlanta. The tall kid banging away on the drums was starting to think his band could really amount to something.

Every one of them knew that the draft could throw a wrench in the plans, and like all young men across the country, they were exploring their options. Roberts's father had seen a lot of combat in Europe during World War II, and he didn't want his son to go through the same thing. They talked it over as Roberts worked with his father during the day in his heating and plumbing business. The older Roberts urged his son to look into the National Guard and the reserve programs that would help keep him out of Vietnam, and Roberts agreed that was a good choice. Whatever he ended up doing in the military, he didn't want to be in a jungle where you couldn't see the people shooting at you. And he had read enough about Vietnam to know that the Vietnamese were using dirty tactics like booby traps. He didn't want to go.

Roberts and one of his buddies started checking into the National Guard and the reserves, but they found that all of the Atlanta units had waiting lists. They couldn't sign up right away, but Roberts made friends with a couple of the recruiters at the naval air station outside Atlanta and started thinking about the navy as an option. When he talked it over with his dad, they agreed that the navy might be his best choice.

"At least you have a place to sleep and regular meals," his father said. "That's more than you're going to get in the army."

Even so, Roberts didn't want to join the navy yet, because the Fugitives were getting bookings and having a good time. He also was studying biology at Georgia State University on a part-time basis. He knew it was risky to wait until he was drafted, so he also hedged his bet by hanging around the naval air station and talking to the recruiters. They treated him to free meals in the chow halls and talked about everything from the navy to the Fugitives. They liked the kid and made it clear that they'd like to sign him up for the reserves if only the list weren't so long already. But they told him they would help if things got desperate.

"If you get your draft notice, come right over here right away," one of the navy recruiters told him. "Don't even go home. Have your mother watch out for it and call you if it comes in the mail, then you come right over here."

Roberts's nineteenth birthday was approaching, and he knew the draft notice could be coming soon. He was worried about what might happen, but he also was excited about what was already happening with the Fugitives. In February 1966, the band landed an audition for a touring rock-and-roll show called "Holiday for Teens." If they could get signed for the tour, the Fugitives would tour the country, which would give them all sorts of opportunities to contact record producers. This was a huge development for a bunch of Atlanta boys, just at the time when nothing was more glamorous for a teenager than being in a rock-and-roll band.

The Fugitives practiced hard in the weeks before the audition. And then just days before the audition, Roberts's mother called him while he was working with his father to say that his draft papers had arrived. Roberts's heart sank, but he did what he had planned. He raced over to the naval air station and told his friends there he had been drafted. Just as they had promised, they bent the rules to get him into the navy reserve program. He'd still have to go in the military, but this way, he got a little more time.

The reserve program required him to sign up right away but he could spend the first year training part-time at the local base. Then he would be assigned to active duty for two years, followed by another year in the reserve. Roberts signed the papers.

Just a few days later, the Fugitives were auditioning for the rock-and-roll tour. They made it and soon found themselves driving around the country in five Oldsmobile Coronados and five Vista Cruiser station wagons plastered with "Holiday for Teens." The tour was a blast, with the Fugitives playing for screaming teens from Miami to Las Vegas. They made a television commercial and were in a parade, and they had girls adoring them. Every time a girl screamed, they were a little more confident that their band had a future.

The tour lasted for a few months and then the band was back home in Atlanta, still playing a lot of shows around town. Roberts still hadn't told his bandmates that he'd signed up for the navy, but now it was time to report to the base for his training. There wasn't very much for him to do, certainly nothing rigorous. Mostly he just learned the basics of navy life, like swabbing a deck and polishing the brass. But the navy made one dramatic change right away. They cut Roberts's hair.

To be in a rock-and-roll band in 1966, you had to have long hair. Roberts and his bandmates had been cultivating their look for a while, and they all had slightly shaggy hairstyles, not really all that long but enough to set them apart from the crisp hairstyles of Middle America. When Roberts showed up for practice one day with his hair trimmed short, the Fugitives were outraged. How could he ruin his hair that way? Roberts couldn't tell them the truth. He was afraid his friends would be angry that he'd joined the navy, so he lied and told them he cut his hair just because he wanted to look good for his college classes. They were mad at him, but he could live with that.

He kept his secret as long as he could—going to his navy training on the weekends and still showing up for the band's gigs—but finally he had to tell them. He was scheduled to go on active duty in February 1967, and after that, the Fugitives would have to find a new drummer.

Roberts didn't know yet that he would end up on the world's most powerful ship. When the *Forrestal* was put in service in 1955, she was the navy's pride and joy, the biggest, best, and most advanced aircraft carrier the world had ever seen. She would soon start collecting a number of historic "firsts" in naval aviation, and before her long career ended. The *Forrestal* ushered in a new class of aircraft carriers that would follow her design and thus be categorized as "*Forrestal* class." She was the first "supercarrier" ever designed, and she represented everything the navy had learned from the pivotal use of carriers in World War II and the years since.

The *Forrestal* was built with more than double the fuel and weapons loads of the most modern *Essex*-class carriers that came before her, and promised to be more useful and versatile than any other carrier on the sea. Her flight deck extended one hundred yards farther than the *Midway*-class ships that had played such important roles in World War II. Built in the early days of the Cold War, it helped fulfill the United States' goal of having the biggest and most powerful military in the world. And it would even carry nuclear weapons at times, ready to deliver them to ground targets within distance of her planes.

Despite her size, the *Forrestal* could move in a hurry. Her four main propulsion engines delivered more than 260,000 horsepower, enough to keep 1,430 1968 Ford Mustangs cruising along at ample speed. Those oil-burning engines powered four propellers that could move the ship at a brisk thirty-three knots, about thirty-eight mph. (A top speed of thirty-eight mph may not sound like much unless you remember that this is a war machine the size of a skyscraper coming your way.) The crew was made up of the sailors assigned to the ship itself, plus the airplane pilots and their own specialized crew. When an air wing was aboard, the *Forrestal* carried a total crew of about five thousand men and about ninety planes.

The *Forrestal* was the first carrier specifically designed to handle jet aircraft. The ship was designed and built at an exciting time in naval aviation, part of the service's huge leap forward in using jets rather than propeller-driven planes. She was the first carrier built with four steam catapults instead of two hydraulic ones, and four deck-edge elevators instead of three. Her flight deck was the first to be designed as a key load-bearing member of the ship's structure, rather than just a flat surface stuck on top of the ship. That change reflected the sophistication of carrier design since the days when they were seen as oddball ships with a runway stuck on top. With the flight deck as a load-bearing part of the ship's structure, the entire ship was strengthened. But there was a cost: if the flight deck was severely damaged, the rest of the ship could be compromised.

Designing such an advanced ship required the very best of 1950s technology. The *Forrestal* was breaking new ground in many ways, and engineers were challenged to come up with new ideas that were difficult to test. Anchoring a ship, for instance, is a fairly simple concept until applied to a ship this big. For such a massive vessel, the anchor chains had to be both heavy enough to hold the ship in place and strong enough not to snap when pulled hard. The engineers designed a 2,160-foot monster weighing 246 tons, each individual link twenty-eight inches long and seventeen inches wide, weighing 360 pounds each. The chain's breaking strain was calculated to be 2.5 million pounds.

Engineers were still refining the ship's design as her keel was laid on July 14, 1952, trying to incorporate the best innovations from the U.S. Navy's own experience with carriers and also the lessons of other countries. The ship was originally designed with the same axial landing deck that most carriers had used up to that point, meaning the "runway" on the deck ran the entire length of the ship from one end to the other. But as the ship was being built, the designers switched to an angle deck design that the British had developed. This method used a landing zone on the rear of the ship that was angled off to the left of the ship's centerline, essentially dividing the ship into a rear landing area and a forward catapult launching area. Previous designs had required the entire deck to be cleared for landings, or necessitated net barriers or similar devices to keep landing planes from running into the other planes parked forward on the deck. With the angle design, the carrier could conduct launches and landings simultaneously, and planes could more easily take off again if they missed the arresting cable. They would continue off to the port side of the ship rather than all the way straight down the length of the flight deck.

The *Forrestal* also was the first ship to incorporate a system of mirrored lights to guide pilots in for landing, instead of the World War II—era method of having a man stand on the deck with signal paddles and wave them at the pilot.

The result was a ship of such strength, size, and endurance that the *Forrestal* was an all-purpose carrier; no other carrier was better at anything. The ship was christened and launched on December 11, 1954, and assigned to the naval station at Norfolk, Virginia. Her total building costs came to $188.9 million.

She also was designed with some previously unimaginable creature comforts. Shelton and Blaskis slept on foam-mattress bunks in cubicles that afforded at least a little privacy, barely realizing this was a substantial change from the bare-bones crew quarters of previous carriers and almost all other navy ships. Another major improvement was the ship's air-conditioning.

Most ships had no air-conditioning at all, and the crew of a carrier certainly could not expect such luxury even when cruising through the hottest climates. But seven five-hundred-ton air-conditioning units on the *Forrestal* provided more cooling power than that used at Radio City Music Hall. The crew could enjoy air-conditioned living spaces twenty-four hours a day, though much of the working space was not cooled. Aviators could even take an escalator up to the flight deck, a more necessary addition than it might seem. Once the aviators were suited up for a flight, they would be lugging nearly one hundred pounds of gear. If they hustled up four flights of steps, they would be perspiring heavily by the time they got to the plane and soaking wet by the time they reached the cold air of high altitude flight.

The *Forrestal* was promoted as the first carrier to try to make the crew reasonably comfortable during long voyages, but the ship's builder explained that the improved accommodations "are not just for luxury, because experts have found that air-conditioning and good recreation and sleeping quarters will make the *Forrestal* a 'happy ship' which will lead to greater crew efficiency."

Though by 1967 she still hadn't seen a single day of combat, the *Forrestal* was known as the very best of naval might. She was the testing site for many new ideas in naval aviation, conducting trials in the 1960s for the introduction of the new F4H-1 Phantom II and A3J-1 Vigilante fighter and attack jets. In one of the most amazing feats, the ship hosted the largest aircraft ever to land or take off from an aircraft carrier: a C-130 Hercules, a fat, cumbersome cargo plane designed to move heavy equipment and troops. The "Herc" is about as different from the sleek carrier-based planes as you can get and still call it an airplane. Just to see if it could be done, the Herc made several takeoffs and landings on the *Forrestal* in 1963 and 1964 with cargo test weights ranging from 85,000 to 121,000 pounds. Though the tests were successful, the navy never again found reason to land a Herc on an aircraft carrier, leaving the *Forrestal* to hold that record.

The ship's size and versatility made her useful as one of the big sticks wielded by American presidents. When a world conflict erupted, the first question asked by American presidents usually was "Where are the carriers?" The *Forrestal* could be moved into position, ostensibly for "training exercises," to remind someone that the United States was the strongest kid on the block. No matter how strong or wild-eyed crazy the other country's leader was, the sight of an American aircraft carrier parked just off his coastline often was enough of a reminder not to mess around too much. To a very large extent, that actually is the purpose of the aircraft carrier in the modern military arena. As part of the American arsenal throughout the Cold War, the *Forrestal* could accomplish much of its mission by simply existing, just sitting in the water and looking fierce. When operating in international waters, an aircraft carrier and its accompanying ships do not need the permission of host countries for landing or overflight rights. Aircraft carriers are sovereign U.S. territory that steams anywhere in international waters—and most of the surface of the globe is water.

That is not to say, however, that the *Forrestal* was all bluster and swagger. The presence of an aircraft carrier off a country's coastline is little more than a curiosity until the residents understand exactly how much power it can aim at them. The *Forrestal* could launch nearly one hundred aircraft in an all-out strike, most of them loaded with the latest, most deadly bombs and missiles. The planes and weapons on the carrier alone often represented more than the entire military resources of the country staring at the big ship on the horizon.

Speed was an essential element of the *Forrestal*'s operations. When the president wanted to intimidate another country, he usually needed to do it quickly. That meant a matter of days, not weeks. That is one reason that modern carriers were designed to be as fast as possible. High speeds, however, are not easy to achieve and sustain when pushing something as big as an aircraft carrier through the water, so they were designed with power plants that are as big as the ship's structure will allow. The *Forrestal* ran on fuel oil, but nuclear power is now the preferred method for powering carriers because it can easily move the ship at the thirty-three knots, or thirty-eight miles per hour, that is considered the minimum top speed for a carrier. Unlike most ships, which are designed only for short sprints at high speed, the navy wants its carriers to be able to sustain a speed of twenty knots, or twenty-three miles per hour, for long distances.

Everything on the *Forrestal* was a wonder to the new sailors on board. When Shelton first reported for duty, he was awestruck by the complexity of nearly everything and every task on board. Simply going from his bunk to breakfast made him feel like a mouse scurrying through a maze in search of the cheese.

One of the first priorities for the young men assigned to the *Forrestal* was to learn just how an aircraft carrier works. This was no ordinary type of ship, and understanding the strange world of a carrier was essential to surviving your time there, much less doing your job well. As the newcomers would soon learn, those two goals often went hand in hand.

The ship could be described as an airport operating under the worst conditions possible. It was like a busy metropolitan airport reduced to just one runway, with planes landing and taking off at the same time, often less than a minute apart. The airport was moving back and forth, and up and down. The airplanes were loaded with some of the deadliest armaments in the world, and live bombs and rockets were stacked all over the runway. Seawater and fuel oil covered everything in sight. There might be an enemy in the vicinity who wanted to destroy the airport. And of course, all the planes taking off that day had to be able to land there in a few hours, no matter what.

Operating an airport under those conditions required a number of special techniques. Taking off from the *Forrestal* was not easy, even for specially designed airplanes. The carriers would always turn into the wind during flight operations, and the crew carefully calculated how to combine the ship's own speed through the water with the existing wind to achieve the optimum wind across the flight deck. With the proper wind speed across the flight deck, planes could much more easily land and take off because the wind created more lift.

Even under optimal conditions, however, airplanes needed a lot of assistance in taking off from an aircraft carrier. The *Forrestal's* flight deck looked huge when you were walking around on it, but it seemed like a postage stamp when trying to land or take off from it. There was no room for the long acceleration run that would be normal at an air base on land, so the planes had to be artificially accelerated. That meant actually shooting the planes off the deck.

The *Forrestal* used a catapult system that attached to the front wheels of planes and, with a tremendous burst of energy, flung them off the deck at high speed. The steam-powered "cats" took a plane from a dead stop to sometimes 150 mph in as little as three seconds and one hundred yards when everything went well. Otherwise, there was a lot of swearing about "bad cats" and "cold cats." The catapult system consisted of long pistons underneath the flight deck, with a shuttle on the deck surface that was a little bigger than a shoebox. The plane was attached to the shuttle with a tow bar, and the crew carefully calculated the amount of power needed to launch the plane. The calculations were extremely important, taking into consideration the type of plane, the total weight, the wind speed, and other factors. With the proper information, the crew could power the catapult with just the right amount of steam and send the plane airborne. Too much power on the catapult would rip the plane apart, the tow shuttle tearing the front wheel assembly right off the plane. The rest of the plane might or might not stay on the deck. But with too little power, a "cold shot," the plane would be slowly dragged to the front edge of the ship and lightly tossed in the water just ahead of the carrier. Aviators had to be ready to "punch out" with the ejection seats during a cat launch; if things went wrong, there wasn't much time to react.

For the aviators, though, the real nail-biting, sweat-drenching operation on a carrier came when it was time to land. The launch did not require a lot of aviators except to sit there and endure the harsh catapult, ready to respond quickly once they were airborne or headed into the water. But when it was time to land, the aviator had to call upon every bit of training, innate skill, and experience. The difficulty of landing on an aircraft carrier is legendary, and for good reason.

The cliché is that landing on an aircraft carrier is a "controlled crash." Cliché or not, that's an apt description. Unlike anything experienced on a commercial flight or a private plane, a landing on the *Forrestal* was an extremely hard, sudden stop. The plane slammed down onto the deck and was stopped by the arresting gear in a matter of just a second or two. That meant that a thirty-ton plane went from its landing speed of more than one hundred miles per hour to zero miles per hour in about two seconds.

There simply wasn't enough room on a carrier deck to bring planes in for a gentle landing and then a leisurely stop. Instead, they had to be snatched out of the air. The planes were equipped with a tail hook, a bar several feet long that could be extended down from the tail of the plane. When the pilot landed on the deck, the tail hook snagged one of the four big cables stretched across the landing portion of the deck. The cables were only the visible part of the arresting gear, attached below deck to massive machines that controlled how much the cable would give when a plane hooked it, and absorbing much of the force exerted by the plane. The arresting cable had some give to it, extending out a few dozen yards when the plane pulled on it, but the tension had to be just right. When a plane was approaching the carrier to land, the pilot radioed how much fuel, armaments, and cargo remained on the plane so that the arresting gear could be calibrated to stop the plane with just enough resistance. Too much and the tail hook could snap right off the plane and cause it to veer out of control. Too little and the cable would stretch out as the fifty-million-dollar plane continued forward off the side of the ship, right into the water. When a plane went in the water, it was gone forever.

When all went well, the effect was an almost immediate, eye-popping stop. If the plane missed the arresting cable with the tail hook, that was called a "bolter." Though problematic, bolters were not at all uncommon. Even great pilots missed a landing once in a while on a carrier. It could happen because the pilot just didn't hit the landing right, or sometimes because he did everything right but the tail hook still bounced right over the wire he was aiming for. (Even with four wires to hit, the angle of approach and where the plane first hit the deck usually meant there was a chance at hooking only one wire. If the plane missed that one, the tail hook wasn't likely to hit any of the others as the plane continued forward.) When a plane missed the wire, the pilot had to take off again *immediately*. There was absolutely no time to waste, because even a slight hesitation would rob the plane of the boost needed to get off the deck again. The plane would then roll right off the edge of the flight deck and into the sea, or perhaps careen into something on the deck. Because there was no time at all for the pilot to react to missing the wire, a carrier-deck landing required the pilot to go full throttle when the plane was just about to touch down. If the tail hook caught a wire, the plane would still stop and the pilot could throttle back when he felt the hard lurch. If the tail hook missed, the plane was at full power and the pilot immediately took off again. The idea was that the pilot would go onto the deck as if he were intending all along to just hit the deck with his rear wheels and then go up again (a "touch and go" landing). That minimized the need to react when, in fact, he didn't catch the wire.

When necessary, the *Forrestal* could "trap" planes for landing as often as every thirty seconds. As soon as they landed, the planes began taxiing away and folding their wings, if necessary, to clear the deck. One crewman, the "hook runner," was always standing by with a long crowbar, his only job to watch the landing and rush forward to disentangle the arresting cable from the tail hook when that happened. Others were in charge of stowing the plane out of the way and chaining it to the deck, a safety precaution that kept planes from rolling off the deck edge in the event of a slight list or a strong gust of wind. The crewmen responsible for chaining the planes down would sometimes challenge one another between landings, conducting little races in which they hustled forward with their heavy chains to see who could complete the chain-down first.

Landings on the *Forrestal* were assisted by a system of landing-signal lights to the left of the deck, known as the "meatball." The meatball was an array of special lights, each about the size of a car's headlight, that the pilot used to determine if he was on the proper approach to the carrier. The lights were configured so that a pilot on the proper glide path would see the middle lens illuminated, but a too-high glide path would show the top lens and a low glide path would show the bottom lens. When a plane was approaching the carrier and given permission to land, the flight controller on the ship asked the pilot to "call the ball." The pilot responded by saying he was "on the ball," letting control know that the meatball was in sight and the pilot was proceeding with landing. If the pilot could not see the meatball, he responded with "Clara."

Besides the meatball, there was the landing signal officer (LSO) to help guide planes in. This person was a descendant of the sailor who used to stand on the deck and wave paddles at World War II pilots to indicate how they should adjust their approach. But with the meatball doing much of that work, the LSO acted more as a coach, offering advice on how to correct a landing and then grading each and every landing or attempt. The LSO was always a highly experienced pilot, and his or her critiques could make or break a naval aviator's career. Too many bad landings and you didn't get to play on the carrier anymore. You had to go back to "the beach," an embarrassing rejection by your fellow pilots.

When the plane was approaching the carrier to land, it was the LSO's voice that came over the radio with commands for improving the glide path. The words were terse, providing only the information needed and not a single word more. A good LSO worked with the pilot's own instincts by telling him what to do, not what was wrong. Since all naval aviators, including the LSO, were egoists who didn't like being criticized, a command for "power!" was received better than the criticism that the plane was "low." When split-second reactions are crucial, such distinctions become important. The LSO watched the lights on the front of the plane to discern whether it was in the proper glide path, and if the plane was too far out of the right path to correct it in time, the LSO hit the "pickle switch" that was always in his hands, and the meatball would signal a wave-off. The pilot had to abort the landing attempt and go around for another try. The LSO also was the one who would warn the pilot when a landing attempt was doomed and the plane was about to crash; sometimes the LSO's experienced eye could see the crash coming a heartbeat before the pilot realized, and that difference could save the pilot's life. The LSO would shout "Eject! Eject! Eject!" to the pilot, who would probably respond without taking a second to doubt the LSO.

There was always one LSO on the radio speaking to the pilots, but there would be several others on the LSO platform just to the left of the landing area, all watching the landing carefully and administering a grade. The biggest part of a pilot's grade was determined by whether he landed successfully and, if so, what wire he hit on landing. Landing without killing anybody or causing damage usually got you an "OK" grade, which was amended by what wire you caught. Catching wire one was considered dangerous because the plane came in too low, and wire four was bad because the plane almost overshot the landing zone. Wire two was acceptable, but the best grade came from hitting wire three. So an "OK three" was the grade pilots were looking for.

The LSOs were the only people on the flight deck not wearing ear protection, because they had to be able to hear the sounds of the incoming jet to know what the pilot was doing with the engines. The LSO platform put them in an extremely vulnerable position if a jet crashed on landing, so there was a safety net nearby where the LSOs would run and jump if they had to avoid flaming wreckage.

In addition to the violence and split-second timing inherent in a carrier landing, pilots had to contend with a runway that was moving up and down, left and right. The pilots had to land on this small, small, small bit of metal in the pitch-black ocean.

One of the pilots taking that challenge nearly every day was a young John McCain, later to become a prominent United States senator and presidential candidate. In 1967, his assignment to the *Forrestal* was a chance to further his family's legacy. Despite a strong family background in the navy, with his grandfather and father both four-star admirals, his attempt to follow in their footsteps did not start well. He nearly washed out of the naval academy, his bad temper and lack of discretion nearly overcoming his highly praised skills as a sailor and even the family connections that greased the rails for him. But by the time he was assigned to the *Forrestal* in 1967, his reputation had changed. Instead of being known as a naval-academy midshipman with a hearty disdain for the rules, he was now known as a *naval aviator* with a hearty disdain for the rules.

There had been some important changes since he left the academy, however. McCain still was a brash young man who knew how to have a good time, and who was willing to give a lesson to anyone else who might be less innately skilled in that area. And when it came to what he considered the less important conventions of navy life, like how well your bed was made, he still didn't care much. But by the time he hit the deck of the *Forrestal*, he also was known as a serious aviator and people were starting to think he might actually live up to his family's reputation. He was a maverick, but he was good. The navy likes that.

McCain already had served aboard the aircraft carriers *Intrepid* and *Enterprise*, and those deployments had been eventful for him. He had been aboard the *Enterprise* when she sailed to Cuba for Kennedy's showdown over nuclear missiles, ready to fly off at a moment's notice when the president declared war. Throughout it all, McCain adopted the standard-issue demeanor for military pilots—calm, maybe a bit cocky, but at all times composed and fearless.

It was during his term on the *Enterprise* that McCain started to think seriously about where he wanted his naval career to go. Though he had been less than enthusiastic about the navy in his younger years, by this time McCain was thinking that he might shoot for the top. Even in his most rowdy days, McCain had always held a deep respect for the notions of honor and service to your country, and as he matured a bit, he saw that he could focus on those aspects of a naval career instead of the meaningless parts he still disdained. The young man who saw no problem with having a water balloon fight in his room and talking back to his superiors at the naval academy was starting to think that he would like to command a carrier someday. Perhaps his service on the *Forrestal*, flying bombing runs over North Vietnam, would be a good step in that direction.

McCain and the other pilots would be put to the test during their time on the *Forrestal*. Flying on and off a carrier strained the skills of even the best, most experienced aviators, not to mention that people might be trying to shoot you down in the meantime. The pilots agreed, enthusiastically, that landing on a carrier deck at night in bad weather was the absolute worst, most difficult, and truly challenging thing they ever had to do. The navy even quantified this challenge during the Vietnam War by attaching biomedical sensors to aircraft-carrier pilots and measuring their physical reaction to different parts of their flights. The sensors showed that the pilots' stress levels peaked when they had to land on a carrier at night, even surpassing the levels registered when they were fighting enemy planes and dodging antiaircraft missiles in combat. It was not uncommon for a pilot to climb out of his cockpit after a night landing on the *Forrestal* with sweat pouring off his pale face, looking like someone who had just barely escaped death.

To make things worse, that challenge was not at all rare. About a third of a navy pilot's landings on the *Forrestal* were at night, partly out of necessity and partly because the navy wanted its pilots experienced in the very worst. Night landings washed out many a pilot who otherwise would have made a fine naval aviator.

The stress level was so high on landing because there was so much that could go wrong. Even with multimillion-dollar airplanes, sophisticated landing systems, and some of the best-trained pilots in the world, landing on a carrier still entailed a huge degree of risk. If the plane came in too steep or too far back, it could hit the "ramp," a slight overhang on the rear of the ship intended to soften the blow a bit instead of having just a hard edge. A ramp strike was the worst landing mistake, a terrible thing to see, as the plane usually broke up and exploded, sending flaming wreckage forward onto the flight deck.

Landing too far to the left or right of the centerline also was risky because the plane might veer off to the side, either rolling off the edge of the deck or into structures and equipment on the deck. Simply coming in too steep or too fast could be deadly as well, causing the plane to smash into the deck harder than intended. Another scenario could occur when the pilot came in too low or received a wave-off from deck control. If the pilot pulled up hard, either trying to correct for a low approach or intending to go around without even touching the deck, the nose could go high enough to throw the tail hook down right into one of the arresting cables. When that happened, the plane was still in the air with no wheels touching the deck but the arresting cable was going to stop the plane no matter what. The result usually was that the plane slammed down onto the deck and pancaked. Even planes specially designed for the rough landings on a carrier could not tolerate such forces.

All of that frenetic activity on the flight deck appealed to some sailors, but Shelton was beginning to doubt his goal of working with the planes. That goal had seemed great until he learned more about how "bird farms" really worked, and realized that flight-deck work meant long hours in very dangerous conditions. By the time he reported for duty on the *Forrestal,* however, he didn't have much say in where he would work, so he assumed he would be out on the flight deck or maybe working in the hangar bays. But one morning he was waiting with some other newly assigned sailors when an officer walked in the room holding seven file folders. He called out the names on the folders, including Shelton's, and said that some of their personnel tests indicated they would perform well in the ship's navigation department. If they wanted to switch to that from their other assignments, they could. Shelton made a snap decision: this was his chance to get out of the aviation assignment. He stood up and accepted the transfer. So did another sailor named Blaskis.

Soon, Shelton and Blaskis found themselves training for duties in the division that supplied sailors to work in the secondary conn, on the main bridge, and in the aft steering compartments. The secondary conn was a spare control center in the very front of the ship, just under the flight deck, that could be used if the main bridge high above the flight deck was knocked out of commission. It was always ready for use in an emergency, but it also was used for storing and updating maps and other navigational materials. When Shelton and Blaskis worked there, they usually spent their time updating navigation charts to indicate changes in the locations of buoys or other landmarks. They also learned to work as quartermaster on the main bridge, the central command center high up in the structure that rose above the flight deck. One of several sailors and officers on the bridge, the quartermaster recorded all activity and orders given on the bridge, creating an official record of the ship's activity. The other duty that Shelton and Blaskis rotated through involved the after steering compartments, little rooms way down in the very bottom of the ship at the rear, near the rudders that made the ship turn. They would work long hours in those compartments, always manned in case manual control of some of the steering devices was necessary in an emergency.

Since Shelton and Blaskis were both new to the ship and learning the same duties, they found it easy to become buddies. They spent much of their free time together, Blaskis frequently teasing Shelton for what they agreed was Shelton's stupidity in signing up for four years instead of two like Blaskis. The friends often worked side by side, and once in a while they would trade shifts when one got an assignment he didn't much care for. Blaskis wasn't too crazy about working on the main bridge, because that meant he had to put on his dress white uniform and be on his feet all day. The bridge was a high-profile workspace, with the captain and other officers eyeballing you all the time, and the easygoing Blaskis didn't care for that. Shelton liked the bridge assignment, on the other hand, because it put him right in the center of the action. When he was on duty on the bridge, he knew everything that was happening on the ship. And it was an air-conditioned space, and out of the weather.

But for Blaskis, the secondary conn was better, since there were no high-ranking officers there to make things tense, and he liked working the steering compartments even more. Many of the sailors in his division, including Shelton, didn't like that steering assignment too much because the steering compartment was small and windowless, below the waterline in fact, and the shift could be boring as hell. Most of the sailors working there always took along a book to read, even though they weren't really supposed to. Shelton knew that was one of the reasons Blaskis liked to work in the steering compartment. He'd rather be left alone with a good book than have the captain looking over his shoulder all day.

Chapter **3**

Young men and old

Few of the men on board intended to make the navy a long-term commitment, but for others, the *Forrestal* was a glorious assignment, the high point in their naval careers. John Beling was thrilled when he learned he had been named the new captain of the *Forrestal*, and he was even more excited when he heard that the carrier was going to Vietnam. Though she was the most fearsome vessel on the water, she had never seen a day of combat. When Beling first saw her tied up at the dock in Norfolk, he thought she was like a powerful horse, pawing at the stable floor and waiting to be set loose. He was eager to see what she could do.

Beling knew the ship could fulfill her mission, and then some. Now that the White House was escalating the bombing campaign against North Vietnam, the navy needed another carrier to join those from the Pacific Fleet. The *Forrestal* had not been deployed yet because she was with the Atlantic Fleet, but the war in Southeast Asia had grown and in 1967 the call came.

Commanding a carrier is the ultimate goal for a naval aviator. There are higher posts to reach late in a military career, but for a pilot, the command of an aircraft carrier represents the absolute pinnacle. In a field as rarefied as flying jets off aircraft carriers, it is a huge responsibility, and an equally huge honor. The captain of an aircraft carrier holds a place of great respect within the naval community, and everyone recognizes that he didn't get there easily. A navy career can lead to advanced positions with more money, privilege, and security, but that's not what a man sits and thinks about when he is old and tired. He remembers what he enjoyed the most and did the best.

In 1967, John Beling had reached such a pinnacle. He knew that his assignment to the *Forrestal* would be the glory days he would remember for the rest of his life. No matter what else might await him, he could not imagine anything more fulfilling than serving as captain of this ship.

But he was much more than captain to the men who served him. To many, he was a father figure of sorts, especially to those still making that transition from boy to man. Beling was the leader of the ship, and the young men looked to him, and to the other older and more experienced sailors, for guidance and reassurance.

When he assumed command of the *Forrestal* in 1966, Beling was forty-six years old, an accomplished naval aviator, and one of the rising stars in the navy. A native of Harrington Park, New Jersey, Beling flew bombers and fighter-bombers in the Pacific during World War II. When the war ended, he studied aeronautical engineering and nuclear physics at the Massachusetts Institute of Technology, and served as operations officer on the aircraft carrier *Intrepid*. Then he was commanding officer of two attack squadrons, and commanding officer of the supply ship *Alstede*. By the time he was assigned to the *Forrestal,* it was clear that the navy trusted Beling with powerful command positions and the lives of many men.

Most of the younger crew on board had only a sketchy knowledge of Beling's background—that is, if they knew anything at all. Some had heard that he was a pilot in World War II and had been shot down, but he rarely told the whole story to anyone. It was typical of Beling to downplay his own involvement in anything noteworthy.

The truth was that Beling had been to Southeast Asia before and almost didn't make it back. He came within a moment of dying in the waters of the Pacific Ocean like so many other pilots and crewmen whose planes went down on raids against the Japanese. Beling was a twenty-five-year-old bomber pilot in 1944, stationed on the carrier USS

Yorktown. One day in July, he and his co-pilot flew their two-seater bomber to a tiny island in Micronesia called Yap. The lush tropical island, located just nine degrees north of the equator, was a beautiful green spot in the Pacific Ocean, surrounded entirely by a broad shallow lagoon and nearly ninety miles of barrier reef. The island was held by the Japanese, and Beling's mission was to hit their installations.

As they got to the island, Japanese fighter planes came up to meet the bombers and their fighter escorts. Beling, in the front seat, took aim at one of the Japanese planes with his guns and, for just a split second, regretted having to shoot it. The target was a "Betty," which the American pilots considered a beautiful plane. Beling zeroed in on the plane's right engine and squeezed the trigger, watching as his cannon shells cut through the plane and started a fire in the engine. But the fire died out quickly and Beling didn't have time to chase the fighter for another shot. The island was almost directly beneath him now and he had to continue on his bombing run.

Beling's escort fighters were taking care of the Japanese planes, so he turned his attention to the island, where antiaircraft guns were filling the air with exploding metal. He was lining up his plane with a good target when he felt a jolt and the whole airplane shuddered. The plane showed no ill effects, so Beling disregarded it and continued to concentrate on the bombing run. He didn't realize that a large-caliber antiaircraft shell had blown through his plane without exploding. Beling squeezed the trigger on his cannons and strafed the island as he lined up his bombing target.

He was low and almost on top of the small island before he realized his plane was on fire. The flames were visible outside the cockpit, but then they died down and Beling thought he might be okay. Then they reappeared inside the cockpit. The plane started to fill with smoke. His co-pilot called for them to bail out, but Beling realized they were right over the island and would land in Japanese hands. Besides, they were too low to bail out.

"No, don't bail yet!" Beling yelled. "Wait! Wait!"

He realized that he still had control of the plane, so he made a big climbing turn under full power to get the plane away from the island and up high enough for their parachutes to do some good. But as he pulled the yoke back hard, Beling felt the fire crawling up his legs.

Within seconds, his legs were completely on fire and he thrashed about the cockpit, trying furiously to put out the flames. Beling screamed in pain. He struggled to pull away from the heat, but the tiny cockpit offered no hope of that. His hands and arms were catching fire as he tried to beat out the flames below. With the fire growing larger every second, Beling frantically decided to jump out of the plane *now,* even though he couldn't tell exactly where he was in relation to the island or how high.

It turned out that he was about one thousand five hundred feet high, enough altitude for his parachute to break his fall. Beling watched as his plane crashed into the ocean, then he landed in about three feet of water about a hundred yards off the island. He never saw what happened to his co-pilot. He thought maybe the other man had gotten out in time while Beling was too distracted to notice.

Beling stood up in the shallow water and looked around. He was in agony from the burns that covered his legs and much of his arms. His flight suit was mostly burned off. As he stood there, he could see that the fighter escorts were strafing the antiaircraft gun that had shot him down. He was close enough to see the Japanese installations on the island, but so far no one was shooting at him. Once the antiaircraft gun was out of commission, the fighters circled over Beling and one dropped an inflatable life raft to him. He knew they would send help if they could.

The bundled life raft landed near Beling and he struggled over to it, every movement causing excruciating pain in his legs. He inflated the small one-man raft and flopped into it. He saw that the landing on the coral reef had torn open the dye marker intended to help rescuers spot him, and the green dye was filling the raft as seawater splashed in. He didn't care.

Beling wanted to get away from the island as quickly as possible, because he didn't know if the Japanese would start shooting at him or send a boat to take him prisoner. After trying a few different positions, he found that lying on his back made the raft the most stable in the breaking waves. So he lay there staring up at the blue sky and paddling with both hands. But he soon realized that the coral reef surrounding the island was making his journey difficult. The waves broke hard over the reef and Beling had to contend with higher and higher surges as he got closer to the reef. Paddling was exhausting, and the pain was growing worse every minute. He had to take frequent rest breaks. When he had to urinate, he saw that the urine was fluorescent green because the dye marker had soaked into his body through the burns on his legs.

After more than an hour, Beling saw a navy seaplane headed his way. Landing inside the reef was too risky for the rescue plane because of the shallow water, so it skittered down just outside. Beling paddled with all his might as the Japanese opened fire on the seaplane with mortars.

That's why they didn't shoot at me. I was the bait so they could get a bigger target.

But the rescue plane did not come alone. Fighter planes had come along for support and they strafed the island while Beling paddled furiously to make it over the reef. The shelling stopped and the rescue plane maneuvered as close as it could get. Once Beling made it over the reef, the pilot on the seaplane stepped out on the pontoon landing gear and urged Beling on. He yelled words of encouragement, partly because he was eager to get away from the island.

The pilot had left the plane's engine revving high so they could make a quick getaway, but Beling feared hitting the props as he got close to the plane. The pilot's weight at the door was making the prop on that side dip low and rock in the waves, so Beling called out for the pilot to get back in his seat and move the plane in a slow circle. Beling rolled off the raft and swam toward the plane, trying to reach a rope that the pilot had left trailing in the water. The young man struggled to follow the plane, every kick of his legs sending terrible pain throughout his body, but he finally grabbed the rope. The plane continued to roar forward and Beling was pulled through the water for a while, desperately clinging to the line. Finally, the pilot pulled the line in and grabbed Beling, heaving him into the backseat. The bare metal of the seat was torture on his burned legs, but he had to endure a long, slow ride back to the plane's home, the cruiser USS *Biloxi*.

Medics on the *Biloxi* began treating Beling's extensive burns, but it would be a slow, painful process of recovery. His flying days were over for a long while, and it was weeks before he could walk again.

Beling was a contrast of personality traits, at once brash and cocky as hell but still humble about his own achievements. He was proud of his work in the navy, but like a good officer, he was more likely to defer all the credit for an accomplishment to the men working under him. Like many military leaders with the authority to get away with it, Beling wasn't at all shy about bending the rules just a little or saying whatever would get the job done. And if he tweaked the military establishment a bit, so much the better. Like most accomplished military men who worked their way up the ranks and earned their position through real work, he harbored at least a slight disdain for the desk jockeys back home.

Beling was a strong leader, quiet-spoken and accommodating to his men when possible, but he expected everyone to meet his high standards. He was a very intelligent, well-educated man with a highly analytical mind. Unlike some high-ranking officers whose training emphasizes just doing everything the one "right" way, Beling was a creative problem solver. A smallish man, like most military pilots, Beling nevertheless exuded great authority. He was well liked by those serving with him, but he was known as a real bulldog whenever he was dealing with something that mattered to him, and most things mattered to him. Officers working with him learned not to bring up any problems or ideas at the end of a meeting when what they really wanted was to just end it and leave. No matter how late the hour and how tired everyone was, Beling would insist on hammering out a solution right then and there.

And the cardinal rule in dealing with Beling was never to bullshit him. If you did and Beling found out about it later, God help you. The best policy was to assume that Beling knew the answer to whatever question he was asking and admit when you didn't know. Beling had quite a temper when riled, and nobody wanted to be on the receiving end of it.

The other *Forrestal* officers also learned that Beling was even more determined than most captains about looking out for the welfare of his men—and most of them also had good intentions in that area. Very soon after he took command, the ship's hierarchy discovered that he was a hands-on captain, someone who wanted to see it all for himself. He was not a captain content to enjoy his own privileges while giving no thought to the lowly sailors working under him. To the contrary, Beling didn't hesitate to get right down to what mattered. And to sailors on a long sea cruise, what matters is food. Beling had a habit of touring the ship in the evening hours, accompanied by another officer or two, just to see for himself how things were running. One evening on the ship's first cruise after Beling took command, he opened the door to one of the big coolers used by the enlisted men's kitchen and found that the floor was covered with cockroaches. That set off a tirade that those present still remember as one of the worst they've ever seen from a navy officer. Beling had the supply-department chiefs rustled out of bed and brought down to explain the mess, which they couldn't. First thing the next morning, the whole area was fumigated and the captain was still hot about the incident when he called the supply chiefs in that day to tell them, in very clear terms, that no such scene should *ever* be found on his ship again.

Beling sampled the enlisted men's meals without any notice to those working the kitchen. He would usually grab a fellow senior officer to go with him, and they would get in line with the rest of the men. More often than not, the senior officer accompanying the captain on those surprise trips to the mess hall was Merv Rowland, the *Forrestal's* chief engineering officer. He was responsible for overseeing a great many of the ship's operations, so he was handy to have around when Beling asked questions or gave orders. Usually, he and Rowland sampled the "night rats," or rations, the meal made available in the middle of the night for men working around the clock. The kitchen sometimes skimped on the night rats, serving a meager or lousy meal just because it wasn't considered as important as the daytime meals. But for those working odd hours, that midnight meal was their primary meal, and Beling knew it mattered a lot to them. The captain's orderly would knock on Rowland's door around midnight and tell him that the captain wanted him to accompany him to the enlisted men's mess, or dining hall.

"Awwwwww, shit. I don't want to do this tonight," Rowland would growl, standing at the door in his underwear and still half asleep.

"The captain says you do, sir," the orderly would reply.

The two senior officers would go through the line with the enlisted men, the suspense in the room building as they approached the servers. They would take trays just like everyone else and then stand right there and taste it. By this time, the mess hall was silent, with all the hungry sailors eagerly watching to see the captain's reaction. On more than one occasion, Beling slammed the tray into a garbage can and loudly declared the food unfit for his men, demanding to see whoever was in charge of handing out that crap.

Rowland would hustle back to his stateroom and get the supply officer, a commander whose stateroom was next to his.

"Sid, the old man wants to see you on the mess deck," Rowland
would tell him. No other explanation was necessary.

"I'll kill that goddamn commissary officer," Sid would reply, referring to the man who was in charge of the midnight meal.

"Okay, but first you got to see the captain."

The supply officer would get dressed and rush down to where the
captain was waiting to give him hell.

"Get rid of this shit and feed these people!" Beling would yell, dressing down the officer right in the mess hall. He would demand that the
midnight meal be just as good as the noon meal, every time. "Goddamn
you, *you're* going to feed them, and *I'm* going to work them. Give these
men something they can eat!"

The mess-hall workers would trash the food that Beling had sampled
and break out something more palatable. Instead of cheese sandwiches,
the men might get pork chops just as the day workers had. As Beling
stormed out, the enlisted men would cheer, but the captain hadn't done
this for the applause. He did it because, by God, nobody was going to
treat his men like that.

Though it was hard to keep up with Beling sometimes, Rowland trusted
him and had great respect for him. They got along well, and each man
admired how the other could get a job done. Rowland had learned to work
with Beling's feisty nature, and besides, he was no cream puff himself.

At forty-eight years old, Rowland was hardly an old guy in the civilian world, but on a ship full of nineteen-year-olds, he was one of the
sages. He was a tough sailor, gruff as they come and able to take charge
of any situation. He'd push his cap back on his round head and start
barking orders, and he didn't take crap off of anybody. But like many
senior officers, Rowland also relied on his paternal instincts, looking
out for the boys as best he could while still getting the job done. The
men working for him knew that if they had screwed up in a bad way, they
should march right down to Rowland's stateroom and tell him about it.
More often than not, they'd leave with blisters on their ears from all his
shouting, but no formal disciplinary action in their records. Rowland
was like an ornery old dad who would never tell you how much he cared,

but who showed it in everything he did. He was tough as nails, but everyone knew he cared about them.

Very few of the men working with Rowland knew what a tough life he'd lived. He was born to a privileged family in Asheville, North Carolina, his father a successful railroad businessman who provided a comfortable home, with a maid and all the luxuries that could be found in the 1920s. He saw a movie every Saturday, and the streetcar that ran down the street in front of his home was a symbol of just how sophisticated his neighborhood was. By North Carolina standards, Rowland was a little rich boy living in the big city. But when the stock market crashed in 1929, Rowland's father lost most of his fortune and the family was forced to move to an old farm where the roads got so muddy that the mail had to be delivered on horseback. The change was a shock to twelve-year-old Rowland and his two sisters, going from the comfortable life of city kids to a run-down farm with no electricity, an outhouse, and water that had to be carried one hundred yards to the house in pails. The kids went barefoot all summer, getting a new pair of shoes only when the first frost hit the ground. Rowland's father struggled through different jobs, trying to put his machinery experience in the railroad to use, and somehow he managed to get all three of his children through high school.

After high school, Rowland struck out with a friend, Lester Millhouse, to find work. Things could not have been much worse for two boys trying to become men. The Depression was in full swing, and there was no work to be found anywhere. Rowland carried letters of recommendation from his doctor, his schoolteachers, the clerk of the court back home, and the county sheriff. They all attested that he was a fine young man, but unfortunately, plenty of other fine young men were out there looking for work.

The two friends hitchhiked all over the Southeast, joining the many others trudging the countryside in search of a few pennies. At one point they took dangerous jobs in a coal mine in Harlan, Kentucky, and worked there for three weeks until the miners went on strike. It seemed everyone there was carrying a pistol during the strike, so Rowland thought he should get out before the shooting started. He and Millhouse hitchhiked to Knoxville, Tennessee, mostly just because that's where the truck they were in was headed. They had seventy-five cents between them.

The two boys spent the night at a Red Cross shelter and then went looking for jobs. There weren't any jobs to be had, so they went to the navy recruiting station, where they underwent preliminary physicals and took written examinations. Millhouse was rejected for being color-blind, and though Rowland had done well on the tests, the recruiter couldn't take him either. You're from North Carolina, he said. You have to go back there if you want to join up.

So the two boys spent twenty-five cents on an all-you-can-eat meal in Knoxville, working hard to get their money's worth, and then they started hitchhiking north. They had a friend in Ohio and hoped they might find work there. But before they got very far out of Knoxville, it started raining hard. They were soaked to the bone when Rowland finally got up the courage to go to a roadside motel and beg the owner to put them up for the night. He was on the verge of tears at that point, tired and cold, scared at what the future might not hold, and the woman gave in. The adventure continued the next morning, the boys slowly hitchhiking north and making their way to Alva, Kentucky, where they got jobs in another coal mine. Rowland and Millhouse were happy to have these jobs, not just because they were desperate for work, but because this was a good mine to work in. Unlike most coal mines, it had eight-foot ceilings, so they could stand up as they worked.

Only three weeks later, these miners went on strike and the National Guard was called in. A friend tipped them off that things were going to get violent soon, and urged them to leave right away. They did. After three weeks of backbreaking work, the boys still had no money in their pockets. They had bought food and work clothing on credit at the company store, but they hadn't been paid yet.

Rowland and his friend stuck out their thumbs again, this time heading back toward Asheville. They survived by eating green apples found along the way. Once they reached Asheville, an uncle put Rowland and Millhouse up for the evening, giving them the first real meal they'd had in days. The next morning, the uncle drove Rowland over to the navy recruiting station, and he signed up. The navy accepted Rowland, but he had to join the long list of other desperate young men wanting to work. The recruiter told Rowland he would be called up at some point, but until then, he was still on his own. It took another six months of waiting, hitchhiking, and scrounging for work before the navy summoned Rowland to duty.

By then, the navy looked like a godsend. For at least a few years, Rowland would have twenty-one dollars a month, a bunk, a doctor, and a dentist. No more green apples.

The navy suited Rowland well, partly because he knew there wasn't much else out there for him. Once he made it inside, Rowland took his job seriously and excelled, soon realizing he could make the navy a lifelong career. He studied engineering as he served on a variety of ships, and when World War II struck, Rowland was right in the thick of things. From Casablanca to Tokyo Bay, Rowland experienced some of the worst.

Rowland made it to the rank of commander, a high-ranking enlisted man. Like Beling, Rowland was a hands-on sort of leader, likely to throw on a pair of coveralls and go crawling through a condensator to find the damn problem for himself. It was his job to keep the ship functioning properly in every way, and he knew the *Forrestal* inside and out. He had his finger on the ship's pulse at every moment, attuned to the slightest changes in her movement, vibrations, and sounds, ready to respond to any problems. When he slept, Rowland dozed lightly. If there was a change in the ship's speed, he could sense it and immediately pick up the phone by his bedside to see what the explanation was.

With Rowland and Beling in charge of the ship, the young men on the *Forrestal* knew they were in good hands. Rowland and Beling, in turn, depended on Washington, trusting their superiors to support the ship well.

The younger men's trust was well placed.

For Beling and Rowland, the *Forrestal*'s deployment to Vietnam was another chance to excel at their life's work. When the orders came for Vietnam, Beling was ready to pull that ship out of Norfolk right then and get going. He was a professional warrior, and this was what they did. There was a war to be fought in Southeast Asia, and Beling was eager to get over there and show the world what the *Forrestal* could do. In addition to his personal stake in performing well, Beling knew that the navy's Atlantic Fleet was looking to the *Forrestal* to do them proud.

She had to prove herself among Pacific Fleet carriers that had been on the job for a while already.

Despite his eagerness to get going, Beling knew that there was work to be done before the ship and crew would be ready for war. The navy scheduled months of training time before the carrier's planned arrival off Vietnam in July. Beling took to the training as heartily as he did everything else, and his determination was contagious among the officers he commanded. Rowland felt it directly. They both had been to war before, so the deployment to Vietnam was nothing new in that sense. In fact, the assignment didn't even rank as especially dangerous for the two men who had been shot at by the Japanese twenty-five years earlier. But they knew they were going into a war zone and that thousands of young men under their command would be facing their first real brush with danger. Like many military leaders, Beling saw a certain elegance in striding off to battle. He was proud to be commanding these men, men he considered a good and well-trained crew, and he was determined to do a good job. At the same time he worried about them, hoping that if he lost any of his crew, it would be for a good reason.

Rowland had similar emotions, remembering the first time he was deployed to a war zone, but comforted by the fact that the Vietnamese wouldn't be attacking his ship the way the Japanese had. The two seasoned officers discussed the situation extensively, and they agreed that the men of *Forrestal* would be ready by July. They would step up the training and drills for the crew, just to make sure everyone was on his toes when they got there, but Beling and Rowland knew they had a good bunch of guys on the ship.

Before Beling ever left Norfolk, he went out of his way to make sure the ship was well supplied for its first trip into a war zone. Every ship has a budget for supplies, and on this occasion, Beling made sure to tinker with the budget so that he could get more emergency supplies. It was only a precaution, but he decided to bring on more medical supplies and firefighting equipment than the ship had carried on previous cruises.

Beling made other changes in the ship's operations. He wanted to replace the ship's doctor before leaving Norfolk, but the new doctor wasn't available yet. So Beling called in Dr. G. Gary Kirchner for a talk. Kirchner had just finished his residency in Rochester, New York, when he was drafted and assigned to the *Forrestal*. He was brand-new to the navy and reported to Norfolk thinking he would be one of four doctors on board, in addition to scores of sailors trained as corpsmen, better known as medics. But when he showed up in Norfolk, Kirchner was called to the captain's quarters for more than the usual welcome.

"Well, Doctor, I've looked over your service record and . . . well, it's pretty thin, isn't it?" Beling said. "You have just gotten in the navy?"

"Yes, sir," Kirchner replied. "I don't really know one heck of a lot about the navy, but I am learning."

"Well, I have a piece of bad news for you," Beling said, putting the file down and leaning back in his chair. "The *Forrestal*'s medical officer has been transferred."

"Oh, will his replacement be here soon?"

"No," Beling replied. "In fact, he won't make it here by the time we will go to Guantánamo for the training and the operational-readiness inspection. I'm going to make you the medical officer. You will be the head of the department and I will provide to you any assistance that you will happen to need."

Kirchner stammered a "Yes, sir" and pledged to do his best, but in truth he was scared out of his wits.

Chapter *4*

Their Greatest Fears

The crew of the *Forrestal* learned early in 1967 that they would be heading to Vietnam later that year. In the meantime, they trained and became more familiar with what was to many still a bewildering and frightening place to work.

The flight deck was a busy place during launch and recovery operations, with planes and people making the most of every small bit of space. Newcomers had to trust that the more experienced hands on deck—some thirty-year-olds were called "old men"—would train them well and guide them through the daily hazards. At any moment, planes might be taking off on one end of the carrier while planes landed on the other end, with dozens of others scattered across the deck waiting their turns or being broken down for storage below. Bob Shelton had the same reaction as most sailors the first time he looked on the flight deck during a launch: it seemed a frenetic melange of men and machinery, even though the trained eye could see that it was a carefully choreographed ballet.

There were scores of men on deck, each one in a color-coordinated outfit that signified his role. Their brightly colored jerseys and headgear gave the flight deck an oddly festive appearance in a navy where gray on gray, with subtle highlights of gray, is the predominant color scheme. Purple indicated fuel handlers, the "grapes" who fueled planes and took care of fuel-pumping stations, while yellow outfits indicated aircraft-handling officers, catapult and arresting-gear officers, and plane directors. Red gear was worn by crash and salvage crews, explosive-ordnance-disposal teams, and others responsible for handling the bombs and other explosives. There were other designations for blue, green, white, and brown outfits.

The color coding resulted in a sea of multicolored dots running around the flight deck, all of them gesturing in carefully orchestrated signals because the incredible noise of jets landing and taking off made it impossible for them to hear one another. Everyone wore a "cranial" that had bulky hearing protection built into a canvas head covering. The cranial cut the noise to a bearable level, but it also had the odd effect of isolating the wearer, creating a lonely effect within a sea of people and activity. For some of the deck crew, the cranial had a two-way radio for communicating with the officers in control areas off the flight deck. But most of them relied on a set of careful, deliberate hand signals, usually large and dramatic gestures designed to be seen and understood clearly. The crew needed to communicate with confidence when moving planes about and conducting various operations that could kill people, so the gestures tended to be sweeping and often were done with a flourish, like those of an old-time baseball umpire adding some drama to his strike call.

When a plane was ready for launch, the pilot saluted the catapult officer, signaling that he was ready to be launched; then the catapult officer, known as the "shooter," would decide whether the plane was ready from his vantage point just outside the plane. From a kneeling position, the catapult officer would then lean forward to signal the launch to the catapult-deck-edge operator, the crewman who actually fired the catapult. Once the aircraft was "cocked" on the catapult, he kept his hands above his head until he received the launch command from the catapult officer. With his hands still over his head, the catapult-deck-edge operator would turn forward and look up the deck to be sure everyone and everything was clear. The catapult-deck-edge operator would then rotate back down the deck to make sure everything was safe to launch the aircraft. Only then would he face his console, lower his hands, and push the catapult trigger. All of this happened quickly, with the plane seeming to fire off the catapult as soon as the shooter leaned forward, the plane's wings just clearing his head by a few feet.

One of the blue shirts on the flight deck was Ed Roberts, the rock-and-roll drummer from Atlanta. He had been assigned to the crews in charge of moving the planes on the deck, a difficult and dangerous job. Roberts had first been given an office job on the carrier, but he quickly decided he didn't like that and asked for a transfer. The office job was easier, but he was really just a gofer and he couldn't stand the piddly-ass work like running down to retrieve laundry and then sorting out everyone's underwear. Plus, he had a fear of being trapped belowdecks if there was any trouble, unable to see what was happening. No one seemed to think there was much risk of the *Forrestal* being attacked, but Roberts had seen enough World War II movies to know that if planes got in to attack his ship, the action would be up top, and that's where he wanted to be.

On the flight deck, one of Roberts's main jobs was to chock the planes, placing heavy blocks on either side of the wheels to keep them from rolling once a plane was parked. He also tied down the planes with chains. The aviators depended on Roberts and the rest of the deck crews to do their jobs well, because the airmen were to a large degree just vulnerable cargo until the plane was actually in the air. Danger was everywhere on the flight deck, and after the aviators were strapped into their jets they depended on the deck crew to move their planes about, arm them with deadly bombs and missiles, and set up the dangerous catapult shots. Each crew had a "plane captain," a sailor who was responsible for that particular plane's preparation, movements, and launch. John McCain's plane captain was a baby-faced twenty-year-old named Robert Zwerlein who, despite his gentle demeanor, gave orders on the flight deck with the kind of authority that was necessary when lives were at stake. Watching him gave no doubt that this young man in the brown jersey could be trusted to get McCain's A-4 Skyhawk in the air. But when he took off his goggles and headgear, he looked more like the quiet soul his mother knew so well.

Like so many of the young men serving on the *Forrestal*, Robert Zwerlein was an example of good, old-fashioned small-town Americana.

Known as Bobby to his family and friends, Zwerlein was the middle child in the family. His father had served three years in the navy, and his older brother also had joined the navy. So when it came time for Zwerlein to make a decision about his future, the navy was an obvious choice.

The Zwerleins were a solid, loving family that stayed close. They ran the local Tastee-Freez stand in the small town of Port Washington, New York, and Bobby and his two brothers worked there after school, handing out ice-cream cones and chocolate sundaes to all the locals. It was the kind of place that everyone in town stopped by every once in a while, and over time, the entire community came to know Bobby well. They watched him grow up, from a little boy barely tall enough to see over the counter to a handsome young man who flirted with all the girls coming in for a cone.

The Zwerleins and their Tastee-Freez were a fixture in the town, and the four men of the Zwerlein family were heavily involved in the community through their volunteer firefighting. Zwerlein's father had been a volunteer firefighter for most of the time that they lived in Port Washington, and he and his brothers hung out with Dad at the firehouse every chance they got. As they got old enough, each one eagerly joined the fire service, making their parents proud that they, too, would want to serve their community. The whole family saw the honor in volunteer service, but Bobby thought that the firehouse was the place to be. It was the Zwerlein men's common hangout, the place their firefighter friends all went to just be with one another, tell stories on one another, and maybe have a beer or two.

The Zwerleins were satisfied that they had raised three young men with good hearts who were ready to take their place in the world as husbands, parents, and whatever else they chose to be. They also knew Bobby didn't relish working at the Tastee-Freez so much; he would be standing at the door when Mom or Dad showed up to relieve him, ready to race out and head to the firehouse. But they knew he was a good kid, like his brothers.

Mom had always considered Bobby a little more fragile than the other two. He wasn't the youngest, but he always got hurt, and always seemed to be sick with one thing or another. He was a sweet kid, never one to raise his voice or lash out. Bobby was the one who seemed just a bit more gentle, and that made Mom worry about him when he joined the navy.

But Bobby saw it as the next big step in his life, the same sort of move his father had made, and his older brother too. It would be a major change to leave his family and the community he loved, but that was part of growing up, and he was ready. Mom wasn't so sure *she* was ready, but she had to trust that he would be okay.

After all, she told herself, he's going to a carrier. And he's got all that training as a firefighter. He can handle himself if anything happens. That was something she repeated to herself over and over again.

Zwerlein's job on the flight deck required him to be right in the worst danger zones, and to stay safe he relied on good communication with the others on deck, as well as a keen sense of his surroundings. Any movements on the flight deck were performed with a deliberate attention to exactly where you were and what was around you, sometimes giving crew members the appearance of operating in slow motion, with a leisurely attitude. But nothing could have been further from the truth. The flight deck of an aircraft carrier often is called the most dangerous workplace in the world, and there are accidents on a regular basis that prove the point. This was no place to let your guard down or daydream. Zwerlein and Roberts both learned quickly that when they were on the flight deck, they had to pay attention at all times not only to operations in their immediate area but also to what was going on elsewhere that might soon come to their immediate area. During landing operations, for instance, their eyes were on the plane coming in if they were not otherwise engaged with their own job. Unless they had something else to concentrate on, they wanted to watch the landing plane so that they knew which way to run if it crashed.

If you were not ever-vigilant, you ran a high risk of being injured or killed on the flight deck. That is why the flight deck was a highly restricted space; no one was allowed there during flight operations without a specific reason. You could not just go hang out there and watch. (There was an area up on the island structure called "vulture's row" that was accessible to most crew interested in watching the operation.) Launching and retrieving planes, and handling deadly bombs and missiles, in such a small space created dangers that were only exacerbated when the crew had to go for speed as well. To make the situation even worse, the crew often had to work in the blazing heat. The carrier was a huge heat sink in the sea, the tons of metal absorbing the sun's rays all day long and not cooling until well after nightfall. Even though Roberts grew up in the heat and humidity of Georgia, never having lived in a house with air-conditioning, he marveled at how hot the flight deck got. He learned to turn his belt buckle to the inside so that it wouldn't heat up in the sun and burn him when he bent over. And when he got caught in the hot exhaust of a jet, he knew that, at least for a moment, his teeth got so hot they would burn his tongue if it touched them.

The heat and long hours quickly could lead to fatigue, and fatigue could kill. The flight-deck crews sometimes had to work twelve hours or more, at physically demanding jobs, and a weary sailor was no match for the hazards that just kept coming and coming.

Ed Roberts and his friend Gary Shaver knew there were dozens of ways to get yourself killed. You could fall overboard, you could be blown overboard by a jet blast, you could be hit by a plane, you could walk into a nearly invisible spinning propeller, an arresting cable could snap and slice you in half, or you could be sucked into a jet engine. The intake of a jet engine posed one of the biggest risks because the crew had to work close by and know just where the dead zone was. A few inches outside the zone, and you would only feel the air being sucked into the engine. Just a little closer, and you would be pulled off your feet and right into the engine before you even knew what was happening. That happened with some regularity, simply because the close proximity of people and jet engines was unavoidable. Surprisingly, the crew member sometimes survived the incident because the strong suction ripped off his cranial and other gear, sucking them into the engine an instant before the person's body would be chewed up. Despite their ferocious appearance, jet engines are delicate machines that can be destroyed instantly by even the tiniest bit of material sucked into the turbines.

With the engines so susceptible to "foreign object damage," or FOD, each flight operation on the *Forrestal* began with what is called an "FOD walkdown." For this vital precaution, off-duty volunteers who rarely got to be on the flight deck because they worked below lined up with the flight deck on one end, shoulder to shoulder, and walked the length of the ship with their eyes cast downward looking for any bit of debris. They picked up anything they found, no matter how small, from an errant screw to a bit of paper. Even a loose bit of the rubbery nonskid surface on the flight deck could be a hazard. During flight operations, the crew was careful to avoid dropping any items that could lead to FOD. Loose items were kept to an absolute minimum on the flight deck, with the crew discouraged from carrying personal items such as an ink pen or spare change.

Roberts had met Gary Shaver when he transferred to the flight deck. Shaver had already been working for a while in the same job, helping move and tie down airplanes. He had joined the navy with some eagerness, looking forward to a job in aviation electronics and thinking seriously about making the navy a career. He was eighteen years old and had started community college in his hometown of Carpentersville, Illinois, when he was hit by what should have been, in a better world, the worst trauma that could befall a young man: his girlfriend broke up with him. Shaver wasn't enjoying college life much and he had already considered joining the navy, so as a way of getting away from a broken heart, he decided to go. Within weeks, he was in boot camp.

Shaver hoped for a job in aviation electronics, but he ended up working on the flight deck as a blue shirt, directing planes as they moved around the deck. It was tough work, but he liked knowing that his job was important, that he had a responsibility to do the job right or else people could get hurt. His crewmates came to know Shaver as conscientious at work, never one to shirk his job or drag ass in hopes that someone else would take up the slack. Shaver and Roberts often worked together, Shaver directing the planes to move about the flight deck and Roberts walking alongside with chocks and chains to secure the aircraft. Shaver had been on the flight deck for a few months already, so he knew just how scary the flight deck could be and he reinforced the main rule of the flight deck for the newcomer: "Be alert at all times. Never let your guard down."

Roberts did his best to stay on his toes, so much so that he started chugging coffee like never before. (The Atlanta boy couldn't get his favorite "Cocola" on board.) At one point, he reported to the sick bay and very reluctantly told the doctor that it burned when he urinated. He was afraid he had contracted one of the dreaded, but common, venereal diseases that the medics lectured about before every liberty call. He was sure he hadn't done anything to contract a disease, but damn if it didn't burn like hell, just like the docs said it would.

The doctor couldn't find any indication of disease other than the burning, but he had an idea what the problem might be.

"Could be a lot of coffee. You drinking much coffee, son?"

Roberts took a minute to think about it and figure out how much he was drinking.

"Fourteen cups so far today, sir."

Roberts hadn't been working on the flight deck long before he found out how scary it could be. Within weeks, Roberts saw a plane blow all its tires on a hard landing, and on two other occasions, he saw Sparrow missiles fall off a plane during landing and go skittering across the deck. And around eleven-thirty one night, as Roberts was nearing the end of his twelve-hour shift and was dog-ass tired, he suddenly found a pilot's life was in his hands. The plane had just landed and been maneuvered into a parking position. Roberts placed two tie-down chains on one side of the plane and then suddenly the ship changed direction, causing the flight deck to lean to one side. Unfortunately, the tie-down chains were on the downhill side of the lean and the plane started shifting. Roberts didn't have time to put the tie-down chains on the other side, and his mind raced as he thought the plane was about to slip off the ship. The pilot was still inside, helpless unless Roberts could do something. He ran for a set of power-assisted brakes, a device used to move planes around on the deck, and quickly attached it to the plane's front nose gear. There was a heart-stopping moment as Roberts wondered if the brakes would hold, but luckily they did.

Shaver, too, had witnessed an accident that reminded everyone just how dangerous a moving flight deck can be. He had just been briefed on the morning's flight operations and was walking out to begin work when he heard an angry voice booming across the flight deck on the public-address system. It was a controller in flight operations yelling for the deck crew to "Get that tractor! Get that damn thing!" Shaver looked across the deck and saw the *Forrestal*'s "crash tractor" rolling across the deck on its own. The tractor was one of many squat, yellow tractors used on the deck for moving aircraft and other needs, but this one was specially outfitted with a bulldozer blade on one end. With that gear, the tractor was useful in emergencies such as, say, a flight-deck fire. An enclosed driver's area allowed it to be driven right into a fire, and the bulldozer blade could be used to push wreckage out of the way or right over the side of the ship.

Moments earlier, the ship had turned into the wind to prepare for the morning launch and the deck had leaned to the right. The deck crew had used the strong tractor to pull away the heavy deck plating around a catapult that was being serviced earlier that morning, and then they had neglected to secure the tractor with wheel chocks or by lowering the blade to the deck. Now the leaning deck had put the tractor in motion. Shaver joined the crowd of crewmen rushing toward the runaway tractor, but it was picking up speed as it rolled toward the starboard side of the ship. No one had time to catch up to the tractor before it rolled over the edge of the deck, bumped over the catwalk, and fell in the ocean. Shaver reached the edge of the deck in time to see the bright yellow tractor float for just a second and then sink into the ocean.

The crew was embarrassed that they had lost such an important piece of equipment, but more important, someone could have been run over or pushed off the ship. Incidents like that scared the hell out of everybody, because they could happen at any moment.

Shaver had been injured himself when a jet-blast deflector, the big shield that rises out of the deck to deflect the jet's exhaust during takeoff, suddenly lowered. Shaver was hit by the full force of the jet exhaust. In an instant, he was knocked off his feet and sent down the length of the flight deck like a tumbleweed. Shaver frantically grabbed at the deck for anything that would stop him, but the jet blast was so strong that he had no hope of hanging on even if he managed to grab something fixed. His mind was rushing through possibilities as he bumped along the deck, wondering what it would be like to suddenly go off the end of the ship and into the water. As he neared the edge of the deck, the jet's engine shut down and he managed to stop before rolling off. He was badly bruised, and his arms and knees were bloody from scrapes.

On days like that, Roberts and Shaver were glad to have their shifts end and get off the flight deck.

But in any sort of emergency on the ship, another hazard was the sheer complexity of the carrier's inner structure. Except for the flight deck and the hangar bays, all the other decks might as well be a maze, even to those familiar with them. An endless series of identical hatches, doorways, ladders, and hallways, the decks all looked the same and there didn't seem to be any rhyme or reason to how it all worked. Even before the ship was ever launched, workmen at the Norfolk, Virginia, shipyard would get lost in her interior mazes. One welder was lost in the hull all day until a search party found him exhausted and frightened. He had beaten his flashlight to pieces, furiously pounding on the hull all day long trying to help someone find him.

The sailors learned some tricks for orienting themselves within the ship, mostly by knowing what "frame" they were near. The frames were structural elements in the ship's design that were numbered sequentially, so if a sailor was at frame 200, he knew which way to go to get to frame 225. The *Forrestal* also had "you are here" diagrams and placards telling a sailor exactly where he was in numerical code. If he knew how to read the sign that read "01-170-3-Q, FR 170-174, X3," he knew his precise location. But in reality, finding your way around a carrier was difficult even for those who lived and worked on the ship for years. It was not unusual for a sailor to get lost and have to ask for directions from a "local," someone who actually lived or worked in that part of the ship.

Even though they were riding on a huge warship that could kill them in hundreds of creative and gruesome ways, the biggest fear for the men of *Forrestal* was of the simplest, most basic hazard—falling overboard into the sea. It was one of the things that Ken Killmeyer feared the most, and he was not alone. Killmeyer felt the fear intensely in his first few days on the *Forrestal,* and the fear stayed with him on the way to Vietnam, even though he managed to push it aside so he could get his job done.

The first time he walked to the edge of the carrier deck and looked over the side, he felt a queasiness in his stomach and felt as if he were falling forward. He stepped back quickly and learned not to do that anymore, but he thought about the danger often. Killmeyer was glad that he wasn't working right out on the flight deck, where it seemed every step threatened to send you into the sea.

Indeed, there was good reason to fear a "man overboard," because it was not an unusual occurrence. Killmeyer's introduction to the *Forrestal* included a lot of sailors yelling at him to watch out, don't step over there. At a great many points on the ship, very little came between the sailors and the open sea—sometimes little more than a guardrail or a catwalk structure. At some spots, there was nothing to keep a man from walking right off the edge. When the seas were rough and the wind was blowing, it didn't take much more than tripping over your feet to send a sailor over a barrier and into the sea. Once a man went overboard, he probably would be seriously injured either by the long fall to the ocean or by hitting some part of the ship on the way down. Once he was in the water, he had to be rescued quickly if he was to avoid death from exposure. When the water temperature was forty-five degrees, for instance, an uninjured sailor could lose consciousness in thirty minutes and die in one hour. If he was hurt by the fall, death could come much sooner.

Killmeyer's work on the *Forrestal* put him right on the edge of the ship during operations to transfer supplies, and he was constantly aware of what could happen so quickly if he let down his guard. Part of the risk, and one of the reasons sailors feared this accident so much, was that you had no chance whatsoever of rescue unless someone noticed you fall. The accident could happen so quickly it was possible for a sailor to go overboard and for no one to see it happen. And with five thousand men on board, it could take hours or even a full day before anyone missed the sailor. By then, the ship could be hundreds of miles away. That is why carriers always have people scanning the water for a man overboard. If they spot someone in the water, sometimes just by seeing an unusual light or form in the dark sea, they quickly sound the man-overboard alarm. Then the bridge will slow the ship and bring it around, while also launching a helicopter to go back and look for the lost sailor. Other ships traveling with the carrier also may aid in the rescue.

Without an immediate rescue attempt, the sailor had no chance. But even with a quick response, the sailor still might never be recovered. Going in the water is such a nightmare that many sailors say the real enemy is always the sea, not the person shooting at them. For instance, it has often been the sailor's custom to rescue enemy sailors after blowing their ship out from underneath them, rather than leaving them to die as soldiers might do on land. Once the enemy is no longer a threat, one sailor will help his fellow sailor in his fight against their mutual enemy, the ocean waters. And though Killmeyer's fear of falling off the *Forrestal* made him feel like a real rookie, it wasn't just young, inexperienced sailors who went overboard. In March 1942, Rear Admiral John Walter Wilcox, Jr., fell off his own flagship, the USS *Washington*. Despite the frantic efforts of thirteen ships searching for six hours, he was never recovered.

Killmeyer's work in supply transfers put him at risk from the heavy cable assemblies that could knock a man off the upper tiers of the ship or pull him out of the big doors on the side. But up on the flight deck, Zwerlein and his fellow workers were in jeopardy because the flight-deck operations made it impossible to put up much of a barrier on the ship's edge. Sometimes a light wire barrier marked the edge, but that was more symbolic than anything, just a reminder that you were close to walking off the ship. If a man was hit unexpectedly by the blast of a jet engine, that wire wouldn't keep you from going overboard, and neither would the safety netting sticking out a few feet just below the deck edge.

The first man to ever fall off the *Forrestal* provided a good example of how such an accident could happen. On November 25, 1958, the ship was steaming off the coast of Spain, scheduled to pull into Barcelona the next day. There were to be two flight operations that Tuesday, with the first launch scheduled before sunrise. Jim Johnson was a plane director on the flight deck, one of several crew members responsible for directing plane movement on the deck, carefully pulling planes out of the pack where they were prepared for launch and then moving them to the catapults. All the normal hazards of the flight deck were exaggerated because it was still dark outside. The first launch would use the catapults at the midsection of the flight deck, the "waist cats," and not the catapults at the front of the ship, so the plane directors who normally worked up front came back to help out Johnson. As Johnson was directing a plane to move forward from the fantail, the very rear of the ship, another plane director was pulling a plane forward from the starboard side. That plane director, being less familiar with the rear portion of the flight deck, got the plane hung up on one of the fittings that house the arresting cable. Rather than maneuvering the plane back and around the obstruction, the plane director instructed the pilot to rev his engine enough to get over it.

As the pilot blasted the engine over the deck obstruction, the plane cocked unexpectedly to one side and the powerful jet blast aimed directly at Johnson, who was farther back on the deck. He started sliding backward in the strong wind.

Because he was so close to the blast, he could not stop sliding even though he got down on one knee. When he realized that he could not stop and was going over the fantail, he decided to run and jump, hoping to clear the fantail and the screws.

Johnson turned his back to the wind and ran right off the edge of the ship and into the darkness, the jet blast helping to propel him beyond the structures jutting out from the ship and the big propeller blades churning the water below.

After surfacing, Johnson was still holding one of the lighted wands he used to direct planes on the carrier deck. He realized that it was a valuable asset in the dark waters, so he held on to it with all his might. As he bobbed in the water, Johnson could hear two jets being launched off the carrier, which was by now becoming a much smaller cluster of lights in the distance. His heart fell because he thought that the continued launches meant no one had seen him go over.

Johnson was wearing only his yellow jersey over a foul-weather jacket. He tried to take off his shoes, as he was trained to do, but he was too scared he would drop the lighted wand so he gave up on that. He tried pulling off the jersey, which was weighing him down, but he feared getting it stuck on his head and just left it on.

Soon, Johnson saw a ship pass about one hundred yards away with its searchlights on. A destroyer was searching for him, so he found the whistle that he used on the flight deck and started blowing furiously. The ship passed him by, and then Johnson saw two helicopters searching for him. Then the destroyer returned and the searchlights landed on Johnson.

That was when he lost his composure and began yelling for help. Men on the deck of the destroyer shouted back that they saw him and would throw a line as soon as they got a little closer. By the time the line was thrown and Johnson swam over to it, a helicopter had reached him and was hovering overhead. When the helicopter dropped a line, Johnson grabbed it and was hoisted up.

The helo carried Johnson back to the *Forrestal,* where he stepped onto the deck still tightly gripping the lighted wand that he had refused to let go of in the water. He had no injuries, so after a trip below to take a shower and rest for a short while, Johnson went back to work. Despite his ordeal, Johnson still showed the dogged enthusiasm typical of the

Forrestal's young men. He had been scared to death while he was in the water, but Johnson showed the attitude of a young adventurer once he was safe. He wished he had stuck with the destroyer's lifeline instead of the helicopter's, because then he would have had to make a daring transfer from ship to ship on a line stretched between the two.

"I could have been high-lined back aboard the *Forrestal,*" he said to a friend. "That would have been quite a thrill."

Chapter 5

JOURNEY TO VIETNAM

In the months before they sailed for Vietnam, the men of *Forrestal* went off on the kind of adventures that make great recruiting posters. As part of the navy's Atlantic Fleet, the *Forrestal* usually ventured to destinations in the Mediterranean—Naples, Rome, Barcelona—as well as all the Caribbean ports of call. In February 1967, the *Forrestal* went on a training cruise to Guantánamo Bay, Cuba, where the men enjoyed shore leave, with the requisite heavy drinking and carousing. Already, the youngsters had stories to tell.

Another physician joined the *Forrestal* when it reached Cuba, and Dr. Kirchner was glad to hand over control of the carrier's medical department. For another four months, the *Forrestal* sailed the Atlantic, stopping in the Virgin Islands and visiting Cuba again. On May 18, the carrier left Norfolk for a roundabout trip to Vietnam. First she had to stop nearby at the Virginia Capes for a one-day "Family, Friends, and Dependents Cruise," a popular day trip in which sailors could invite their loved ones on board to see where they worked and to watch carrier operations up close. These cruises were always fun for the crew and their families, and this one was especially important. Everyone knew the *Forrestal* was heading into danger, at least in theory.

The next day, the carrier was all business. She sailed on to Saint Thomas, in the Virgin Islands, to pick up a group of navy officials so they could conduct an "Operational Readiness Inspection," the final test to see if the *Forrestal* was ready for war. The navy inspectors studied the ship and its crew for three days and awarded a grade of "Excellent" before disembarking again in Saint Thomas.

Plans called for the *Forrestal* to take a southerly journey to the other side of the world, all the way down and around the Cape of Good Hope, at the bottom of Africa. Going through the Panama Canal was not an option for such a huge ship; she wouldn't fit. As she worked her way south, the *Forrestal* crew looked forward to crossing the equator on June 19. Rowland took a lot of flak from the crew for insisting that they not grow beards on the voyage, even though it was common for navy commanders to bend the rules on facial hair when crossing the equator. But a beard prevents an oxygen-breathing apparatus (OBA), the full face mask that supplies oxygen during a fire, from making a tight fit. The complaints made their way to the captain, and he called Rowland in.

"Captain, there ain't no damn way in hell that a man can fight a fire with an OBA and a beard," he insisted. As a compromise, Beling had agreed to let the crew grow beards until the ship crossed the equator but then everyone had to shave.

Crossing the equator is cause for celebration on a ship. The crew was excited about observing the naval tradition of initiating all those who had never crossed the equator before, the pollywogs, with an elaborate and messy ritual that would make them shellbacks. Those who were already shellbacks would mercilessly haze the others with age-old cere-monies on deck. The shellbacks faced a logistical problem, however. There were only about five hundred of them versus nearly five thousand of their intended targets. Normally, most of the sailors on a ship were shellbacks and they took advantage of their numbers to force the others through a gauntlet of abuse that included paddlings, elaborate cos-tumes, and kissing a fat man's belly.

The night before the crossing, the pollywogs organized a revolt. They wanted to become shellbacks, but they knew the numbers were on their side. Instead of submissively following orders for the hazing, they turned the whole initiation into a good-natured free-for-all and forced the shellbacks to go through some of the same rituals with them.

Four days later, the carrier anchored off of Rio de Janeiro, Brazil. The crew knew that this would be the last big liberty call for a while, so they practically stampeded off the ship. Rio welcomed them; the city was full of nightlife and the kind of entertainment that leaves a young sailor broke and happy at the end of the evening. Rio also turned out to be one of the few episodes that cheered Ed Roberts's view of his stint in the navy. Soon after coming aboard, Roberts joined one of the bands made up of crew members, and they played for various parties and recreational activities while at sea. Playing drums for the Dynasties made him feel a little better about leaving the Fugitives behind, particularly when they played in Rio de Janeiro. The Dynasties occasionally played for local crowds at their ports of call, and the Rio locals loved them. The rock-and-roll hits that the Dynasties played hadn't made it to Rio yet, so the crowd roared when they played songs by the Doors or Paul Revere and the Raiders. The Dynasties played up their rock-star roles, with Roberts getting furious on the drums. He even had a favorite move where he jumped up, kicked his stool away, and went nuts. He didn't let on that it was just for show and he couldn't really play the drums standing up.

The stop in Rio seemed to provide everyone with a chance to create a memory. Shaver, the blue shirt who worked with Roberts on the flight deck, took full advantage of his opportunity. Drinking with some buddies at a little bar in Rio, Shaver found one of the specialties was a mixture of whiskeys in an unusual flask with a spout at the top. He was already pretty far gone when the bartender challenged him. If he could chug an entire flask of the whiskey concoction, the bartender would give him the flask to take home and another free one to share with his buddies. Shaver was game and managed to swallow it all down, but he was completely shitfaced by the time his buddies dragged him through the dark streets of Rio back to the small boat that would return them to the *Forrestal*. Hey, no problem. All he had to do was get back on the ship, find his bunk, and sleep it off. But the seas were a little rough in the port that night, and Shaver faced one last challenge. He had to leap off the boat onto the little platform floating by the ship, and then onto the ladder that would take him aboard. It required a bit of timing even in good conditions, and Shaver most certainly was not in good condition. He miscalculated one of the jumps and went right into the water. The cold water instantly sobered him and he felt a big marine reach in and drag him up by the collar. He still was holding on tightly to the flask he'd won in the bar.

On another night in Rio, Shaver and some of his pals took pity on a friend who had been unable to get liberty that night. They couldn't stand the idea of him sitting bored on the *Forrestal* while they were having a good time in Rio, so they decided that if he couldn't get to the local flavor, they would bring some of the local flavor to him. It took a little scheming, but they managed to get three prostitutes from Rio aboard the *Forrestal* and deliver them to their very appreciative friend.

After three memorable days and nights in Rio, the carrier hoisted its anchor and continued on its journey. The rituals at the equator and the time spent exploring exotic cities, not to mention the long days at sea, helped the group of strangers bond. They began to form friendships, to get to know people from different parts of the country and people who were very different in some ways. They settled into the daily life aboard ship, learning from some of the more experienced hands who knew more than the basics taught by the navy. Spill fuel oil on your work clothes? Don't send them to the laundry. They'll never get all that stuff out. Just tie a rope to the jeans and throw them overboard. Let them trail in the carrier's wake for a little while and the churning seawater will clean them right up.

The *Forrestal* sailed around the Cape of Good Hope at the tip of Africa. The trip past South Africa was not an easy route, exposing most of the crew to their first big storm on an aircraft carrier. The ship ran into a storm with huge waves, big enough to bat it around like a little boat on a three-hour cruise. It takes quite a rough sea to send a carrier lurching from side to side, but on that night, mashed potatoes and gravy went flying and covered everything in the dining halls.

Then the carrier headed north of Australia and passed close by the tiny island of Yap, where Captain Beling had been shot down years earlier.

After a stop at Subic Bay in the Philippines, the *Forrestal* would go on to Yankee Station.

Though the *Forrestal* crew partook of liberty calls just as much as any other ship's crew, their cruise to South America and other destinations involved a great deal of training, both in standard, everyday operations and in emergency operations, like firefighting and man-overboard drills. When the crew was not being trained and drilled on specific operations, the daily tasks of running an aircraft carrier still amounted to practice in procedures that could be vital later on. Ken Killmeyer had been aboard for only a few months, but already he had a number of assignments on board. Though some were as boring as cleaning his crew's sleeping area, others put him right in the middle of the action. Killmeyer served as a messenger on the ship's bridge, standing by to answer the phone and relay messages to others on the bridge, or running messages elsewhere on the ship. As with Shelton and Blaskis, that position put him in the brain of the ship, standing within feet of the captain and making him privy to everything on the bridge. And it also gave him a terrific view of the flight deck.

When he wasn't working that job, Killmeyer was involved in resupply operations, in which a supply ship would pull alongside the carrier and transfer goods along cables suspended between the two. It was a complicated and potentially dangerous operation, but it had to be done frequently, because a carrier requires quite a lot of everything to keep going. The supply ship might provide fuel oil for the ship's engines, jet fuel, food, mail, bombs and other armaments, or just about anything else found on board. Killmeyer was a "phone talker" for the operations, standing on a small deck jutting out from the side of the carrier and communicating to the carrier's crew and also the other ship's crew, helping coordinate the delicate operation. The two ships would remain in motion for the entire operation, carefully matching each other's speed and movements to keep a steady distance between them—about two hundred feet separating them at twelve knots, or about fourteen miles per hour. The maneuvering was a challenge to the captains of both ships, but it was better than bringing both ships to a halt and letting the seas push them around. At least when they were in motion, they had control over where the ships went.

The operation began with the carrier crew firing a line over to the supply ship with a device similar to a shotgun, then both crews would rig the lines for transferring the goods. If fuel was being transferred, the carrier crew hauled over the big hoses from the supply tanker and coupled them to the carrier's intake pipes. With other goods, big crates and wooden pallets stacked with supplies were hauled over. It was customary, however, for the captains to first exchange small gifts. The first package sent over the high wires might be a box of cigars or some cookies made specially by the ship's cook. It was typical for the transfer to last several hours.

Resupply operations were routine, but on a carrier, routine never means safe. There was ample opportunity for error in the operation, especially if the ships did not synchronize their movements precisely. Straying a little too far away from the other ship might mean breaking the transfer cables and dumping the supplies in the ocean, not to mention the danger of high-tension cables suddenly snapping and whipping back toward the crew. Mismatched speeds could have the same results. But if one ship veered in toward the other, there could be a disastrous collision, probably to the detriment of the smaller supply ship. Such accidents happened despite the efforts of captains and crews who performed this operation regularly, sometimes several times a day for the supply ships, because the sea didn't always cooperate. When a sudden wind or current shoved the ship in the wrong direction, or if steering control failed on one of the ships, a captain would call "Emergency breakaway!" and the two ships quickly disconnected their lines and veered away from each other. Lines went flying, fuel gushed from severed hoses, and sometimes a ship got way too close for comfort. Killmeyer had seen a few of those, and they were always scary. One supply ship, the USS *Caloosahatchee*, had two breakaways with the *Forrestal* on successive days. The first day, the supply ship lost steering control and went wild in the water, causing Captain Beling to veer sharply away while the crews slammed sledgehammers on hook assemblies to send the hoses leaping off. Fuel oil covered everything, and one crewman was hit in the head by a flying pulley assembly. The ships tried the transfer again the next day, but the *Caloosahatchee* again veered off too far from the carrier, causing the hose teams on the front of the carrier to abandon the transfer and release the hoses. The crew on the back of the carrier, however, was determined to complete the transfer. They hung on as the rear of the tanker swung in close and its front swung away, popping the other team's hoses.

On the same voyage, the *Forrestal* crew also saw firsthand how dangerous magnesium flares could be. Pilot Ken McMillen was sitting in his A-4 Skyhawk one evening, waiting to be launched off the ship. The deck crew was completing the preparations for arming the plane with bombs and magnesium flares, when suddenly the world lit up behind McMillen. A brilliant white light reflected off the pilot's rearview mirrors and into his eyes.

Nearly blinded, McMillen frantically looked around his plane. He couldn't make out what was happening, but he knew the only thing that could produce such blinding light was one of the flares. But McMillen didn't know for sure if it was from his plane or another nearby. If it was from his plane, was it still on his plane and burning a hole into the fuselage? The pilot twisted around in the tight seat, one way and then the other, desperately trying to see what was happening to his plane.

Out on the deck, the unexpected flare had confused the crew, not to mention blinding those who had been working in the dim light on the deck. No one knew exactly what to do, and crew started giving conflicting directions to McMillen. One person signaled him to pull forward, and then another signaled him to push back. McMillen kept calling the control tower to ask what was going on. "Is it my plane? Is it my plane?"

The tower never responded and McMillen knew that if the flare was burning white hot on his own plane, it could ignite his fuel and everything else aboard. Even if it were on the deck nearby, it still could be a danger to him.

McMillen responded the way most carrier pilots would. He stayed with the airplane. Aviators on an aircraft carrier are trained to stay with their airplanes at all times, and for good reason. The deck of an aircraft carrier is a tightly choreographed stage, and no one wants an aviator moving around on foot when he could be safely out of the way in his cockpit. And more important, the aviator needs to be with the plane in case it has to be moved. So the rule was this: Don't go topside until your plane is ready, then go immediately to your plane and stay there. When you leave your plane, get off the flight deck as quickly as possible. The aviators may have been the glory boys of the aircraft-carrier set, but no one wanted their feet on the flight deck.

McMillen knew the rule, but he still spent several frantic minutes debating whether to leave the airplane. Finally, a petty officer grabbed the flare by its parachute and flung it into the sea. The incident was over quickly, but it gave McMillen a good scare. He never found out if the flare came from his aircraft, and sitting helpless in the cockpit had tested his resolve about staying with the plane. He wondered if he would have the nerve to do that again, or even if it was wise.

Robert Zwerlein and Ken Killmeyer had gotten lucky with the lottery of work assignments. With five thousand men on board the *Forrestal,* not everyone could have a glamorous job, but they at least had not gotten the worst. Zwerlein was in an enviable position with a job as John McCain's plane captain. He had a great deal of responsibility, with McCain relying on him to make sure that everything was in order before they shot him off the ship. It was a high-profile job for Zwerlein, and he loved it. He wrote home to his parents often, telling them how exciting it was to work on the flight deck, how demanding the job was. He told his mother that he enjoyed the fast-paced atmosphere, that it was satisfying to be part of such a great crew.

There were things he didn't tell his mother, though. Zwerlein never mentioned that the flight deck was the most dangerous place he could be on the carrier. Mothers don't need to hear that when their boys are so far away from home. They need to hear that the ocean is beautiful and their boys are having a great time. But the danger was on Zwerlein's mind. He saved those thoughts for when he wrote to buddies back home, knowing they also would not trouble his mother with his fears. The letters Bobby sent them contained plenty of excitement just like the ones he sent to Mom, but he also confided in them that the flight deck was a place where men died.

Paul Friedman, on the other hand, had ended up in an assignment not so directly in the path of danger. He was not pleased with his assignment. He had expected to become a munitions technician, loading missiles onto airplanes. That would put him on the flight deck, or at least up in the hangar bays. Instead, he was assigned to be just another hand working in the kitchen, pretty much the lowest job around. His superiors told Friedman it was only a temporary assignment, something that a newbie might have to do for a while, but he wasn't so sure.

He just knew that he didn't want to peel potatoes every day when he could be up in the middle of the action.

Shelton also was not so happy with life aboard the *Forrestal*. He was trying hard to make the best of it, but the Texan used to big open spaces just couldn't stand being crowded on the ship with thousands of men. The carrier was huge, but the living spaces were small. And though he realized that the *Forrestal* had amenities many other sailors would envy, that didn't make it any more pleasant to stand in line every time he wanted to buy a postage stamp. Still, Shelton was a bit of a pragmatist. He didn't enjoy the everyday life on the carrier, but he knew he had it a damn sight better than the guys who had to work down in the belly of the ship every day. And the guys who ended up in the jungles . . . no comparison.

Roberts felt the same way as Shelton about navy life. He didn't want to be here, but he wanted to be in the jungles of Vietnam even less. He kept telling himself that every day when he went to work on the flight deck, but it didn't make him much happier to be out there in the sun, sweating furiously and working harder than he had ever worked in his life. He wasn't used to a cushy life, having done a lot of physical labor for his father's business back home, but working on the *Forrestal*'s flight deck was more demanding than anything he had experienced. In just a few weeks of working on the flight deck, the six-foot, two-inch Roberts dropped from 205 pounds to 175. The quick weight loss left him looking a bit gaunt and feeling less than energetic. In addition to the hard work, he knew that he'd lost weight partly just because he didn't have time to eat. With the long work hours every day, his free time had to be divvied up between sleeping and eating. When he came off the flight deck after twelve hours, covered in soot and grease, he often found he wanted sleep more than he wanted food. At least he didn't have to stand in line to get some sleep.

Another newbie, Frank Eurice, had become a machinist's mate in the engine room, just as he expected. He wasn't thrilled about being on the *Forrestal*, but it wasn't like he'd been ripped away from anything great back home in White Marsh, Maryland. He had been laid off from his job at the local Montgomery Ward department store, where he was the store's expert in drilling holes in bowling balls. When he went home after being laid off, his mother was already crying when he walked in the door.

Eurice asked her what was wrong, but she couldn't speak through her sobbing. She just pointed to the mantel over the fireplace, and when Eurice looked that way, he immediately knew what was going on. Perched on the mantel was a telltale envelope from the United States government. Eurice didn't have to open it to know that he had been drafted.

When he was assigned to the *Forrestal,* he was glad to be on a big carrier. It turned out that for him and Roberts, the rock-and-roll drummer from Atlanta, their assignment to the *Forrestal* would spark childhood memories.

Eurice remembered the mighty *Forrestal* from when he was eight years old. The carrier had just been launched and was hailed as the most magnificent warship afloat. The little boy in parochial school saved ten cents per week from his milk money until he had three dollars to buy the plastic model of the *Forrestal.* He lovingly assembled the *Forrestal* and kept it displayed in his bedroom for years.

Roberts remembered the Christmas when two of his neighborhood pals received the *Forrestal* model from Santa and he didn't. He was terribly disappointed.

Now, at eighteen years old, Eurice was actually controlling that ship's propulsion, receiving orders from the bridge to rev the engines up or down. He was the kid with his foot on the gas pedal of an aircraft carrier.

The training cruises had assured Beling that his crew was in good shape, but he knew that there was no way to anticipate what might happen when the *Forrestal* went to Southeast Asia, so he tried to prepare his crew for the very worst. He was amply supported in that effort by Merv Rowland.

On the voyage around South America, he and Rowland stepped up the routine drills and exercises. Rowland convinced Beling that the ship should have "general quarters" drills for two hours every evening. General quarters was an emergency condition that sent each sailor racing to his preassigned station when the alarm sounded, ready to handle whatever was happening. It was used as an all-purpose response to combat or just about any other kind of threat to the ship. The idea behind general quarters was to get all points on the ship manned, but especially those positions that might be crucial in an emergency. Some sailors might be assigned to combat tasks such as manning the defensive guns on deck, while others went to firefighting stations, medical-aid stations, or important engineering work. Others simply reported to certain areas of the ship and awaited further instructions. Even when a position was already occupied by a sailor on regular duty, someone else might rush in to take that position for general quarters because the very best person for each task was to be at the station for general quarters. If the ship was threatened in any way, general quarters assured that the ship's best helmsman was steering the ship, for instance, and not just whatever helmsman happened to be on duty at that time.

Some drills and exercises were carried out all the time, but the pace was increased dramatically on the way to Vietnam; two hours of general-quarters drills every night was much more than the usual routine. And to make the drills even more useful, Rowland decided to simulate damage to the ship. Each department head judged a different zone in the ship each night, making notes of any deficiencies during the drill. The next night, the crew tried to correct those deficiencies.

The crew tired of the constant drilling, but Rowland could not be deterred.

"We're going in harm's way, and repetition is a damn good instructor," he replied. "You go over it and over it, and then when it comes time to do something, you can do it by reflex. You don't have to stop and think or ask somebody. You do it."

Beling and Rowland knew that warships are complicated and, by their very nature, replete with deadly hazards. Over the years, the navy had found that its ships were susceptible to serious accidents at any time, including fire, collision, and grounding. Between 1900 and 1967, the U.S. Navy experienced at least seventy major accidents resulting in the loss of life and substantial damage, as well as hundreds of smaller incidents. Sixty men were killed in 1905 when a boiler exploded on the gunboat *Bennington,* while she was moored in San Diego. Fifty years later, a carrier also named the *Bennington* suffered an explosion and fire that cost 103 lives. The accidents often led to important changes in operations for the navy, with the tragedies providing vivid lessons in what men could do better. And in more than a few instances, such as those involving the grounding of ships in shallow waters, the accidents publicly humiliated the commanding officers and threatened their naval careers.

Of all the accidents that could befall a navy ship, though, fire was at the top of the list. Fires were common, and they were serious. The prospect of a major fire was terrifying to sailors for one obvious reason: there was no way to escape, short of abandoning the ship. The crew could not simply exit the building and wait for firefighters to show up. When a major fire broke out on a navy ship, the crew immediately had to engage it with the same determination they would wield against an enemy firing shots at them. If they didn't, the fire would quickly consume their ship and, at best, they would have to abandon it and take their chances in the sea. At worst, there could be massive loss of life on some of the big ships, with thousands of crew crammed into them, not to mention the tons of volatile materials that could blow the ship out of the water. Some sailors had specialized training in firefighting, but in truth, every sailor was a firefighter. They had to be.

The navy's major lessons in ship fires started just months earlier, on October 26, 1966, when flames broke out aboard the aircraft carrier *Oriskany*. She had already taken a role as a major player in the war in Vietnam, mounting over twenty thousand successful sorties against land targets earlier that month. She had been at Dixie Station off of Vietnam for much of her work, but late in the year she moved to Yankee Station in the Gulf of Tonkin, another ocean grid from which she could launch air strikes on a twenty-four-hour basis.

The crew of the *Oriskany* was planning to launch six Skyraiders and seven Skyhawks on an attack just after midnight. But the weather had turned nasty, so the launch was rescheduled for 7:30 A.M. that day. The rescheduling meant that the crew had to remove and stow much of the ordnance that would have been used, because it was unsafe for it to sit on the flight deck or on the airplanes for more than seven hours.

The attack had been planned for the early-morning darkness, so the ordnance included a lot of Mark-24 Model 3 flares. When activated and dropped from a plane, this parachute flare could provide up to two million candlepower of light for three minutes, lighting up ground targets. The flare created its tremendous light through a combination of magnesium and sodium nitrate, chemicals that were kept separate in the flare until a sharp pull on its lanyard mixed them. When ignited, the chemicals combined and burned furiously at a temperature of four thousand five hundred degrees Fahrenheit. Furthermore, the chemical composition of the flare resisted all firefighting efforts; once ignited, a magnesium flare would burn white hot for its allotted three minutes, and there was practically no way to stop it. Though the pyrotechnic flare was not designed to kill directly, it was one of the most dangerous items on board.

The *Oriskany* had thousands of the flares stored belowdecks, including some in a storage locker in the forward hangar bay just below the flight deck. That storage locker had not been officially declared safe for the dangerous magnesium flares, but the crew used it because it was so much closer to the flight deck than the other designated flare lockers farther belowdecks. What they didn't consider, however, was that the more convenient storage locker was directly above a row of officers' staterooms.

When the crew cleared the flares from the thirteen planes, they started putting them in the unofficial storage locker on the hangar-bay level. Large skids stacked with the magnesium flares were moved down to the storage locker and then the flares were placed individually inside. The night crew left a large pallet of the flares sitting outside the storage locker when they quit for the day, and when the day crew came on at 7 A.M., there was still a big stack of flares to be moved inside. This was a lousy way to start the day, because it meant a morning full of back-breaking work. To make matters worse, the *Oriskany* was scheduled to receive a transfer of armaments later that day. More hard work ahead.

To speed the job, the one sailor responsible for the storage-locker area convinced another sailor to help him move the flares inside. They moved the skids as close to the locker door as they could get it, and then one started passing the individual flares to the other, who stacked them inside. This method worked fine on the first skid parked close to the door, but as they finished with a skid, the sailor outside the locker moved back to another skid and the distance between the two men grew a little farther. Soon, they were tossing the magnesium flares instead of handing them off.

It didn't take long for the accident to happen. As the sailor outside tossed the flares to the man inside the locker, the lanyard on a flare got caught on something. The outside man instinctively tugged on the flare to free it, and both men heard the loud "pop!" as the flare activated. The sailor dropped the flare to the deck, and almost instantly it began to shine with a tremendous light, the heat radiating out to unbearable levels, and toxic fumes spewing forth. The man who activated the flare immediately panicked and ran away, leaving the other sailor in the locker filled with the deadly flares.

That sailor also began to panic, recognizing the deadly heat produced by the magnesium flares and the danger of fire aboard a carrier. He ran out of the flare locker to a place near where the flare lay burning on the steel deck. In the heat of the moment, the sailor's urge to respond to the accident served him poorly, and he did the most illogical and dangerous thing possible.

Though intensely hot and dangerous, the flare could have been left to burn on the steel deck for its three minutes, after which the incident would have been over unless something else had ignited. Or the sailor could have thrown the burning flare overboard into the sea. Instead, the sailor managed to pick up the burning flare by its parachute and fling it into the flare storage locker where 650 magnesium flares were already stacked. He then slammed the door shut and secured it tightly. Then the sailor ran into the hangar bay shouting "Fire!"

Predictably, the white-hot flare ignited others in the locker, and soon there was a ferocious chemical fire consuming the forward portion of the *Oriskany*. The flares generated massive amounts of toxic fumes that spread through much of the ship via the ventilation system. The fire spread quickly. By the time the hangar-safety petty officer arrived on the scene, the locker was already buckling from the heat and spitting clouds of deadly fumes. He immediately ordered the crew to throw the remaining skids of flares overboard.

The bridge sounded the fire alarm and then shortly thereafter the general-quarters alarm that signified a serious emergency. Explosions rattled the ship as the fire spread from one compartment to another. The captain maneuvered the ship to help clear the smoke, turning first one way and then another. The ammunition magazines were flooded with seawater to keep them from exploding, a possibility that surely would have meant the end of the *Oriskany*. The fire ravaged the ship for nearly two hours before the crew brought it under control, and then it broke out again with a new vigor when fifty-five-gallon drums of paint in an elevator shaft exploded. The crew continued fighting the fires until 11:58 A.M.

Once the *Oriskany* was under control again, the death toll was terrible. The fire killed eight enlisted men and thirty-six officers, including twenty-four veteran pilots who had survived many combat missions over Vietnam.

The navy conducted a major investigation of the *Oriskany* fire and concluded that it could be traced to the unsanctioned use of the storage locker in the hangar bay, poor training in the handling of flares, and poor performance by the two seamen moving the flares. The navy also cited the *Oriskany*'s executive officers for poor leadership related to the other problems. In addition, the investigation determined that the fire spread as quickly as it did partly because there was not enough fog-foam equipment for firefighting. A number of policy improvements and technical changes in aircraft-carrier operation flowed from the *Oriskany* fire, viewed at the time as one of the worst ever on a naval vessel.

Some of the safety improvements derived from the *Oriskany* fire were put into place on the *Forrestal*, such as the emphasis on adequate fog-foam firefighting equipment. But the navy still had a lot to learn about aircraft-carrier fires as the *Forrestal* made her way to Yankee Station.

The aviators weren't spared from the drills. They didn't get much flight time during the six-week voyage, but their leaders decided the time should be put to good use anyway. They reminded the aviators that they had to be in good shape if they expected to outrun "Charlie" if their plane went down, and so they required daily exercise regimens in the tropical heat. On many days, the fliers could be seen running laps around the flight deck, huffing and puffing in their heavy flight gear.

There were general-quarters drills, firefighting drills, and man-overboard drills, far more than the crew was used to on a normal basis. The men spent many hours fighting pretend fires and rescuing pretend victims from the water, with many others standing around waiting to be counted as part of the man-overboard drill. Counting heads was a major part of the drill, or a real event, for a man-overboard. When the alarm sounded, every single person on the ship had to be counted and then representatives from the different divisions reported the numbers to an administrative officer. If everyone was accounted for, the alarm could be canceled. If not, the count should reveal who was missing.

Killmeyer hated the man-overboard alarms because they reminded him of the risk of falling off the ship, and he couldn't help thinking about the poor guy out in the water if it wasn't a drill. And besides, a man-overboard alarm was always a major headache for everyone. Captain Beling was never happy about going to all that trouble for a false alarm. If a man were recovered, he was likely to get a lecture about staying on the damn ship.

On the trip to Southeast Asia, the *Forrestal* had a number of false alarms for men overboard, plus some incidents in which men actually went overboard, at least one of whom was thought to have committed suicide, a mess cook who jumped overboard on the first day out of Norfolk. Word spread on the ship that some of the crew were getting anxious about going to Vietnam, losing some of their confidence in the safety of an aircraft carrier, and apparently one or more decided to jump. Even in peacetime, it was not unusual for an aircraft carrier to have individuals panic at the thought of going to sea for a long stretch. Sometimes only the prospect of leaving home for a few months of hard work at sea was enough to make men take desperate measures.

All the false alarms and men overboard tried Beling's patience. He declared to the crew one day, over the public-address system, that if anyone else fell off the ship, he wasn't stopping. Other ships would look for the sailor, but the *Forrestal* was continuing on. There were no more false alarms after that.

Beling and Rowland were also mindful of the *Oriskany*'s experience at Yankee Station, when the magnesium flares set off a terrible fire. The possibility of fire was on their minds, and Beling wanted his crew to know what happened on the *Oriskany* and what lessons might be learned from the experience, so he requested a summary from the navy. Nothing was available. Seeing no better option, he ordered reprints of a *Reader's Digest* story and distributed them to everyone on board.

As the ship sailed toward Subic Bay in the Philippines, the last stop before Vietnam, many of the crew were beginning to question some accepted procedures, especially now that they were going into combat for the first time. The men knew they were about to be challenged, and they were as prepared as possible. Even beyond the normal demands of working on an aircraft carrier, a combat situation would put extraordinary stress on standard procedures and the crew's ability to complete all their assigned tasks. The *Forrestal* was about to go into a "high tempo" combat operation, which meant that planes would be launched in large numbers and in a very small time frame, straining the already tense flight-deck operations. Unlike training exercises in which time was not necessarily a critical factor, the launch of aircraft for an air strike against land targets required precision timing and speed, speed, speed. The planes had only a limited amount of fuel and they all had to be in the air simultaneously to carry out a coordinated attack. While they were launching one group of planes, another group might be returning from a mission, low on fuel and eager to land once the deck was cleared. That meant getting planes launched as quickly as possible.

With the need for speed a paramount concern, the crew of the *Forrestal* reassessed some standard procedures. Unfortunately, two separate groups were both contemplating a safety shortcut that, though technically not allowed, they thought would be fine because other safety measures were in place. The weapons systems on the *Forrestal* had redundant safety measures in place so that if one failed, the other could still prevent a disaster. What the two groups didn't know was that each one was relying on the other's safety rule to cover the one they were about to circumvent.

One group, the Weapons Coordination Board, was composed of representatives from the air wings on the ship and others directly involved in arming the planes with rockets, bombs, and other weapons. On June 29, 1967, on the way to Vietnam, the Weapons Coordination Board decided that the *Forrestal* crew could ignore a navy rule regarding "pigtail connectors" in the arming system of rockets on the planes. Called a pigtail because it was a curly cable resembling a telephone handset's cord or a pig's tail, this device connected the triple ejector rack (TER) to the launcher used for various rockets on the planes. Simply put, the TER was a component underneath the plane that ejected and fired the rockets when the pilot activated the system in the cockpit. But the TER could not fire the rockets unless the pigtail connector was attached between it and the actual launching device for the rockets.

Navy regulations clearly stated, "The pigtail connector shall not be plugged into the launcher receptacle until just before takeoff." There was no dispute that "just before takeoff" was when the plane was sitting on the catapult, only seconds before being launched off the deck. This was meant to keep the rocket-firing systems disconnected until the very last moment to prevent a rocket from being accidentally fired while the plane was still on the deck.

There was another rule to achieve the same goal. The firing system also used a device called a TER electrical-safety pin, or just a TER pin. (It also was called an intervalometer pin.) This small device, which was plugged into a receptacle in the rocket-firing mechanism, interrupted the electrical system and prevented a firing command from reaching the rocket. Navy regulations clearly stated that the TER pin was to be in place the whole time the plane was armed on the deck, and the crew was supposed to remove it immediately before launch, as the plane was sitting on the catapult.

The pigtails and the TER pins were a double layer of protection against human error or even an electrical malfunction that could fire the rocket. Without the pigtail in place, the electrical signal could not reach the rocket. Even with the pigtail in place, the firing command still could not reach the rocket because it could not get past the TER pin.

The only problem was that waiting to fully arm the rocket on the catapult was not the fastest way to get planes off the deck and in the air. Everything had to move quickly and smoothly when launching planes, and once the plane was on the catapult, any last-minute steps would just slow the system down, especially if there was a problem. A plane having difficulty on the catapult would delay every plane in line behind it. It was better to take care of as much as possible while the plane was back "in the pack" waiting for takeoff.

So the Weapons Coordination Board decided to circumvent the rule about pigtails, giving the crew permission to plug in the rocket pigtails while the plane was back in the pack. The board acknowledged that this was a deviation from standard practice, but said the rockets would still be safe because the TER pin would be in place. But unbeknownst to the board, other members of the crew had gotten in the habit, without any official approval, of removing the TER pins while the planes were still being prepared for launch. They operated on the same theory that it was much more expedient to remove them before the plane got to the catapult. Those crew members thought the shortcut was acceptable because the rocket pigtails would not be plugged in until the plane was on the catapult. There was a breakdown in communication, one that led to the *Forrestal* inadvertently causing rockets to be fully armed while the planes were sitting on the rear of the ship, bunched up and pointed at one another while being loaded with explosives.

The weapons board's decision to circumvent the pigtail rule was never forwarded to the captain. No one with authority to overrule the weapons board ever saw the board's report, and no one realized the conflict with the habit of removing the TER pins early.

The pigtail decision did not go unnoticed, however. Ken McMillen, the pilot who had the frightening experience with the magnesium flare, heard from an ordnance crewman about the decision. The crewman was responsible for loading the planes in McMillen's division with bombs and rockets, so he was familiar with why the pigtail shouldn't be plugged in early. He expressed some concern to McMillen, who also acted as a safety officer within the squadron. McMillen, in turn, went to his friend and fellow pilot Jim Bangert, who was a safety officer one step up in the chain of command.

"Hey, our people are having some problems with this new thing about arming the rockets while we're still in the pack," McMillen told Bangert one day. "You think that's really safe?"

Bangert said he had wondered about the new policy, too, and said he would look into it. A few days later, after checking with the Weapons Coordination Board, Bangert went back to McMillen and said that was indeed the new policy. Bangert apparently had no idea of the conflict between the pigtail and TER pin shortcuts.

"That's what they say we're doing now," Bangert said. "They say it's the only way to get all the planes launched fast enough."

Chapter 6

ON YANKEE STATION

The *Forrestal* reached Subic Bay in the Philippines on July 18 and then sailed off four days later for her assigned post at Yankee Station, in the Tonkin Gulf south of Vietnam. She was almost there.

Back home, most people had not paid much attention at first to the buildup of hostilities in Vietnam and the United States' growing presence in Southeast Asia. But by 1967, the country's involvement had reached the point that average Americans were concerned, though not always in the same way. The old guard was worried about the spread of communism and saw North Vietnam as dangerous, generally going along with the Kennedy and Johnson administrations' explanations that U.S. involvement was unfortunate but necessary. The younger generation wasn't buying it.

In 1967, the antiwar movement had not reached a fever pitch yet, but the opposition was making its voice heard. The men of *Forrestal* saw some of the protests before leaving for Vietnam, and on the trip over, they heard about more of it from their friends and family back home. Most of them saw the protests as an affront. Even if they weren't crazy about going to Vietnam or had even thought through the politics enough to disagree with the U.S. involvement, they didn't like being criticized by a bunch of college kids. A great many of the sailors fell in the ranks of Middle America, not necessarily supporting the war but uncomfortable with longhaired kids denouncing their country. It was unpatriotic.

The media were bringing home some images of the war by 1967, and that was starting to turn the tide in the opposition's favor. In April, opponents of the war marched in protests across the country, including two hundred thousand who gathered in New York's Central Park. About 150 young men burned their draft cards at the rally, openly defying the law and signaling a new vigor to the movement. The protestors screamed for Lyndon Johnson to bring home the half a million troops in South Vietnam.

The president was feeling the heat, but not just from the protestors. He could dismiss them as a bunch of misguided college students, naive at best and traitorous at worst, but he could not deny the reports from his own advisers. A year earlier, even those who had pushed for the bombing and ground combat had produced one report after another showing poor results and poor prospects. After two years of the world's strongest country throwing its military might against a supposedly backward jungle nation, victory was nowhere in sight. Johnson was willing to bomb the North Vietnamese mercilessly, but apparently the North Vietnamese were willing to take it and wait for the Americans to leave.

Military leaders pushed Johnson to expand the campaign against North Vietnam, a move encouraged by Secretary of Defense Robert McNamara. He is considered the leading architect of the bombing campaign in Southeast Asia, though by late 1966 he and other civilian leaders had also concluded that the effort was futile. Known for his aggressiveness in pursuing the military effort in Vietnam, McNamara was reluctant to tell Johnson and others in the administration that the Vietnam War might not be winnable. Some other resolution might be necessary, but the question was how to get out.

The buildup in Vietnam had been long and progressive, and the Johnson administration could not back down without losing face. Since July 1965, there had been a steady escalation in the bombing of targets in Southeast Asia, accompanied by a buildup of ground troops. By the end of 1966, the United States had more than four hundred thousand ground troops in Vietnam. After a brief bombing pause in 1966, the administration expanded the bombing again, targeting North Vietnamese supply lines. The bombing moved closer to the major cities of Hanoi and Haiphong, and also to the Chinese border. In 1967, the United States flew 122,960 attack missions in Southeast Asia, hitting 5,261 motor vehicles, 2,475 railroad cars, and 11,425 water craft. Some 3,685 land targets were hit by carrier-based planes.

Fewer than one thousand four hundred Americans had died in Vietnam in 1965, but the figure had jumped to five thousand by 1966 and would reach nine thousand total by 1967.

America's huge military presence in Vietnam came at a high cost, with the country spending millions of dollars every day. The daily bombing runs over North Vietnam pushed the military's supply efforts to the breaking point, and by 1966 there simply weren't enough bombs. Pilots reported going out on bombing runs with only half of what they needed to do the job right, and others were sent out with other types of ordnance, like rockets, that were inappropriate for the mission. The U.S. military couldn't keep enough bombs in the supply line, and the pilots' grumbling was working its way back to the White House and the media back home.

On January 25, 1966, the White House received a cable from Bangkok, Thailand, in which a number of leaders in the American military structure in Southeast Asia assessed the war effort and its future prospects. The cable represented the conclusions reached by General William Westmoreland and Admiral Ulysses S. Grant Sharp, the commander in chief of the U.S. forces in the Pacific, whose carriers had been largely responsible for the bombing runs. Also represented by the cable were General Dick Stilwell, regarded as a slick spinmaster in Saigon who worked hard to suppress negative reports in the media, and several ambassadors: Henry Cabot Lodge, the ambassador to South Vietnam; William Sullivan, ambassador to Laos; Graham Martin, ambassador to Thailand. This was not a whiny complaint from an antiwar crowd; these were the administration's point men for the war effort.

The message they sent to the White House was problematic, especially because it came at a time when the public was starting to question the war effort.

"As far as air actions are concerned, we recognize that the sortie [bombing run] rate may have to be curtailed because of existing and foreseeable shortages in the supply of iron bombs," the cable said. "Iron bombs" refers to unguided, high-explosive bombs, what the public thinks of as simply a bomb rather than something like a missile.

The shortage of bombs was troubling to President Johnson, but more so to McNamara. Though he would soon seek alternatives to the bombing campaign, in early 1966 he still was in favor of it. The intricate plans for demoralizing the North Vietnamese and interrupting their supply lines could not be carried out unless the United States had enough bombs in its supply lines. McNamara was rankled by the cable from Bangkok.

He met with President Johnson in late January to discuss whether to resume the bombing campaign, which had been halted as part of peace negotiations. McNamara expressed his concern that "further delay on resumption of bombing can polarize opinion in this country. I feel we should resume, and send the execute order tonight."

McNamara clearly did not want to slow the bombing campaign for any reason, because he felt that doing so might give the antiwar protesters a foothold. And if it were slowed due to a shortage of bombs, the country would look weak in its enemy's eyes.

McNamara declared that there was no bomb shortage. Years later, he sticks by that assessment, writing in his 1995 memoir *In Retrospect* that he and the military leadership "did our utmost to keep U.S. troops in the field as well supplied and well protected as possible. As the war heated up and passions increased, some critics of the Johnson administration alleged that matériel shortages had compromised our soldiers' safety. This was not the case." He goes on to quote a 1966 letter from General Bus Wheeler, who wrote that "there have been no shortages in supplies for the troops in Vietnam which have adversely affected combat operations of the health or welfare of the troops. No required air sorties [a sortie is an attack mission by one aircraft] have been canceled."

Those who were actually in Vietnam knew the truth was different. Admiral Leighton W. "Snuffy" Smith, Jr., flew over 280 missions in Vietnam during three tours as a navy pilot, during which the military structure in Vietnam encouraged him to do whatever was necessary to send positive reports to Washington, including lying about the success of bombing runs. One day, an intelligence officer told him he should report hitting a target bridge when he had in fact missed it. He felt that an air of deceit had worked its way down from Washington.

The more Smith saw of the lies, the angrier he became. He saw Secretary McNamara on a news report saying, "There's not a shortage of weapons," and soon after he was assigned another mission to bomb a bridge. At the pilot's briefing, Smith was informed that he would be armed with 2.75-inch rockets instead of the five-hundred-pound bombs that he expected.

"Why in the world are you assigning me this target with this weapons load?" he asked.

"That's all we got" was the reply.

Smith complained, and he was not the only pilot unhappy with the shortage of bombs, but the complaints fell on deaf ears in Washington. Sitting in the White House, McNamara and the others controlling the war effort could not be troubled by details like whether there actually were enough bombs to carry out the instructions they sent down the military chain of command.

The White House ordered more bombing. The navy would have to do whatever it took to get enough bombs on those planes.

Like the entire military structure during the Vietnam War, the United States Navy constantly found itself pitted between the directives coming out of the White House and the realities of what was happening in Southeast Asia. The directives from Washington often bore little relationship to what military leaders in combat, or even those sitting in the Pentagon, knew was necessary to fight the war.

Naval officers with both the practical insight and enough authority might have resisted instructions that needlessly put their men at risk, but they needed the right information. As the *Forrestal* would soon demonstrate, the necessary information could be lost in the navy's vast bureaucracy.

The *Forrestal* depended on other ships. Despite her size and strength, or actually because of them, the *Forrestal* did not sail off on her own. Instead, she was accompanied by destroyers and other smaller ships that provided various types of support. They helped defend the carrier from any water-based threats because they were far more maneuverable and carried more weaponry for close combat. Together, the carrier and her support ships were known as a battle group.

The battle group, in turn, was supported by supply ships that rendezvoused with the *Forrestal* and the other ships to transfer all manner of goods. Some ships supplied fuel oil or jet fuel, and others provided food or other goods. And some ships like the USS *Diamond Head* provided ammunition. Among navy ships, the *Diamond Head* was an outcast of sorts, the dangerous cousin that still had to be invited to family gatherings once in a while. Far from glamorous, she was a utilitarian cargo ship that hauled tons of ammunition from storage depots all over the world out to the ships that needed replenishment. At any time, her holds might be chock-full of bombs, rockets, grenades, black powder, small-arms ammunition, and pretty much anything else that could explode. (The irony was that, even with all that ammunition on board, she had only two small guns mounted on the deck to defend herself. One of them usually worked.)

The *Diamond Head*'s task was to load up and then steam out to where the other ships were in transit or already stationed for duty. The work was dirty, especially in a navy that often makes a sailor seem like a fastidious housekeeper with nothing better to do. On the *Diamond Head*, the dangerous cargo was usually dirty and greasy, and there wasn't much hope of maintaining the spotless appearance that other navy ships required. Hard physical labor was routine, with the young men manhandling bombs and other explosives as they moved them on or off the ship. The worst part of working on the *Diamond Head*, however, was knowing that you were on a floating powder keg. All of the sailors knew that they were riding a massive bomb in the ocean, liable to explode with little warning if something went wrong. And with all those tons of high explosives on board, there would not be much left to find. It was a fear that shook many of the 160 sailors when they were first assigned to the *Diamond Head*, but after a while, they became resigned to the possibility of their ship exploding underneath them. Still, there were idle moments on the long voyages out to meet another ship when a sailor's mind could start wandering: *If this thing blows up, what will be the last thing I see? Will I see the deck actually coming up at me?*

The fear was very real for these *Diamond Head* sailors because their ship was not exactly a showpiece. She was old and, though she could still do her job, she was plagued by electrical problems that occasionally started small fires on board. Fires on any ship are serious, but the danger was nightmarish for a supply ship stuffed with explosives. When a fire broke out, the *Diamond Head* sailors had to attack it quickly, and ferociously, because they didn't have a second to spare. The risk of fire and explosion aboard ammunition ships was so serious that they were shunned by navy ports. When the *Diamond Head* docked at a naval base, either to pick up ammunition or just to let the sailors off for shore leave, she was not allowed to pull up alongside the other ships. She had to dock far away, sometimes a forty-five-minute bus ride back to the base, or anchor out in the deep water and send her men to shore in small boats.

The *Diamond Head* shared a small honor with the *Forrestal*. She was the first ammunition ship from the navy's East Coast fleet to go to Vietnam, and the carrier was from the East Coast. When the *Forrestal* set sail for Vietnam in June 1967, the *Diamond Head* was already in the area servicing the other ships there. She had settled into a routine of visiting naval ports to pick up ammunition and then running out to where the other ships were at work. She supplied everything from the carriers to the little gunboats that worked their way up the rivers in Vietnam. Most of the time, the *Diamond Head* picked up ammunition at the Subic Bay Naval Base in the Philippines, not far from Vietnam, and then sailed for about three days back to where the other ships were stationed. Once there, she traveled around the area, fulfilling orders for ammunition. The *Diamond Head* might supply six or seven ships in one day.

In the months before the *Forrestal* arrived, the *Diamond Head* sailors had grown accustomed to the routine of docking far out in the undeveloped part of Subic Bay and then driving back to the naval base. With help from Filipinos hired by the naval base, they trucked tons of ammunition back to the *Diamond Head* and loaded it on board. When they stopped for their pickup in July 1967, the sailors were surprised at some of the ammunition they were taking on board. It was old and was clearly not in good shape—dirty, rusty, even leaking. The sailors didn't necessarily know much about the ammunition they worked with every day, but they could tell that this batch was different. Some of the bombs looked different in design, and they clearly hadn't been stored well. When the crew asked the local sailors about this, they learned that the bombs had been sitting in open-air Quonset huts in the Philippine jungles for years, exposed to the humid weather and the occasional storm. No one was sure just how long, but from the grime layered on the bombs, it had been more than a few years.

The *Diamond Head* sailors asked why they were taking on such old matériel, bombs that looked like they should have been destroyed long ago. The local sailors working at the base said they had an order for one-thousand-pound bombs, and these were the only ones they had in that size.

These weren't the first old bombs the *Diamond Head* had loaded in Subic Bay, though the condition was especially noteworthy this time. The sailors had gotten used to loading filthy bombs that had sat out in the jungles. On one recent trip, there was a commotion on the pier as the bombs were being loaded onto the *Diamond Head*. The Filipino workers were shouting and scrambling around one of the stacks of bombs and then, much to the amazement of the *Diamond Head* crew, they pulled out a snake that was long enough to require four men to hold it. The snake had been living in the bomb pallets, apparently for quite a while. On other trips, the crew had found large green tree frogs living among the bombs, a few of which inevitably made their way into the officers' quarters as a prank.

But this ammunition was frightening, even to the *Diamond Head* crew, who were accustomed to the prospect of blowing up at any moment. The young men on the ship were not weapons experts, but they knew that such old and poorly maintained bombs could be overly sensitive, liable to explode with the slightest mishandling. To make matters worse, these were thousand-pound bombs, which were big enough to destroy the ship on their own. The crew didn't like having the old ammunition on their ship, but that was what the navy told them to pick up. At least they could get it off in just a few days when they met up with the *Forrestal*.

As the *Diamond Head* was picking up the old bombs in Subic Bay, the *Forrestal* was just arriving at Yankee Station. The carrier steamed into position on July 25, sixty-seven days after leaving Norfolk.

Yankee Station was a spot in the water off of North Vietnam that looked like any other—except the navy had declared it a staging area for launching air strikes against North Vietnam. Located in the Gulf of Tonkin, about seventy-five miles east of Mui Ron Ma in Ha Tinh Province, North Vietnam, Yankee Station was eighteen degrees above the equator. For sailors on a big steel ship sitting out in the water, Yankee Station guaranteed hot, humid days interrupted only by the occasional rainstorm. Captain Beling was glad to be there, having brought the *Forrestal* for her first days of combat ever, and his first day of combat as the commander of an aircraft carrier. Plus, there was the matter of upholding the honor of the navy's Atlantic Fleet. The carriers from the Pacific Fleet had been on Yankee Station for some time already, and now the new kid on the block was determined to show the other carriers what she could do. The *Forrestal* joined a number of other navy ships assigned to Yankee Station, including the aircraft carriers *Oriskany* and *Bon Homme Richard*. The carriers would cruise around the Yankee Station area almost constantly, rarely coming to a halt for any reason.

When the ship arrived at Yankee Station, Captain Beling was confident that his crew and his ship were ready for combat.

For the first four days on Yankee Station, all seemed well. Hundreds of planes were launched in those four days, the crew working fast and hard to meet the demands of high-tempo combat operations.

On their fourth day at Yankee Station, the crew started gearing up for what they knew would be a major air strike the next morning. Two launches were scheduled for the next day, making up the biggest air strike the *Forrestal* had launched so far. Though the specifics were not passed on to much of the crew, they learned enough to know that this one would really test their skills.

The pilots always knew a lot more about the missions than nearly anyone else on the ship, so twenty-year-old Rocky Pratt knew the target for the alpha strike was a rail line north of Hanoi. Pratt flew A-4 Skyhawks like Ken McMillen and John McCain, but he was not going out on the alpha strike the next day. Instead, he had been assigned to stay back on the ship and wait for others to report on "lucrative targets" they had spotted while on their missions. Instead of those pilots deviating from their flight plan, Pratt would take off and attack the targets they had spotted. Because he wasn't a primary pilot for the alpha strike, he had not attended the briefing for that mission. But by the time he meandered through the *Forrestal*'s big hangar bay that evening, he had spoken with his buddies enough to learn that the planes would hit a rail line—*hard*. He had marveled at how big the air strike was going to be, and he noted that his buddies were excited about the target. The rail line was just south of the Chinese border, in an area that previously was off-limits to air strikes. But now the *Forrestal* had been given the honor of plunging deep into the previously forbidden territory, with the aim of disrupting supply lines to the North Vietnamese. The way Pratt heard it, the plan was to lay bombs on the rail line itself, but also to lob bombs at a mountainside in hopes of causing an avalanche to cover the railroad. The planes were to carry thousand-pound bombs, bigger than the ones they usually carried on such raids.

Pratt was thinking about the mission as he entered the hangar bay, noticing right away that the carrier was taking on some sort of cargo from a supply ship alongside. The other ship was the *Diamond Head*, which had rendezvoused with the *Forrestal* to transfer four hundred tons of ammunition, including the thousand-pound bombs and other armaments for the big alpha strike the next morning. The two ships were cruising alongside each other with lines strung between them, their crews hoisting large wooden pallets stacked with bombs and rockets, cargo nets crammed with rocket fins and other nonexplosives, and box after box of other ammunition.

Pratt watched the transfer for a moment, the careful operation of the two ships always a wonder to anyone nearby, and he strolled past the big open hangar doors to get a better look at the ammunition ship and the operation. As he did, he could hear one of the ordnance officers pitching a fit. The officer was an older man, about fifty, whom Pratt knew casually, so he was curious about what had set him off so badly.

Pratt moved a little closer until he could hear what was going on.

"These are comp B bombs!" the older sailor yelled. "These are goddamn comp B bombs and they're old as hell. Why are we getting this shit?"

The ordnance officer was yelling at two other officers, and all three seemed upset at what they were seeing. Pratt didn't want to get involved in any trouble, and he didn't really know enough about weapons to be sure what all the fuss was about anyway, but he stepped in close enough to take a look at what the officers were yelling about. He saw bombs that looked like nothing he had ever seen before.

They were big and fat, thousand-pound bombs sometimes known as "fat boys" because of their appearance. They looked like the kind of bomb you saw falling out of World War II planes in old black-and-white movies, not the sleeker bombs he usually carried. He also noticed that the bombs were in wooden crates that looked very old, and some of the crates were even rotting. Pratt could read a stencil on one of the crates indicating the bombs had been manufactured in 1935.

Nineteen thirty-five? Geez, that's before I was born!

The older, seasoned sailor was growing red-faced with anger as he talked about how dangerous the bombs were.

"These damn things get real sensitive when they get old and start degrading like that," he said. By then, a group of sailors had gathered around to see what all the commotion was about. "Hell, they'll go off in a fire, and they'll go off just from a bad vibration. There's no telling what could set these damn things off."

The crew working on the arms transfer was used to handling bombs and other ammunition, so they knew the officer was saying that the bombs were far more sensitive than the other ones they used. In normal conditions, a bomb is not extremely sensitive to heat and vibration. In fact, the newer H-6 variety was designed to withstand high temperatures without blowing up at full strength. If exposed to a fire, they would melt and burn, or they might detonate at far less strength than intended. They wouldn't blow up at "high order," the way they were intended to blow up on a target, and they could be trusted to survive some length of time in a fire without any detonation at all.

But the old, decaying bombs sitting on the *Forrestal*'s hangar deck were an entirely different matter.

"Goddammit, these things get a lot more sensitive to heat when they get old like this," the officer explained to anyone close enough to hear. "A fire will sure as hell set them off, and I don't know if they can even take the vibration of a launch. The plane's damn catapult launch might set off the bombs right there."

The ordnance crew was beginning to understand why the officer was so upset, and Pratt was close behind. They were looking at a stack of bombs so old and faulty that nearly anything could set them off, and the blast would be enormous. And of course, the bombs weren't sitting safely in a warehouse somewhere. They had just been delivered to a ship where it was nearly impossible to keep them from exposure to the kind of things that could set them off unexpectedly.

The officer was getting livid, and others in the hangar bay were noticing the commotion. The men working under him were getting scared to handle the bombs, and several suggested tossing them over the side of the ship. The officer considered that option for a moment but then said no. He wasn't sure he could authorize jettisoning ordnance like that without being sure there was an immediate danger. He *was* sure the damn things were dangerous, but making his case with the higher-ups was a different matter. Clearly, the navy had sent these old bombs because the *Forrestal* needed them for its mission the next day. The officer knew that the navy had been short of ordnance for the past couple of years, making it hard to carry out its bombing raids in Vietnam. Throwing these bombs over might make them short on thousand-pound bombs the next morning, and *he* would have to explain why.

The weapons officers passed word on to Captain Beling that the bombs were too dangerous to keep, and he radioed over to the *Diamond Head* to straighten things out.

"Take these damn things back and give us something we can use," Beling told the *Diamond Head* captain. "Sorry, can't do that," the *Diamond Head* skipper replied. "That's all we have for you."

Beling was angry, but he had orders to carry out the next day and he couldn't do the job without thousand-pound bombs. He'd have to keep the damn things, but he wasn't happy about it.

In the hangar bay, the situation didn't look right to Pratt either, but this wasn't his business. He moved on as the men continued arguing. One of the last things he heard as he walked away was one of the ordnance officers saying, "These goddamn things are not going down in my weapons storage!"

Pratt was curious about the incident, but he had no intention of pursuing it. As a pilot, he didn't get involved in much that didn't directly involve his airplane, and he certainly wasn't an expert at weapons handling. But when he bumped into the ordnance officer later that night, he was still curious about what he had seen. They were friendly enough that Pratt could bring it up and ask why everyone had been so upset.

"Rocky, did you look at those bombs?" the man replied, starting to get agitated all over again.

"Yeah, they looked weird," Pratt said. "What were they?"

"Those are old comp B bombs. Composition B."

"Well, what's that?" Pratt asked, still not seeing what was so wrong.

"Rocky, they don't make those bombs anymore. The H-6 bombs were built and designed to replace comp B. They're a different type of explosive."

"Yeah, I didn't think they looked like what we usually carry."

"Did you notice that they're banded bombs? You have to put a band around it to hang the damn thing on the airplane!"

"What does that mean?" Pratt asked.

"That is World War Two. Those things have come off an ammunition dump somewhere. They should have been disposed of, and somehow or another here they are in the damn system. And we don't know what to do with them."

"So that's what all the excitement was about? You wanted newer bombs?"

"Rocky, composition B was *very dangerous*," he explained, more than a hint of impatience in his voice. "Did you notice that it was dripping?"

"No."

"Well, if you had looked you would have seen a few spots on the deck. The stuff drips as it ages. That's dangerous because it's a fire hazard. Number two, composition B becomes sensitive to heat and sensitive to vibration when it ages, and it becomes more powerful."

The ordnance officer went on to explain that the old bombs could increase their explosive power by 50 percent under the right circumstances, meaning the thousand-pound bomb could explode with the force of a fifteen-hundred-pound bomb. A huge explosion. That's fine if it blows up on target, but not if it blows up on the ship, he said.

"Did you see the markings on those things?" he asked Pratt. "I know you're not going to believe me, but those dates . . . Damn it, one or two of them were dated 1935! And I know the rest of them have to be nearly that old. They've been sitting in some goddamn disposal area in a weapons depot all this time. They shouldn't be on this ship. That's what the argument was about."

Pratt had gotten the message, and he was concerned. Even if he wouldn't go out with those bombs strapped underneath him tomorrow, his buddies might.

"Well, what the hell are they going to do with them?" Pratt asked.

"I'm not sure. One group wanted to wheel them right across the hangar deck and throw them off the other side of the ship. But I don't know, they're going to need all the big stuff for that strike tomorrow, so it looks like we're keeping them. The captain talked to the skipper of the ammunition ship and they said that was all they had to give us. The captain didn't seem real happy about it, but he said we just have to keep the stuff.

"The weapons officers wouldn't let them down in the magazines with everything else, so they're moving it all topside and just storing it out on the deck."

The conversation upset Pratt, but he still wasn't sure if he had any role to play in the problem. He wondered if he should get involved by telling his superiors, but then he saw the ordnance officer again that same night. This time, some of his fears were allayed.

"Well, it looks like they've decided these things won't go off from the vibration of the catapult shot, so they're going to put them on that big launch tomorrow. We'll just get rid of them as fast as we can."

The ordnance officer seemed less upset, resigned to having the bombs on board for as short a time as possible. Pratt took his word that the bombs would be fine stored up on the flight deck. Hey, with those things, his buddies might have a good shot at bringing that mountainside down tomorrow.

Pratt settled down for the evening, and many of the rest of the ship's crew joined him. There were still men working all over the ship, as there always were at night, and some of the crew were still finishing up the ammunition transfer from the *Diamond Head*. Once the four hundred tons of ammunition was all on board, it still had to be put away, so those men would not be able to call it a night for quite a while. But for a lot of the crew, the day's work had come to an end and they were settling down for a late-night snack, maybe even a game of cards before they hit their bunks and fell asleep.

For others working late into the night, they would not be able to hit their bunks until much later, 2 A.M. for some. Once they did, they fell asleep quickly, exhausted from the night's hard work. Most of them would have to get up early the next morning for the big air strike, so the few hours of sleep were precious.

At 3:15 A.M., the quiet throughout most of the ship was shattered by the man-overboard alarm. Every single man had to get up and assemble in his division for a head count, standing in his underwear or whatever he could throw on, half asleep and barely standing erect. They had done this a hundred times before, but it was especially maddening when it happened in the middle of the night. The men were held in assembly for more than an hour as the division heads counted repeatedly to determine if anyone was missing. Others throughout the ship had to scramble to their stations to aid in the rescue attempt.

One man was missing. Word spread quickly that this was no false alarm, which shook some of the men out of their stupor. After a while, they heard that the man had been spotted in the water but not recovered. That immediately spawned questions. Why couldn't they pick him up? It was nearly dawn before the men were allowed to return to their bunks and try to get some sleep. They went back to sleep, but many were bothered by the sudden loss of a shipmate. Most didn't know the man, or even know who he was, but they knew they had lost their first life on Yankee Station.

They cared because he was a fellow sailor, and they cared because it just as easily could have been one of them. It also was a bad omen, a lousy way to start their long deployment on Yankee Station.

Chapter 7

FIRE ON THE FLIGHT DECK!

The morning of Saturday, July 29, 1967, began early for some of the men, but not all. Even though two launches were scheduled for that morning, much of the ship's crew was given the unusual permission to sleep a bit later than usual to make up for all the late hours. The ammunition transfer had been hard work for much of the crew, and the man overboard had kept anyone from getting rest in the late-night period when the bulk of the crew was off duty. Even on an aircraft carrier where men work around the clock and long days are nothing unusual, the officers still tried to compensate if the crew had been put through an extended period without rest.

A nice gesture, but it didn't help Ed Roberts any. Flight quarters, the call rousting the crew to begin preparations for the day's launches, was sounded at 4 A.M. Roberts and Gary Shaver were already awake, never having gotten back to sleep after the man-overboard alarm. As soon as they heard the alarm, they knew they wouldn't get any more sleep. By the time flight quarters sounded, Roberts had already dressed and started making his way to the flight deck. He was groggy as hell, regretting his decision last night to eat dinner before going to bed. He could have had an extra hour's sleep.

Roberts joined Shaver and the rest of the crew on the flight deck, working in the dark for a long time, testing the catapults and arresting gear, waiting for the sun to rise over the horizon and bring them closer to another full day of combat.

Bob Shelton was on the coffee-break area outside the bridge, still trying to settle down from his second night of sleep interrupted by the nightmare. He was badly shaken and waiting for the sun to rise. Shelton was looking over the sea with a coffee cup in his hand when his buddy James Blaskis appeared.

"Hey man, how's it going?" Blaskis asked, cheerful as usual. Then he saw Shelton's face and gave him a quizzical look. "Geez, what's wrong with you? You look like hell."

Shelton nodded his head and said he wasn't surprised, that he hadn't slept much at all in the past two nights.

"Yeah, that man overboard. I hear they didn't find the guy either."

"Even after that," Shelton said. "I . . . I just couldn't sleep. That's all."

Shelton was still thinking about the nightmare and wondering why he suddenly had such a problem. But he didn't want to discuss it with anybody, not even Blaskis. Too weird.

"Well, almost eight o'clock, about time to go. Where are you today?" Blaskis said.

"I'm in port aft," Shelton said, referring to the port-after steering compartment in the belly of the ship. "Guess I better get going . . ." And then he realized that he was wearing his white uniform as if he were going to work on the bridge that day. He'd put on the wrong uniform and never realized it until then.

"Yeah, I thought you might be. I'm supposed to be on the bridge. Wanna trade?"

Shelton hesitated and Blaskis asked again. "C'mon, you've already got the whites on."

Shelton agreed and he could see that Blaskis was happy to have a quiet day ahead of him instead of working on the bridge. He must have been pretty confident he could make the trade, too, because he was wearing his denim work clothes.

Blaskis called out goodbye to Shelton as he hustled down the ladder, the first of many on his long trip to the port-after steering compartment. As he left, Shelton could see that he had a paperback book shoved in his back pocket.

Shelton was still bleary-eyed, but it was time to go to work. The rest of the ship was getting busy too. On the *Forrestal*'s fifth day in the Vietnam War, the first air strike had been launched at 7 A.M., and that meant that the air crews, pilots, and flight deck crews had made an early start. The second launch was scheduled for 11 A.M. This was the mission Rocky Pratt had heard about the night before, the big assault on the rail line that would require launching most of the *Forrestal*'s planes as quickly as possible.

The mission needed heavy firepower, so the ordnance crews loaded the old composition B bombs that came aboard the night before—anything to get rid of the dangerous ordnance. If all went well, the old bombs would be off the ship by 11:30 A.M. and wreaking havoc over Vietnam. The pilots were never told they would be carrying old World War II–era bombs that were so unstable they scared the dickens out of the *Forrestal*'s ordnance crew.

The day promised to be a beautiful one on the sea, reaching eighty-seven degrees Fahrenheit by midmorning, with 74 percent humidity and calm seas. Cloud cover was scattered at two thousand feet, and once the sun rose, the sailors could see for ten miles. The sea was glassy, as flat and calm as a mountain lake.

All indications were that the *Forrestal* would serve another relatively uneventful day launching and retrieving airplanes in this, its fifth day of combat in its entire history. The previous days' operations had gone smoothly and today's operations shouldn't be any different. Still, the crew knew that nothing on an aircraft carrier was routine or certain.

The ship was set at material condition Yoke, a midpoint status required by the fact that air strikes were being prepared. If the ship were to completely stand down, material condition would be set at X, meaning that the ship is essentially "open" with free access throughout the ship for authorized personnel to travel from one area to another. When the ship was set at material condition Yoke, certain hatches and passageways were closed off as a protective measure so that the ship could be compartmentalized quickly in an emergency and any problems could be isolated. In a worst-case scenario, the ship could go to condition Zebra, sealing off most of the ship into tight portions that help compartmentalize fire, water, and dangerous gases.

A number of other navy ships in the area were providing support or conducting their own activities that morning on Yankee Station. The USS *Oriskany* and the USS *Bon Homme Richard,* two aircraft carriers, were nearby, as were the destroyers USS *Mackenzie, Rupertus,* and *Tucker,* and a number of other smaller vessels. The ammunition ship USS *Diamond Head* was still at Yankee Station after supplying the *Forrestal* with arms for the day's air strikes. Yankee Station was a central work area for navy ships supporting air strikes in North Vietnam and other land-based activities, so a number of ships were always in the area. Once in a while Roberts would look out toward the rising sun and see a ship's silhouette.

Shaver was on the flight deck with Roberts, but Shaver wasn't doing his usual job. He had broken his hand earlier in an accident when he and some other crew were lifting a piece of equipment on the flight deck. His hand was caught between the equipment and a railing, and severely crushed. Dr. Kirchner in the sick bay had put a cast on the hand and then Shaver was reassigned to duties he could perform with limited use of the hand. On this Saturday, he was working with the crash crew, ready to respond in an emergency, and he also was driving one of the tractors that helped start the planes. As he worked that morning, Shaver noticed that some of the bombs looked unusual.

Damn things look like antiques, he thought. *Those things look old as hell.* But ordnance wasn't his job. So what the hell. Work to do.

Roberts was in a foul mood already, angry that he'd gotten so little sleep the night before and feeling like he'd been on the flight deck for days without a break. He knew how tired he was and he knew that put him at risk for an accident, so he tried hard to concentrate. Just recently, before Shaver broke his hand, the two of them had witnessed a grisly accident on the flight deck. Shaver was directing an F-4 Phantom onto a catapult when someone frantically signaled him to stop the plane. The man normally didn't have anything to do with plane movement, so Shaver was puzzled at first. When the man continued his frantic signaling, Shaver ordered the pilot to stop and signaled for the wheels to be chocked.

That's when he noticed crew running toward the rear of the plane, on the other side, out of Shaver's view. He felt a knot in his stomach as he saw crew members with white shirts and red crosses running toward the plane. When he stepped around to see what was wrong, Shaver saw a red shirt on the deck. While working on the ordnance hanging from the plane's wing, trying to make the last-minute adjustments so the plane could be launched quickly, the man's red shirt had become snagged on a rocket-mounting bracket. The plane continued to move forward, and the man was pulled off his feet. The man was dragging helplessly as the plane continued forward, and in his thrashing to free himself, one of his feet got caught under the plane's wheel. No one could hear the man's screams over the deafening sounds of the flight deck. Before anyone could react, the plane had rolled all the way up his leg and one side of his body.

Shaver was horrified. Blood was everywhere and Shaver could even see that the man had bitten through his tongue. Shaver suddenly realized that he had directed the plane forward and over the man's body. He took a few steps back, then ran behind the island and fell to his knees, vomiting on the deck. Falling forward, he pounded on the deck in a rage, so upset that he couldn't go back to work that day.

Roberts had also seen the accident up close and the image stuck with him. Now, as he worked to prepare the 7 A.M. strike, he knew the same thing could happen to him if he wasn't careful as he put the chocks under the wheels of aircraft. He had to be alert, no matter how crappy he felt.

There was another big reason Roberts was in a bad mood. Just a few weeks after shipping out on the *Forrestal,* Roberts had received a Dear John letter from his girl back home.

After finishing his work on one plane, Roberts was walking back to another when he saw a couple of crew members writing messages on a bomb hanging under a plane's wing. An old tradition, the messages usually were some sort of taunting toward the enemy. One of the crew was finishing up his message: "Suck on this, Ho Chi Minh!"

Roberts walked over and asked if he could borrow the chalk. With his greasy, gloved fingers, he carefully wrote out "Fuck you Janet."

The 7 A.M. launch proceeded with no problem. By 7:50 A.M., thirty-seven aircraft were launched against North Vietnam, and while the crew waited for the planes to return, they began preparations for the second launch, scheduled for 11 A.M. Roberts and the rest of his team of blue shirts had just finished positioning a plane on one of the catapults and were waiting over by the island for their next task. Their crew leader came over, motioning for them to crowd in closer to hear him. He shouted over the plane noise.

"Do you guys want to break for chow now?"

Roberts and the other crew were surprised because their team didn't usually take a break for another hour. Crew 4 usually went to chow first, but Roberts's crew leader explained that the other team wanted to switch for some reason. Didn't matter to Roberts or his fellow crew members. They shrugged their shoulders and headed off. Roberts was glad to get out of the noise and the wind, not to mention the stench of the fuel and exhaust. They filed around the island structure to the hatch that led them below, walking single file. As they went below, they stopped in their "coffee locker" to stow their gear. The locker was a small area with a coffee urn, used as a general break area and a place to hang your helmet and gloves. As they tossed their gear aside, Roberts pulled a cigarette out of his pocket and then pulled out his lighter. He snapped open the Zippo and sparked the lighter in one smooth move, a motion meant to look so utterly casual but one he'd practiced over and over when no one was looking. Unfortunately, the lighter didn't ignite, causing a few of his buddies to chuckle.

"Damn thing's out of fluid," he said. It probably wasn't, he realized, but he had to save face. "Better see if I can get some av-gas."

Roberts headed down the passageway to one of the fueling stations, where big black hoses were used to pump aviation fuel, or av-gas, up to the flight deck. Checking first to see if any of the purple shirt fuel guys were around, Roberts unreeled a couple feet of hose and squeezed it enough to make a few drops flow from the nozzle and into his lighter. Then he headed back to the coffee locker, where a few guys were still waiting before heading to chow. He started to head out with them, but he was so tired he decided a little sleep was better than food.

"Hey, Dan," he called out to one guy. "I'm not going to chow. I'm going to get some sleep back here in the fuel station. Wake me up when you get back, okay?"

Dan said he would, so Roberts turned around and went to the fuel station again. He stretched out on the floor there, resting his head on his arm and his headgear, and quickly fell asleep.

As 11 A.M. approached, some of the crew belowdecks were just getting into their day because of the late start. Ken Killmeyer had gone to breakfast and then went to pick up the day's mail for his division.

He returned to his berthing quarters, passed it out to the men in his division who were still there, and then stashed the rest to distribute later. Killmeyer's assignment for the morning was dull and laborious, like a great many of the jobs on board an aircraft carrier. While the glamorous work was being done up on the flight deck, Killmeyer was far below cleaning his division's berthing compartment. But before he got to that, he had to read his mail. Killmeyer had received a letter from his six-year-old sister Patty back home in Pittsburgh, and he immediately sat down to write her back.

Like so many others who had worked the night shift and were on their rest period, Gary Pritchard and Paul Friedman were sound asleep in their bunks, ignoring the constant cacophony that would wake anyone who wasn't used to sleeping with airplanes landing on a metal deck just feet above his head.

Captain Beling was still in his stateroom preparing to address the crew about the previous night's activities. Other officers usually handled the preparations for a launch and then Beling would step onto the bridge just before the planes were ready to go. The captain had been on the bridge for the launch of the aircraft in the 7 A.M. strike, but he then retired to his nearby sea cabin before resuming the rest of his working day. He was nearby and ready to take command if necessary, but Captain Beling wanted to take advantage of the lull between flight operations to address the crew about the previous night's man overboard. Losing a man overboard was particularly frustrating for Beling because it was always an unnecessary, wasted loss of life. Some purpose might be found in losing a man to combat or an unavoidable accident, but losing a man overboard was inexcusable for Beling.

As work continued on the flight deck and throughout the ship, Beling's voice got the crew's attention through the 1MC, the public-address system that penetrates every part of the ship. Killmeyer paused when he heard the 1MC crackle to life, putting down the letter he was writing home.

Beling began with the three words that he always used when addressing the crew.

"Men of *Forrestal*, this is the captain. As you know, we just launched our midmorning strike. Pretty soon we will be recovering some of our aircraft. But right now, I want to talk to you about something very, very serious. It is what happened and why it happened, that man overboard that we had early this morning at 3:15 A.M. At that time, a man named Warren saw someone fall overboard from elevator number one, which at that time was at the hangar-deck level. A few seconds later, the alert starboard lifeboat watch, two of them, saw a man in the water. Without hesitation, they threw in a life ring and notified the bridge.

"The life ring had a light attached to it and they put it in the water about twenty yards from the man and heard him shout for attention the word 'Hey!' The starboard quarter watch ran next; a seaman in Fourth Division also was alert. He didn't happen to see the man, but he did see the life ring and the light that was alertly thrown from the bridge. Within minutes HC-2 number twelve [a helicopter], piloted by Lieutenant Gregory, was launched. *Forrestal* maneuvered into position for rescue and stopped dead in the water about five hundred yards from the man's spotted position. A very black night."

Killmeyer listened carefully to the captain's story. Even way down in the port-after steering compartment, Blaskis put down his book to listen. They were curious to learn exactly what happened the night before, and why the man was not recovered.

"There were two destroyers in company, the *Rupertus* and the *Tucker*. They came in close to help. It took the helo about thirty minutes, with the destroyers' help and the ship's help, to find the man in the water. The helo then maneuvered into position over him for rescue and then lowered its rescue seat. The man involved grabbed the seat. However, as the seat was raised just a little bit, a foot or two or three, the man immediately lost his grip and disappeared into the water. *Forrestal* remained on the scene with the two destroyers until daybreak and departed without finding him. We have left the *Tucker* to continue searching. However, there is in my judgment no chance whatsoever that this man will be found.

"Now by taking our muster and subsequent close checking, we have established who the unfortunate individual is. It is Seaman Dyke of the First Division.

"Now some of the rest of this. Seaman Dyke fell from number-one elevator. At this time he was not assigned to the working party on that elevator. Accordingly, he had no business there. Second, three other shipmates appear to have been engaged in horseplay. The man, who must remain at this time nameless, who was fooling around with Dyke was observed to have made a punching motion at him, fooling around. Dyke backed up, lost his balance, and fell over the side.

"Now the rest of this is that horseplay cannot be conducted anywhere at all on a ship like this. It is all very well to give your life for your country, but it is not very smart to foolishly fall over the side.

"On a ship like this there are dangers on every side, and unless one keeps his eyes open and thinks ahead a little bit, we are going to have much more of these needless losses. Let's play heads-up ball and our losses then, if any, will come from the enemy, not from ourselves."

The 1MC fell silent again, and throughout the ship men went back to what they had been doing. The captain's address had captured everyone's attention, partly because it was the first time that most of the crew had gotten the whole story on the man overboard. Word had passed quickly that the man was not recovered, but most of the crew did not know until Beling's address who was lost, or how it happened. Some of the crew were not content with the explanation that the man could not be recovered; they wondered why the helicopter crew did not send a swimmer in to pick up the man, who would have been weak and probably hypothermic after thirty minutes in the night sea.

The planes from the first air strike were recovered without incident and then the deck was configured to launch the second air strike. Because an aircraft-carrier deck is both huge and tiny at the same time, depending on what you're trying to do with it, preparing a launch always required a great deal of planning and meticulous positioning of aircraft. To get all the planes launched as quickly as possible, so that all of the air strike's planes were up at once, the deck crew positioned planes around the edges of the flight deck to go through all the start-up sequences and safety checks that were necessary before flight. Then each plane was taxied forward to one of the four catapults for launch.

John McCain, Jim Bangert, and the twenty-five other pilots were ordered to their aircraft at 10:25 A.M., climbing into their cockpits with the aid of their crews and then proceeding with the sequential steps necessary to get a jet engine up to speed. As the pilots worked in the cockpit, dozens of crew were working around the aircraft to load bombs and missiles, conduct safety checks, and perform various other duties. The flight deck was a sea of colored shirts, with sailors maneuvering around aircraft and other equipment in the deliberate motion designed to avoid the many dangers lurking everywhere on deck. The sound was deafening as twenty-seven jet planes were readied for takeoff.

At 10:46 A.M., moving along at a brisk twenty-seven knots—about thirty-one miles per hour—the *Forrestal* turned so that the pilots would have enough wind over the flight deck to provide lift. The total wind speed over the flight deck was thirty-two knots, blowing from forward to aft of the ship, the equivalent of a thirty-seven-mile-per-hour wind.

Before the 11 A.M. launch of the attack planes, the deck crew launched a KA-3B tanker plane. This was standard procedure for any air-strike launch; tanker planes were always put in the air first so the attack planes could refuel as necessary. This enabled the fighters and bombers to take off with less weight and to fly longer missions than would be possible on just their initial fuel stores. An EA-1F Skyraider was also launched to provide electronic countermeasures that would help protect the other planes.

By 10:51 A.M., all of the flight crews had manned their aircraft and some of the planes had been started. Another KA-3B fuel tanker was being readied for launch, as was an E-2A Hawkeye, a prop plane with a large rotating dish on top that would be used for monitoring the attack planes' flights.

The pilots were in the final stages of their preflight tasks. Bangert was in the forward cockpit of his F-4 Phantom jet. He'd just started his starboard engine and was about to switch from external to internal electrical power. Bangert was a seasoned pilot, so much so that he was the senior landing-signal officer (LSO) for the carrier air wing, a position that made him responsible for guiding other pilots on their carrier-deck landings and also for issuing a grade on each landing. His mission for the 11 A.M. launch was to suppress any ground targets providing anti-aircraft flak. Lawrence McKay would be riding in the second seat behind Bangert, acting as the radio intercept officer.

Bangert was informed five minutes before climbing into his aircraft that he would be carrying Zuni rockets rather than the 2.75-inch rockets more commonly used by the F-4 Phantom. Bangert had never flown with Zuni rockets, and during the five days the *Forrestal* was in combat, only 3 aircraft out of 379 planes launched with ordnance had carried Zuni rockets. The change was spurred by some technical problems that made it difficult to load the 2.75-inch rockets on the Phantom, which had been flown just that morning on the 7 A.M. strike and had come back with a five-hundred-pound bomb that had not disengaged properly. The commanding officer of the air wing briefed Bangert about a few flight procedures that needed to be altered because of the Zuni rockets—such as changing the target-sight settings—but apparently the Zuni rockets did not alter the original flight plan much. The MK-32 Zuni rocket could be used by naval aviators for a variety of tasks because of its versatility in both air-to-air and air-to-ground applications. For missions over North Vietnam, it was used almost exclusively against ground targets, often in an effort to suppress antiaircraft fire. Various types of warheads and fuses were installed on the Zuni, depending on the desired effect. On Bangert's plane that morning, the Zuni rockets were equipped with VT proximity fuses that caused them to detonate at treetop level. That made them effective against ground troops, whereas other fuse and warhead configurations could detonate the warhead on contact with a target, or as a "bunker buster" with a delayed-action fuse to detonate the explosive below the surface. At about six and a half feet long and five inches in diameter, the Zuni was long and sleek. Fins on the tail of the rocket were folded into the body until it was fired, and then they popped out to provide aerodynamic stability. Unguided once it was ignited, the Zuni was basically a point-and-shoot type of weapon. The rocket used a solid propellant that burned for about 1.5 seconds. Produced in Belgium, millions of Zuni rockets were fired in combat in Vietnam and in other conflicts.

Only two months earlier, a Zuni rocket had misfired from an F-8A Crusader on the aircraft carrier *Hancock*. Several crewmen near the plane were burned by the rocket launch, but the Zuni did not hit any-thing on the deck and caused no serious damage.

Bangert's plane was outfitted with twenty-four Zuni rockets, two Sidewinder missiles, and two Sparrow III missiles. The other aircraft on the flight deck were loaded with a variety of weapons, including Shrike and Sidewinder missiles, and many of the bombs that had been transferred to the *Forrestal* the night before.

In all, the planes sitting on the deck were loaded with sixteen of the old, World War II—era bombs weighing 1,000 pounds each, four newer bombs weighing 750 pounds each, and sixty newer bombs weighing 500 pounds each, in addition to missiles, rockets, and twenty-millimeter ammunition. There also were 150 tons of bombs and missiles sitting on the deck on pallets, and more below in storage.

Bangert's Phantom was positioned on the starboard side, at the extreme aft portion of the flight deck, with six more Phantoms parked to his right along the edge of the deck. Looking at the flight deck from overhead, this put Bangert's plane at the extreme lower right of the long flight deck, pointing across the deck at about a forty-five-degree angle. Other planes were positioned along the other deck edges, wingtip to wingtip, with a few looking straight up the flight deck toward the front of the ship, and others across the deck from Bangert, pointing back almost in his direction. The effect was to have the ship's deck ringed in planes, with an open space in the middle so that individual planes could be moved out and then forward to the catapults for launch. In addition, a dozen other planes were bunched up just aft of the island structure and on the two elevators in that area. Those planes included a KA-3B Sky Warrior fuel tanker loaded with twenty-eight thousand pounds of JP5 jet fuel.

Most of the jets on board required an external power source to start them up. Shaver was driving one of the tractors that help start the planes, and he had been working at the very rear of the flight deck before being called to help with some planes farther forward. As he drove his tractor forward, he passed his good friend Lonnie Hudson on a tractor going in the opposite direction. Gary Shaver's tractor had the longer hose needed by the RA-5C Vigilantes that were forward, so he knew that Hudson was going back to do the F-4 Phantoms at the rear. They were swapping places.

As they passed each other, Hudson nodded his head and gestured at Shaver as if to say, "Hey, what's up?" Shaver responded with a friendly shrug of the shoulders and moved on. He had no idea that switching positions with his friend Lonnie would turn out to be such a pivotal moment.

Bangert's plane was being readied by still another crewman in a squat, bright yellow tractor. He hooked up his tractor to the plane's electrical system and hit the juice when Bangert gave him the signal. The crewman then sat back on his tractor and watched Bangert go through the rest of the preflight preparations, much of which involved coordinating his cockpit checks with the crew outside arming his plane with the missiles.

Two of the crew members working with Bangert's plane were busy checking the missiles and rockets to ensure that they were properly installed and that the systems were safe. One man began conducting stray voltage checks on the weapons systems, to make sure the electrical system was not malfunctioning in a way that could accidentally trigger the weapons. He found no stray voltage in any of the systems on the port side and then went to the starboard side to conduct the same tests. Having found no stray voltage or other potential problems with the weapons systems, he plugged in the "pigtails," cable connectors that linked the rockets and the plane's launching device. This was the short-cut approved by the ship's administration for the sake of speed. Plugging in the pigtails armed the weapons on the port side.

At 10:51:21 A.M., Bangert had just started his starboard engine. With the engine running, Bangert reached out to press the button that would switch from the external cart's power supply to the plane's internal system. As his gloved finger hit the button, Bangert and McKay both felt a mild explosion shake the plane. Bangert looked up in time to see a small rocket flying across the deck with a yellow-orange exhaust flame.

Oh my God, what was that? Was that from my plane? Frantically, Bangert immediately rechecked all his weapons switches and found that they were in the proper position. *I couldn't have fired a rocket! What happened?*

All over the deck, other pilots who had glimpsed the missile's path were frantically checking their own cockpit systems. They all shared that heart-stopping moment of uncertainty, the blood draining from their faces as they looked to see if they were responsible. None of the pilots found their switches out of place. An electrical surge had fired the rocket on Bangert's plane without anyone hitting a firing switch.

The single Zuni rocket had fired from one of the three launchers installed on the port wing of Bangert's F-4 Phantom. Ironically, Bangert was the safety officer Rocky Pratt had consulted about the pigtail shortcut, the officer who said there was nothing to be done about the safety risk.

In an instant, the firing of the rocket initiated a long journey of pain. Two crew members were kneeling under the port wing of Bangert's Phantom when the rocket fired. The one who was checking the weapons systems was burned on the left side of his face, left hand, and his wrist, and he felt like his jersey was on fire even though there were no flames. Several other crewmen working around the Phantom were knocked down by the rocket launch, which happened so quickly that no one actually saw the rocket leave the plane. They all looked back at the Phantom to see smoke rising from one of the rocket pods on the port wing, and small bits of debris fluttering in the wind.

The rocket was flying across the deck at chest height, at hundreds of miles per hour, headed toward a fuel chief who was standing just behind the number-four arresting wire, pretty much in the middle of the deck between Bangert's plane and those parked on the other side of the ship. He was knocked off his feet by the rocket as it passed without touching him.

Another sailor on deck was much less fortunate. An ordnanceman, he was walking along the flight deck in front of a group of A-4 Skyhawks when the Zuni rocket hit him in the shoulder, passing through and instantly severing his arm but leaving him standing.

The rocket then continued on, its course altered to the right by the collision with the ordnanceman. Having traveled about one hundred feet, the rocket then struck the A-4 Skyhawk piloted by John McCain. Like most pilots, McCain was a bit superstitious, and his parachute rigger, Tom Ott, a crewman responsible for the pilot's equipment, had begun a little preflight routine. Ott was carefully wiping McCain's helmet visor clean before handing it to him in the cockpit. This was to make sure McCain could get a clear look at the antiaircraft missiles coming at him over North Vietnam, but the act had taken on more significance over time. It had become an important gesture of friendship, a reassuring, last-minute favor for a pilot who was about to risk his life in combat. Ott had just wiped the visor clean and handed the helmet back to McCain, and then Ott shut the plane's canopy.

Ott gave McCain a thumbs-up signal, and McCain probably returned it with a smile that Ott could not see under the pilot's face mask. That was the last time McCain ever saw Ott.

Nearby, Robert Zwerlein was getting McCain's plane outfitted and ready to move forward to the catapults. Standing just a few feet away, he was focused on the plane and never saw the rocket fire on the other side of the deck.

McCain felt a huge impact as the Zuni rocket tore through his plane on the right side and exited the left side, ripping open his fuel tank with four hundred gallons of JP5 jet fuel. Two crewmen nearby were set on fire as the hot rocket exhaust passed by them. They were already rushing forward toward the island before the jet fuel spreading over the deck ignited.

Just below the flight deck at the very rear of the ship, Edmond McGrew was on man-overboard watch, keeping his eyes trained on the water in his sector, looking for anyone who had fallen overboard. As McGrew watched the water on the port side of the ship, another sailor had joined him on the fantail for a cigarette. Now they both saw the Zuni rocket hit the water on the port side, never exploding. They could tell that the object was not a man overboard, but they had no idea what it was.

The fuel poured out of McCain's torn plane, spreading to the rear of the ship rapidly as it was pushed not only by the thirty-seven-mile-per-hour wind but by the exhausts of at least three jets positioned immediately in front of McCain's plane. The jet fuel was ignited soon by fragments of burning rocket propellant, but there was a delay of a second or so as the fuel spilled from the plane, giving some crew members enough time to realize the danger they were in. With a sudden, deafening "whoomp!" sound, the fuel ignited and soon engulfed all of the A-4 Skyhawks parked on the port side. In a heartbeat, scores of men were in a horrible situation. Some men, like Robert Zwerlein, were doomed by their close proximity to the initial fire. As the fire flashed, he had no chance to escape and was caught in the blaze.

The pilots strapped inside their planes needed help to get out. As they looked out of their canopies, they saw nothing but flames and black smoke, which was so thick that some of them could not see well enough to tell what awaited them if they opened their canopies. And others who could see knew that they were surrounded by a burning lake of jet fuel. In that instant, dozens of crewmen around those planes found themselves soaked in burning jet fuel. Several men stumbled out of the fire scene, covered head to toe in flames. One pilot jumped out of his plane and made his way out of the fire, his entire flight suit in flames. Once he got out of the fire and headed toward safety, he inexplicably turned around and walked back into the fire. Probably disoriented, he disappeared into the heart of the fire and never came back out.

The fire had erupted so quickly that no one had a chance to warn those on the rear portion of the deck to run toward the safety of the center deck and the island structure. The men trapped in the fire had little or no opportunity to escape the huge fireball that grew ever larger as the fuel poured out of the planes, each one adding hundreds of gallons of fuel to the fire.

The rocket's flight was almost caught on film by the plat camera, a television camera located on the island structure. The plat camera was used to record all flight-deck operations for future study, and also to provide images of flight-deck activities to monitors throughout the ship. When the rocket and the subsequent fire caught the camera operator's eye, he was focused farther forward on a plane about to be launched off a catapult. He immediately swung the camera back to the rear of the ship and trained it on the fire, where it remained for hours, but he missed the actual launch of the rocket. The camera operator had to abandon his post after a while because of shrapnel penetrating the space, but the camera continued to record the events. Later analysis of the film showed the reflection of the rocket in a window as it traveled across the deck.

Aviation machinist's mate Robert Mitchell was on routine patrol in his temporary duties with the master of arms that day, and he had stopped by the plat-camera location to watch some of the flight-deck operations as the 11 A.M. launch approached. Mitchell was watching one of the monitors in the area when he saw a flash on the screen and immediately felt a concussion of the ship. When the plat-camera operator swung around and showed the aft portion of the flight deck in flames, Mitchell hastily headed toward the master of arms's office.

He knew the fire was immediately above the office, and his friends there probably didn't know the danger they were in. He hurried down the island structure to the hangar bay below and then sprinted to warn them, himself rushing into an area that would soon be in extreme danger. He was constantly shouting "Fire on the flight deck!" as he was running, to alert everyone he saw. Having seen the magnitude of the fire with his own eyes, Mitchell was not waiting for orders to act.

On the level just below the flight deck, Airman Charles Price was in the squadron storeroom and had just finished his duties in preparing the VA-46 squadron for the 11 A.M. launch. At 10:51, just before the accident and before any alarms sounded over the 1MC, Price informed the other squadron members that he'd finished his work in preparing the launch and was going to go to lunch. To get to the mess hall, Price left the squadron storeroom and went to a catwalk that runs along the port side of the ship and up to the flight deck. Price climbed four steps up the ladder leading to the flight-deck level and was facing the front of the ship when he heard a sudden whoosh as the jet fuel erupted. Price turned around toward the sound and found himself facing a wall of flame.

Near the number-two arresting wire on the rear portion of the flight deck, close to McCain's plane, crewman G. L. Reynolds was making a visual check of the aircraft starts in the A-4 Skyhawks lined up on the port side. The warrant officer in charge of the planes, Donald Hugo, was nearby and about to make a check of his headset communications with Reynolds. Both had their backs to the McCain plane, so neither saw the rocket hit, but at that instant, they both heard the fuel erupt and felt a massive shock wave from the explosion. They turned around to see McCain's Skyhawk in flames and men running away from the fire. They also saw others crawling away, their clothes and bodies on fire. Instead of running away from the obvious danger, Reynolds and Hugo both rushed toward the planes on the port side to "break down" the aircraft by releasing the chains and chocks holding them in place. If the pilots were to have any chance at maneuvering the planes out of harm's way, someone had to release them first. After releasing several planes, Reynolds directed one to taxi forward and away from McCain's plane. Hugo then rushed to the rear to help with the initial firefighting efforts.

Overhead, Leonard Eiland was at the controls of Angel 20, the helicopter flying "plane guard" for the 11 A.M. launch. The *Forrestal*'s helicopters were out of commission for the morning because of scheduled maintenance, so the aircraft carrier *Oriskany* had sent Angel 20 as a loan for the morning. For any aircraft launch, navy regulations require a helicopter to be circling in the air near the ship and ready to rescue any fliers who go down. Most days, it meant just flying in circles until the launch was completed, so the pilot, David Clement, let his co-pilot Eiland have the controls.

Angel 20 was commencing yet another turn from nearly a mile out when Eiland caught something out of the corner of his eye and looked toward the *Forrestal*.

What the hell is that?

Eiland saw splashes in the water followed by a large burst of black smoke on the rear portion of the flight deck. He motioned to Clement, who looked toward the carrier and saw the problem.

"Looks like a plane down, maybe some men overboard," Clement said. "Taking control . . ."

The pilot took over from Eiland and turned Angel 20 sharply toward the *Forrestal*, kicking the helicopter into high speed to close the distance. He called back to the *Oriskany* to report what he had seen, and alerted the two rescue swimmers in the back to prepare for a water rescue. In fact, the first splashes they saw were from the Zuni rocket and debris from the initial ignition of the jet fuel. It also is likely that some men jumped overboard at that moment to escape the flames.

On the *Forrestal*'s bridge, Lieutenant Commander James Bloedorn was in charge while the captain was away. When the fire started he was standing by the windows on the left side of the bridge overlooking the flight deck with a young sailor named W. T. Burgess. Bloedorn had looked away from the flight deck, and when he turned back, he saw Burgess pointing toward the rear of the ship. The young man's eyes were huge white saucers and he couldn't get any words out of his mouth. Bloedorn looked and saw the fireball.

"Plane on fire on the flight deck, aft!" Bloedorn called out.

Bob Shelton immediately glanced up at the clock in front of him and wrote in his logbook: "1052: Aircraft fire on the flight deck." It didn't excite him especially; it was just another fire. The ship had plenty of small ones all the time.

Bloedorn ordered Burgess to sound the fire alarm over the 1MC public-address system. Burgess was a native of Macon, Georgia, with a heavy Southern drawl, and one of his jobs on the bridge was to pass on announcements from the bridge officers to various others throughout the ship. He hustled over to the intercom system and first sounded a whistle tone to call for attention. Then he called out, "Fahr on the flight deck! Aeeyft. Fahr on the flight deck! Aeeyft. Man all foam stations on the double!"

Then after a short pause, Burgess came back on the 1MC to call, "All repair crews man your GQ stations!" A bit of a misnomer, "repair crews" referred to the emergency crews specially trained for firefighting and rescue, as well as actual repairs of damage inflicted in combat, for instance.

Shelton looked up when he heard Burgess call the fire alarm, because he thought Burgess seemed a little too excited for a routine fire. Belowdecks, Killmeyer had written nearly two pages of the letter home to his little sister when Burgess's excited alarms came over the 1MC system. Killmeyer and Burgess were in the same division and were close buddies, so he was used to Burgess's thick Georgia accent. The scratchy public-address system, combined with Burgess's accent and his excitement, made it difficult for some on board to understand his initial fire call. When he called, "Fire on the flight deck. Aft," in his heavy accent, the words were a bit muffled and many crewmen did not understand the initial fire warning. Killmeyer did, however, and he also noticed a change in Burgess's usual calm demeanor. He knew that Burgess was a quiet, mild-mannered guy who never even cursed. Killmeyer thought of him as the kind of guy you want to marry your daughter, maybe. But now Killmeyer immediately noted a sense of urgency in the fire call and began to worry.

Immediately after the first fire alarm, Bloedorn could see that the fire was serious and out of control. He called out, "Sound general quarters!" right after the fire started but then several seconds passed and he still hadn't heard the alarm. He looked back toward Burgess, who was standing directly in front of the general-quarters alarm, and realized the young man had not heard him.

"Sound general quarters!" Bloedorn shouted again, more urgently, and he simultaneously lunged toward Burgess's station to hit the alarm himself. Burgess heard him that time and reached up. As soon as he hit the lever, the ship was filled with a sound that chilled most sailors to the bone, while simultaneously triggering a tremendous adrenaline rush. At 10:53 A.M., sixteen alarm bongs rang out—it seemed an eternity as the bongs sounded and the anticipation grew—and then Burgess called, "General quarters! General quarters! All hands man your battle stations!"

If the first announcement did not get everyone's attention on board the ship, and it didn't, the general-quarters alarm certainly indicated that the ship was in trouble. Sailors throughout the ship dropped whatever they were doing and hustled to get to their general-quarters stations, creating near pandemonium as people rushed to get through the crowds clogging passageways. Killmeyer shoved the letter under the pillow in his bunk and started racing toward his general-quarters station, the magazine-handling room for the five-inch port guns aft and below on the fourth deck. He headed up a ladder and to the port side of the ship because GQ procedures called for sailors to run aft and down on the port side and run forward and up on the starboard side, in an effort to expedite movement.

Not everyone was in position to hear the announcements clearly, however. Frank Eurice, coming off of a long watch on the engine's throttles, had decided to take advantage of his midday break to get some sun. While the 11 A.M. air strike was being readied, Eurice and a friend he knew only as French had made their way out onto the starboard-side gun-mount sponson, a structure that juts out from the side of the ship just below the flight deck to hold the big five-inch guns. This was to be a rare opportunity for Eurice to see sunlight, because normally he worked far belowdecks.

There were huge stacks of potatoes in crates out there, so Eurice and his buddy just spread their beach blankets on top of them. They were enjoying a fine morning up there, oiled down and suntanning, just watching the Tonkin Gulf roll by. Local boats were off in the distance, and the water was as flat as a lawn, making for quite a picturesque scene. The guys were really enjoying the time outside, and Eurice rolled over to get some sun on his back. That's when he noticed the black smoke.

Eurice wasn't concerned at first because from his vantage point he couldn't see exactly where the smoke was originating. The *Forrestal* normally produced a nearly invisible exhaust, but as a machinist's mate, Eurice knew the boilers could churn black smoke if the technicians, known as BTs, didn't get the oil-and-air mixture just right.

"Those dumb BTs," Eurice muttered, looking up at the stack. That's when he noticed there was no smoke coming out of the stacks. *What the hell?*

Eurice called to his buddy, "Hey French! What do you think this is?" They both sat up and lifted their sunglasses to take a better look at the smoke, by now rolling off the deck and down toward the sea. They just sat quietly for a moment and watched the smoke, unable to imagine anything that would cause such a scene.

Up on the bridge, the officers in charge immediately notified Captain Beling of an obviously dire situation. The fire message was delivered to the captain in his sea cabin, his working quarters about twenty feet from the bridge. (The captain's regular quarters were farther away and below-decks, but the sea cabin allowed the captain some privacy and rest without being too far away from the action.) Having overseen the morning's first launch and then addressing the crew about the man overboard, Beling had retired to his sea cabin to finish getting dressed. As the time approached for the second launch of the morning, he was just finishing the routine that on most mornings he would have done earlier. He was showered and had put on his crisp uniform pants and shoes, but he was still standing in his white T-shirt in the bathroom after shaving. He had just wiped the last bits of shaving cream off of his face and was reaching for his khaki uniform shirt when he heard the phone ring.

The ringing of the phone immediately told him something was wrong because the captain's sea cabin is considered a refuge where you don't bother him without a good reason.

Beling hurried over to the phone by the bedside and grabbed it. He immediately heard someone exclaim, "Captain, we have a big fire on the flight deck!" Without any other response, Beling quickly put the phone back in its cradle and rushed out the door and straight to the bridge. He arrived in a few seconds, still in his T-shirt, and found a terrible scene awaiting him. He took his seat in the high captain's chair on the left side of the bridge, simultaneously giving him a clear view of the flight deck and putting him in the position that most clearly evidenced his authority.

Beling could see that his officers were understandably excited and frightened by the scene below them. There was a noisy din of voices shouting orders, asking questions, and yelling into microphones to be heard in other portions of the ship. The adrenaline was flowing, and Beling knew it had to be contained if he and his officers were to respond well. Beling immediately established order by taking command of the ship.

He calmly stated, "I have the con." Acknowledging that Beling was officially in control of the ship, Bloedorn called out, "The captain has the con!" and the helmsman repeated, "Aye, aye, captain has the con." Shelton noted in his log that the captain was in control.

Instantly, Beling could see that his ship was facing a major threat. One look out the windows aft showed him a huge fireball and billowing black smoke, with men running out of the curtain of flames, their clothes burning. Others were running toward the fire to help.

Officers and crew were bombarding Beling with information about the fire and the ship's status, but his own voice overcame any others when he gave an order. His first concern was to reduce the wind flowing across the deck so that the flames would not be fanned unnecessarily. "Emergency full back!" Beling called out, ordering the ship's engines slammed into reverse and to full speed. This was a radical move, akin to throwing a car into reverse while cruising down a highway, but Beling wanted to slow the ship very quickly. The ship shuddered as the order was executed, and soon the ship's speed was cut from twenty-seven knots, or thirty-one miles per hour, to about nine knots, or eleven miles per hour. That eliminated the strong wind that was whipping the flames ever higher. But Beling soon ordered the ship forward again at a slower pace. He did not want to come to a dead stop, because a slight wind would help keep the fire from moving forward from its current location.

Other officers on the bridge were busily giving orders to the crew on the flight deck and were communicating with other key individuals throughout the ship, all the while keeping Beling informed of what they were learning and what they were doing. In the first moment of the fire, the bridge was a hectic but highly organized focal point for the men of *Forrestal*. Shelton, the quartermaster in charge of recording everything happening on the bridge, scribbled furiously in his logbook as every order was given and every report called out over the din of voices. Though the first call of "fire on the flight deck" didn't excite him, Shelton began to realize something very serious was happening. He worked hard to concentrate as orders and reports swirled around him.

On the other side of the bridge, Captain Beling was sitting in control, but he was still half dressed. Having taken care of the most pressing duty in slowing the ship, he took a moment to calm his officers and bridge crew. He reminded them that they all had a job to do and that they should all keep a calm head. The men on the bridge paused to hear the captain's reminder and then went back to their duties.

At that point, the captain turned to the marine orderly who was always nearby to assist him. "Go get my shirt," he ordered. The orderly quickly returned with Beling's uniform shirt, which he then put on.

Now I feel like a captain, he thought, and returned to giving orders.

Word was spreading quickly throughout the ship. Commander Merv Rowland, the chief engineering officer, was in his stateroom belowdecks when he first heard the 1MC calls for fire on the flight deck and then the general-quarters alarm. Rowland had been up most of the night like the rest of the crew for the man overboard, but then he was up even longer because there had been a problem with an evaporator. As chief engineering officer, Rowland was responsible for practically every piece of machinery on the ship, so he had stayed awake all night supervising his crew as they made the repairs. Rowland didn't *have* to be there; he had a good crew working under him that he trusted, but he knew it would be helpful for the old man to be there in case they needed a word of advice. Rowland was far from a softy, but he understood that young sailors can be reassured and encouraged by the mere presence of an older, more experienced hand.

The evaporator repair was completed successfully, and then Rowland headed back to his stateroom for some rest. He had just undressed and crawled into his bunk when the fire alarm sounded. Like others familiar with the frequency of small fires on board a carrier, Rowland did not immediately react to the fire call. He lay in his bunk for a moment, waiting to hear further announcements or the ringing of his bedside phone. He knew that if the situation was serious, the bridge would notify him quickly. But Rowland would be long gone by the time his phone rang. Immediately after the alarms, Rowland's Filipino steward rushed into his stateroom, out of breath. He knocked on the door quickly and then opened it without waiting for Rowland's permission. Having seen the fire on a television monitor, the steward rushed to notify his officer.

"Commander, Commander! Fire! *Bad* fire!" he shouted.

As chief engineering officer, Rowland would play an important role in any disaster aboard the *Forrestal,* directing damage control and repair efforts and reporting directly to the captain about the progress of the problem and the remedy. Like Captain Beling, Rowland was not dressed when he got the alarm. He rushed out of his stateroom wearing nothing but his boxers and a T-shirt, headed toward his GQ station at central control, but then he turned back and got his shoes because he thought the deck might get hot.

As he was putting his shoes on, Rowland felt a mixture of anger and determination.

Here I've done twenty-eight years in the goddamn navy, been in wars and on all kinds of ships, and I come out here and a bunch of goddamn gooks are going to finish my career. Goddammit!

But then his innate ferocity surged within him. To no one but himself, he stood up and exclaimed, "Bullshit! Let's put out this fire!" Rowland raced out into a passageway already crowded with sailors rushing to their stations.

Back on the flight deck, less than a minute had passed since the rocket fired from Bangert's plane and hit McCain's plane. The fire had already engulfed most of the planes parked on the port side alongside McCain, with the JP5 jet fuel spilling aft, toward the rear of the ship. Aviation bosun's mates Robert Menery and D. W. Maxwell were standing near elevator number two, forward on the port side, when Menery spotted the fire. The scene on the deck was already reaching hellish proportions, with a huge wall of flame obscuring the rear of the ship and the dense black smoke billowing hundreds of feet into the air. Like dozens of other men who were well out of the immediate danger zone forward on the flight deck, Menery and Maxwell started running toward the fire to help their shipmates. At the same time, those who were trapped in the fire were running and crawling out of the inferno, fellow sailors and aviators helping them along and struggling to carry injured men out of danger.

Airman T. J. Hunt was also running aft from the same area as Menery and Maxwell, and when Hunt got closer to the fire area, he encountered young Bobby Zwerlein trying to move forward with his clothes burning. Hunt aided Zwerlein, putting him on the deck to help extinguish the flames on his body and then dragging him toward the island structure where men were starting to gather for safety and first aid. As he was aiding Zwerlein, other sailors brought forward the man who had been hit by the rocket as it flew across the deck. His face was badly burned and beginning to swell, but he was not bleeding badly even though his left arm was missing. He was reaching across with his other hand to grab the wound, and crying, "Help me." The sailors laid him down on the deck behind the island, where other wounded were gathering, and then they could see that his trousers were on fire and his abdomen was open. He was conscious and worried that he would lose his arm, not realizing it was already gone.

The aviators strapped into their planes were facing tough decisions, without much time to think. For those parked on the starboard side, near Bangert's plane where the rocket originated, the response to the fire was easier because it did not engulf them immediately. Those aviators were able to see how bad the situation was, but they also could tell that the fire was not in their immediate vicinity.

The first reaction of pilots near the fire or engulfed in it was to stay with the plane as they had been instructed, waiting for the deck crew to extinguish the fire or rescue them. They also had no idea some of them were sitting on top of old bombs that would explode in the fire far sooner than anyone expected. Most of the pilots paused before trying to escape, a pause that cost some of them their lives. The most fortunate pilots escaped from their cockpits with the help of their plane crews on the deck and, like everyone else on the flight deck, they alternately ran for the cover of the island and headed back toward the flames to help others escape. All of the twelve aviators parked to the rear on the right side of the deck, including Bangert and McKay, whose plane had accidentally fired the rocket, managed to escape their planes without serious injury. But beginning immediately to the left of Bangert's plane, on the very rear of the flight deck, and all the way beyond McCain's plane on the left side of the ship, the pilots were in serious trouble.

To the left of McCain's Skyhawk, David Dollarhide had been in his cockpit awaiting the launch when he heard a muffled explosion. As he looked out to the deck, he saw burning JP5 fuel rolling out and to the front of his plane. Initially he was concerned but thought the situation might be handled quickly. Within seconds, however, Dollarhide saw five or six men rolling out of the fire, in flames and writhing on the deck.

Dollarhide reacted quickly, knowing he had to get out of the plane before it was totally engulfed by the fire. He unbuckled his harness, opened the canopy, and stood up in the cockpit, feeling the heat from the flames already growing closer. Before trying to extricate himself, he took the time to pull down the "head knock" on the ejection seat. The ejection seat of a jet plane is an extremely dangerous device that can kill when accidentally activated, so the pilots were taught to carefully deactivate the seat when leaving the plane. The "head knock" was a handle that pulled down from the pilot's headrest, deactivating the ejection system. (The pilot would knock his head on it if the seat were left in the safe mode, reminding him to arm the ejection seat.) Though his plane might be blown to shreds in a few minutes, Dollarhide followed proper procedure in disarming his ejection seat so it would not be a danger to others.

Without his plane crew to help him out with the ladder he normally used, Dollarhide could see that he faced a dangerous leap to the flight deck, which was rapidly being covered with burning fuel. The aviators had not been trained to escape a ground fire surrounding their planes, so he had to improvise. Dollarhide decided that the best way to escape was to go directly forward, over the part of the canopy that jutted up from the front part of the cockpit like a short windshield. If he could get out of the cockpit and up on the nose of the plane, he might be able to leap past the flames.

But the cockpit of a Skyhawk leaves very little room for maneuvering; it is known as one of the tightest cockpits ever made. So the best Dollarhide could do was stand on the seat and lunge forward. He fell awkwardly over the front canopy, landing hard on the nose of the plane and immediately slipping right off onto the deck ten feet below. Dollarhide landed hard on his right hip and elbow. Barely making it past the fire line, Dollarhide lay on the deck stunned from his fall, hurting badly and unable to get up. He lay there on his side for a moment, in pain and feeling the intense heat radiating from the fire, waving his arms to call for help. A few yards away, Airman Price, the one who had stepped up the ladder to the flight deck on his way to lunch and encountered a wall of flame, saw Dollarhide on the deck. Price climbed up onto the deck and ran to Dollarhide, helping the aviator to his feet. Dollarhide took a few steps and fell again, this time into the arms of a green-shirted crewman. Price and the green shirt both helped Dollarhide toward the safety of the island, dragging him eventually.

All of the pilots on the port side were engaged in the same struggle for their lives. Back on the fantail on the port side, Lieutenant Commander Herb Hope's Skyhawk was parked on the extreme back corner of the flight deck, behind where the fire started. He heard a sudden "whoomp!" as the fuel ignited, and as he looked forward to the fire, he saw an orange-red fireball before the sky suddenly turned black. The thick, oily smoke was being blown directly back over Hope's plane, engulfing him in a black cloud that shut out any other indicators of how bad the fire was or what Hope should do in response. Before the black cloud completely engulfed Hope's plane, he looked to his left and saw his friend Lieutenant Commander Gary Stark in the cockpit of the Skyhawk just forward of Hope's plane. Stark's canopy was open, like many others on the flight deck, because the pilots got very hot sitting in their flight gear in the blazing sun. They usually did not put the canopy down until the last minute. Hope had closed his cockpit canopy early because he was annoyed by jet exhaust blowing right into his face, but Stark was sitting exposed in the open cockpit with no gloves and his oxygen mask off.

As the flames crawled up Stark's plane and into the open cockpit, he had no protection. Hope could see Stark react by raising his hands and crossing his arms over his face. That was the last time anyone saw Stark alive. Others would report seeing him later, seeming to sit calmly in his plane as it burned, but he was already dead.

As the black smoke caused the bright Tonkin Gulf morning to turn dark for Hope, he quickly considered his options. No one was nearby to help him, and even if there were, Hope would not have seen them because of the smoke. The fuel from McCain's plane was rushing to the rear of the flight deck, directly to Hope's corner of the world, and he could see flames already beginning to leap up toward his plane. He quickly decided to get out of his plane and make a run for it, but as all the other pilots were learning, getting out on your own is no easy feat once you're strapped in for a carrier launch. The easiest way to get out quickly was to jettison the canopy, actually blowing it off the plane instead of raising it manually, which could be awkward without help. The Skyhawk was capable of blowing the canopy off the plane with explosive charges, as part of the sequence required to use the plane's ejection seat. But even in the heat of the moment, Hope was thinking like a good aviator.

I wonder if popping the canopy will put this plane ACOP, he thought, meaning "aircraft out of commission for parts." Normally, he wouldn't want to put the plane down for repairs because he blew the canopy, but that thought only lasted a short second.

Hope put his head down to protect himself from the blast and pushed the button to jettison the canopy. Instantly, the canopy went flying up and away from the plane, allowing the cloud of smoke to wrap around the pilot. Wasting no time, he used the same maneuver that Dollarhide had attempted in getting to the front of the aircraft, but he managed to get over the front canopy and onto the nose without falling off the plane. Then he wiggled his way out across the nose to the refueling probe, a long metal tube that sticks straight out alongside the nose of the plane. Hope grabbed the refueling probe and swung his legs down, hanging from the probe to get himself close enough to the deck to jump down safely. As soon as he was down, Hope ran a short distance to the edge of the flight deck and leapt into the safety net that juts out a few feet. A little lower than the flight deck and as far away from the fire as he could get for the moment, the safety net looked like temporary safety from the fire and the shrapnel that Hope knew would be flying soon. Hope never slowed down when he got to the edge and threw himself at full speed into the safety net, where he landed right on two green shirts who had had the same idea a moment earlier.

Forward at the origin of the fire, McCain was making the same decision as all the other pilots who found themselves trapped in the fire. Like the others who would survive, McCain wasted no time in getting out of his plane. McCain flipped the switches to shut down his engines, and at about the same time, he heard two loud clanks as the thousand-pound bombs fell off his plane's belly and hit the deck. McCain opened his canopy and threw himself out on the nose of his airplane. He walked out onto the narrow refueling probe and jumped down onto the deck and directly into the burning fuel from his plane. He rolled through the fire to the forward edge of the inferno, tumbling out with his flight suit on fire and covered in fuel. He quickly rolled and patted out the flames on his clothes, then jumped to his feet, wasting no time in running away from the scorching fire and toward the safety of the island. McCain ran as fast as he could, glimpsing Dollarhide lying on the deck and being aided by others. He saw another pilot leaving his airplane in the same way he did, jumping into the fire and rolling clear. That pilot's flight suit was in flames.

All over the flight deck, crewmen were rushing to drag hoses from the fire stations toward the fire. Of the seventeen fog-foam stations on the deck, hoses from eight of them were being led toward the fire within the first minute after it started, one station aft was engulfed in flames, and three were inoperable for mechanical reasons. Belowdecks, sailors were manning the foam-generation stations that fed foam up to the deck. They activated the large pump stations that mix a simple detergent solution with pressurized seawater, creating a foam that the firefighters can use to smother the fire. The twenty seawater firefighting stations on the flight deck also were being manned quickly, with hoses from eight stations led aft in the first minute, two engulfed in flames, and one not functional.

Most of the crewmen were trying to help in the firefighting, even if they initially had sought cover from the fire. Sailors ran to the nearest firefighting stations and dragged the hoses toward the fire as others helped to get the fog foam or seawater flowing. Some difficulties occurred right away, as sailors untrained in the operation of the systems did their best to get them working. The fog-foam generators required activation, and some sailors did not know the procedure, fumbling with the switches and buttons to get the system operational. At most stations, however, the fog foam began flowing quickly, within forty-five seconds.

In the crash-crew shack in the island, William Brooks and Richard Sietz were discussing who would take the next launch and who would take the plane recovery. They were part of Repair 8, the team of firefighters and rescuers who stood by ready to spring into action immediately in the event of a crash or other emergency.

The crash shack was located on the rearmost corner of the island, and the only way you could get into it was from the right side. Various firefighting equipment was kept in the crash shack, along with the silver "hot suits" that allow the firefighters to stride right into burning airplane wreckage and rescue a pilot. But they were not yet geared up for the launch, wearing only the standard pants and jersey worn by all the deck crew, as they sorted out assignments for the 11 A.M. launch. Protected as they were by their position inside the crash shack and hearing nothing of the commotion outside, their first sign of trouble was the call of "Fire on the flight deck!" over the 1MC. When they heard the fire alarm, Brooks and Sietz ran out of the crash shack and were stunned by what they saw. They started to break out fire hoses on the starboard side as aviation chief Gerald Farrier ran by them with a fire extinguisher in hand, headed toward the flames. Farrier was the crewman in charge of Repair 8, and he responded immediately to the fire by charging right into it.

Nearby, Shaver had been hooking up his starter tractor to a plane when he heard a muffled explosion behind him. He turned and saw a plane in flames, and then instantly remembered he was working on the crash crew. Shaver dashed to the crash shack and grabbed a large "purple K" fire extinguisher. Along with several others, Shaver and Farrier ran directly into the fire scene. They were met by a surge of people coming forward, some of them badly burned. Shaver and Farrier struggled to move quickly with the unwieldy, heavy extinguishers, Farrier firing a test shot of the CO_2 extinguisher as he approached the flames. The white cloud was immediately blown into the fire in front of McCain's plane, with no effect.

Farrier's first concern was the pilots trapped in their planes, knowing that they would have more difficulty than the others in getting free of the danger. In the confusion of the fire's initial moments, there was no way to know which pilots already had escaped and which ones were still trapped in their burning planes. Farrier charged forward, taking the lead both physically and in his role as chief firefighter. Shaver wasn't surprised to see Farrier putting himself at risk. He knew Farrier was a good man; they were friends and their wives went shopping together back home. If there was a fire to be fought and men to be saved, Farrier's men knew that he was going to be right in the thick of it.

Dozens of crewmen and aviators saw Farrier rush right to the worst of the fire around McCain's plane, with no more protection than anyone else on the deck, and less than some. Shaver was nearby, struggling to activate the fire extinguisher with his broken right hand. He had to put the extinguisher on the deck and crouch down, holding the metal canister between his legs as he squeezed the lever to spray the purple powder. In what seemed an instant, the canister was emptied.

As Farrier got to McCain's plane, he saw that the two thousand-pound bombs had dropped from its belly and one had rolled about six feet toward the center of the deck. These were two of the old composition B, World War II—era bombs that had so upset the ordnance crew the night before—the ones that they said had decayed so much they were extremely sensitive to heat and vibration. They had said these bombs would explode in a fire, rather than just burning like the more modern bombs. And they would explode with the power of a fifteen-hundred-pound bomb because of their age.

Farrier had no idea. Lying in the flaming jet fuel, the huge bomb was quickly heating up. A longitudinal split had already formed in the outer shell of the bomb.

Other crewmen and aviators alternated between running for their lives and fighting their way toward the flames to help their buddies. About a minute and a half into the fire, dozens of crew members were still in the vicinity of McCain's plane and the fire farther aft, and some pilots were still strapped into their planes. The Repair 8 crew was training hoses on the burning Skyhawks, along with other crewmen who grabbed the first hose they could find, and charged into the danger zone.

Just feet from the flames, Farrier did what he could with the wholly inadequate fire extinguisher. He sprayed clouds of PKP into the flames with little effect. He could see that the situation was reaching a point where it was far too dangerous to have so many rescuers this close by, and he started waving off the other crew, telling them to run for safety. Shaver looked up to see Farrier frantically waving at him and other crew members.

"Go! Get out of here!" he yelled over the roar of the fire. "Get out!"

Some men dropped what they were doing and ran, but many continued to play their hoses on the burning planes. Shaver's fire extinguisher was empty, so he started to get up.

Farrier stayed on the job, never leaving the men he knew were trapped beyond the curtain of fire, doggedly training a portable fire extinguisher on a bomb that was rapidly approaching its cook-off point. As the thick black smoke billowed and swirled, Farrier and Shaver could see that the thousand-pound bomb with the ugly split in its casing had begun to glow a bright red.

Chapter **8**

ONE MINUTE AND
THIRTY-FOUR SECONDS

One minute and thirty-four seconds into the fire, the thousand-pound bomb from McCain's plane exploded with a fury not felt on the deck of a U.S. aircraft carrier since World War II.

The detonation of a thousand-pound bomb on an armor-plated aircraft-carrier deck is a nearly unbelievable force. At that moment, the bomb's high explosive is converted almost instantly to a gas at very high pressure and temperature. The pressure causes the metal casing to fragment, and the surrounding air is compressed into a shock wave that feels like atmospheric pressure of two hundred times or more. The temperature in such a blast can be ten thousand degrees Fahrenheit even before anything nearby is ignited. The blast of this weapon, designed to take out huge numbers of ground troops or fortified installations, was concentrated on the 1 3/4-inch steel-armored deck of a ship crowded with men already fighting to escape the flames and suffocating smoke. Even though the ship was designed to withstand direct hits from some of the most fearsome of military weapons, the point-blank detonation of such a massive bomb was too much for any armor. In an instant, the bomb blast sent a colossal fireball high in the sky while destroying everything in its immediate vicinity.

Shaver was looking at Farrier and had just started to get up from his crouching position behind the fire-extinguisher bottle when the blast hit. In the tiniest fraction of a second, Shaver saw Farrier thrown into the air and then simply disappear. And at the same instant, he felt the force of the bomb lifting him up and pulling at his body in a thousand different directions. Time slowed to a crawl and he felt as if his body itself were exploding, every part of his body pulling away from the rest. He was aware that he was flying through the air, and he could see yellow and red flames boiling up from the deck. He knew he was on fire. He felt the shrapnel tearing into his guts. Shaver would survive the explosion, but it began a terrible ordeal for him.

In the first milliseconds of the blast, Shaver was protected in part by the fire-extinguisher canister he was crouching behind. Most of the crew members closest to the bomb vanished in an instant, killed immediately by the force of the blast and the intense heat, never to be seen again. The shock wave from the bomb was like an invisible freight train rolling across the deck at lightning speed, hitting everyone and everything in its path with a ferocious force that knocked men to their knees if it didn't send them flying.

The ship shook and rattled at its very core from the bomb blast. The bomb eruption was so ferocious that it was felt throughout the entire ship, down the length of the huge vessel and to the very bottom of the hull. Those who were belowdecks and still unaware of what was going on felt it rocking the ship, signaling serious trouble overhead.

Up on deck, the blast deafened everyone for a moment, and dozens of men were dazed, lying where the explosion had thrown them and trying to get their bearings. Others were scrambling to run and crawl from the blast area, desperately trying to move forward from what had become a hellish scene of death and destruction. The detonation of the bomb had turned an already bad situation into one of absolute horror. It was clear now that the fire was wildly out of control and the *Forrestal* was losing many men.

There had been thirty-five crew members near the bomb when it detonated. In a heartbeat, twenty-seven of them died or received fatal injuries. That twenty-seven included Farrier and five of the other eight members of Repair 8, the specially trained flight-deck firefighters. Most were killed instantly, along with eighteen other crew members, as they fought to contain the initial fire and cool the bombs that were heating rapidly in the burning jet fuel. The three Repair 8 firefighters not killed by the blast were seriously wounded. One minute and thirty-four seconds into the fire, the *Forrestal*'s firefighting team was gone.

All the while, shrapnel and burning debris fell all over the deck, forcing the men to dodge and weave as they ran for cover. The initial bomb blast had been deadly, but that first split second was only the beginning of the death it would rain upon the men of *Forrestal*. All over the flight deck, men were being hit by bits of debris, some raining down from overhead and some moving horizontally like a speeding bullet. Red-hot, jagged bits of airplanes, tractors, and bombs were flying across the deck, some as large as aircraft wheels, taking down men who had been far enough away to survive the primary blast of the bomb.

John McCain had taken only a few steps out of the fire when the blast hit him. He had turned to look back at the fire and the other men, which meant he was blown backward as bits of metal fired into his chest and his thighs. A larger piece of shrapnel slammed into the radio that hung from his neck, right over the center of his chest. McCain was momentarily stunned by the explosion, staggering backward and ducking to avoid more of the shrapnel, airplane parts, and even body parts that were flying toward him. A headless body flew through the air and thumped down next to him.

Roberts had been awakened from his nap in the fuel station just below the flight deck by the fire-alarm call. He and another man from his crew were headed up the ladder to the flight deck to see if they could help with the fire when the first bomb exploded. The other man had just started out onto the flight deck when the blast blew him back onto Roberts, the huge rush of wind pressing the clothes tight against their bodies. After pausing for a moment, they proceeded onto the flight deck. Once they stood up, they could not believe the hell in front of them. The raging fire drew their attention first and then Roberts saw a man stagger forward and slump down on the deck. He had no face. It looked as if his entire face had been surgically cut off. The man also was burned, most of his clothing gone.

Roberts was terrified at the sight but felt compelled to help the man. He bent down and put his arm around the man's shoulders, supporting him as he sat in a tangle of metal equipment and debris. It was only then that he saw the tattoo on the man's arm. "Justin." Roberts remembered when his friend Justin had gotten that tattoo on shore leave.

"You'll be okay, here, Justin!" he shouted over the noise. Roberts quickly waved over a couple of medical corpsmen with a stretcher basket. They bent down to take Justin, and Roberts patted him on the shoulder. "You'll be okay!"

But that was all he could do for Justin. He felt a wave of nausea building in him and leapt up to get away from it. He then saw two men helping his friend Scotty toward the island. A small, baby-faced eighteen-year-old who was new to the crew, Scotty was considered a mascot of sorts; everyone liked him. Roberts could see that Scotty had lost most of one foot. Still amazed at what he was seeing on the flight deck, Roberts kept looking up in the sky for the attacking planes.

Where are they? If we're under attack, where the fuck are the planes?

He was sure the Vietnamese had managed to attack the carrier with fighter planes, strafing the deck and lobbing bombs. That was the only explanation that made sense. That was the only thing that could cause this kind of shit.

While he was looking around, Roberts noticed a figure lying amid all the tow bars and other apparatus behind the island. It was his own crew's plane director, Kenneth Strain. The man's face was blackened, and the rest of his body was severely burned. Roberts had to fight the urge to run away from the sight, but he went closer and called out to his crewmate.

"Strain! Strain! Come on, let's get you up and outta here!"

The man did not respond, so Roberts tried to grab him under the armpits and drag him closer to the island, farther from the fire. Roberts pulled, and the burned body gave way, his hands slipping on waxy, slick flesh. He fell back hard onto the deck.

"Motherfucking shit!" he screamed. Roberts was overcome with a mix of anger and revulsion. He looked at his hands and couldn't believe what had just happened. He went back to Strain and tried again, this time locking his arms behind the man's back, trying to tug him toward the island. Once again, the slick body slipped through Roberts's hands and he fell back.

"Goddammit!" he yelled. Then he got down closer to Strain's face and yelled at him. "Don't die! Don't die! I'll get you some help!"

Feeling light-headed by now, Roberts got back on his feet and looked around for help. Men were running in all directions. And there were still no planes overhead. Even in the midst of so much horror, this frustrated him greatly. If people were killing his friends, goddammit, he wanted to see them. He stood and looked up at the sky.

"Where are the sorry motherfuckers doing this to us?" he screamed.

When the initial wave of fire and smoke from the first blast died down slightly, those on the bridge and forward on the flight deck could see that the bomb had devastated the entire area near McCain's plane. Where there had been planes and dozens of men fighting the fire, nothing was left but a roiling ball of fire and a cloud of thick, oily smoke. Captain Beling looked down from his perch high above the fire and was astounded. *My God, we've got bombs going off. What the hell is going on here?*

James Bloedorn was still on the bridge after handing control over to the captain, and he too was dumbstruck by the first explosion. Just weeks earlier, he had been in an ordnance-training class that included a film about how modern bombs were supposed to be fire resistant. The film had shown a thousand-pound bomb suspended over a fuel fire, and the instructors said the bomb would last at least ten minutes before exploding. *Why the hell did we have a bomb go off? This fire just started.*

Bob Shelton had walked over to the port side of the bridge in the first few moments of the fire to see what was happening. Along with several others on the bridge, he had been peering down through the armored glass at the fire when the explosion hit. They instinctively ducked for cover as the first bomb went off, feeling the thump as the bomb's concussion hit the armor plating on the bridge and the air exchange as the explosion forced air into the compartment and then sucked it out again. They slowly stood up to look again at the sight below. The officers and crew on the bridge looked down to see no one standing where before dozens of crew had been training hoses on the fire. Instead, men were running toward the island, heading forward on the flight deck, and more than a few were doing so as their clothes burned, trailing blood behind them and desperately crawling or staggering away from the searing heat on their backs. One crewman or aviator could be seen pulling himself slowly along the flight deck, doggedly clawing his way out of the fire and toward the safety of the island, his legs blown off at the waist.

In the worst of the fire and explosions, the men were desperate to get to the island, home base on the flight deck, the only area on a flat ship that represented any real shelter from the hell blowing all around them. The island represented safety, and perhaps more important, it represented the command structure of the ship. These sailors desperately needed to get away from the fire, but in this moment of terror, they also were running and dragging themselves home, to the one spot on that deck they knew as a safe haven. Many would not make it home.

Sailors and aviators were down all over the deck, and the blasts wounded some fliers as they sat in their planes. Others had been blown off the ship by the blast, thrown into the sea by the explosion, sometimes with serious injuries that made their water survival unlikely. Sailors on the other ships in the vicinity could see fireballs falling away from the *Forrestal* flight deck, into the water, and most did not immediately realize that those fireballs were men, engulfed in flames and either leaping into the sea or being blown off the deck by an explosion. On the *Forrestal* deck, Lieutenant James Campbell stood transfixed beneath an F-4 Phantom, stunned by the explosions and unsure where to go or what to do. In the havoc, he could see fireballs hopping and tumbling across the deck. He just stared at them. It took a short moment for him to realize they were men.

Campbell and scores of other men rushed to the burning men and flung themselves on them, rolling around on the burning men, desperately trying to put out the flames. Campbell managed to extinguish the top part of one man's body but saw that his legs were still burning as the medics quickly carried him away. The burned men were screaming.

As those on deck struggled to their feet, they could see that the *Forrestal*'s firefighting crew was gone. Chief Farrier and his men had vanished, leaving charged fire hoses flapping wildly on the deck, most of them shredded by the force of the explosion.

Despite the horror of seeing so many men killed and injured, and the horrific fire that awaited them aft, the men of *Forrestal* headed back to fight the fire and help those who were injured and stranded close to the fire. With burning debris still raining down on their heads, they raced back toward the very area where dozens of people had just been destroyed. Various crew members picked up what remained of the hoses left by the Repair 8 crew and began to fight the fire again, while others started to bring more hoses to the scene.

Nine seconds after the first bomb blast, a second bomb exploded behind the wall of fire with even more violence than the first. This explosion hurled bodies and debris as far as the bow, more than three hundred yards away. Looking down from the bridge in shock and disbelief, Captain Beling watched as a man was lifted up in the air and thrown the entire length of the deck, his body sailing helplessly like a rag doll. An officer standing on the front of the ship, as far away from the fire scene as one could possibly be, was killed instantly when a piece of shrapnel hit him in the heart.

Beling felt particularly helpless to have to sit there in the captain's chair and watch those men out on deck while he was relatively safe up on the bridge.

The first bomb blast had spread the fire significantly, and now the second bomb greatly extended its reach. No longer was the blaze contained mostly to the rear port corner of the ship. Now it had spread across the deck to the starboard side, even approaching dangerously close to the island structure. When the second explosion ripped across the ship like another scythe, the crew on deck realized that the ordnance on deck was cooking off and that the first explosion was not a fluke. *There are hundreds of bombs out here!* Some of the men were surprised that the bombs had started going off so soon into the fire, but they had no time to consider why. The two blasts in quick succession had made it clear that the carrier deck was a deadly place to be. Without any orders being given, the crew realized that they had to take cover while the bombs wreaked havoc on the flight deck. For the moment, simply surviving the explosions was of primary importance. Fighting the fire would have to wait.

The crew members sought shelter wherever they could. Some were trapped out on the deck, seriously injured from the fire and the explosions, missing limbs and suffering from the terrible wounds caused by flying debris and ammunition. Other crew members did their best to help the injured to safety, but in the chaos of the moment, and with the dire need to get out of harm's way, not everyone could be helped. Men crowded around the island structure, seeking shelter behind its thick walls, with some huddling in the Repair 8 crash shack. Others looked at the "bomb farm" directly behind the island on the starboard side, the area where bombs were stored to keep them out of harm's way, and decided they did not want to hide behind thousands of pounds of explosives. They kept running forward.

All across the deck, men were seeking shelter however and wherever they could, diving into catwalks, down ladders and hatches, anything to seek refuge from the hell on the aft end of the flight deck.

Most of the men were in the full throes of a terror-induced adrenaline rush. The mind raced and time slowed. If you leapt into the air, it seemed to take days before you came down. The exertion and excitement made their mouths unbearably dry. And the men worried.

Oh my God, I'm never going to see my momma and daddy again, Roberts thought. *I'm never going to smell fresh-cut grass again.*

The admiral on board the *Forrestal*, Rear Admiral Harvey Lanham, had not been summoned immediately when the fire first broke out. Though the *Forrestal* was his flagship and he controlled the overall operations of the carrier, the air wings, and the accompanying ships, Lanham did not actually command the ship on a daily basis. That was Beling's job. Lanham was in his quarters when the fire broke out, but when the first bomb went off, he realized there was a serious problem and that he should see for himself.

He dashed for the bridge, knowing from practice drills that he could make it in one minute and fifty seconds. He felt explosions rocking the ship as he made his way. When he got to the bridge, the admiral could see that Beling was already in charge. Lanham surveyed the flight deck and was amazed to see the damage that already had occurred.

As he stared out the window in shock at what was happening, his marine orderly rushed over and roughly grabbed his arm.

"Get away from that window!" the marine yelled. "It's not safe!"

The young man yanked the admiral down to the floor just as another explosion shook the ship. A large piece of shrapnel crashed through the thick Plexiglas where the admiral's face had just been. Captain Beling ordered everyone to stay away from the left side of the bridge where he was, closest to the explosions, but he stayed in his chair looking right out the window.

Things were even worse in pri-fly, the primary flight-control center, one deck above the bridge but sixty feet farther back toward the fire. This was where the ship's air-crew officers controlled flight operations on the deck from a windowed room that looked similar to the bridge. The big windows on three sides of the room provided a clear view of the entire flight deck, but now with the bombs going off, those windows made pri-fly a dangerous place to be. The officers and crew there were ducking for cover as the bombs went off on the deck, and the two crewmen standing watch on the catwalk just outside pri-fly rushed in to take cover from the explosions. They found that pri-fly offered little sanctuary, however. One of the watch sailors made it into pri-fly, but by then, some of the thick, battle-ready windows had been blown out by the blasts and those inside were looking for a way out. As officers and crew started to scramble for a way out, the watch sailor was hit hard by a shock wave from one of the bombs on deck and thrown over some chairs, against a distant wall, and onto the deck. As soon as they could get out, pri-fly was abandoned.

Each explosion rocked the ship, rattling the metal framework and breaking windows. All over the flight deck, men hid behind whatever they could find, but they were also trying to administer first aid to the wounded. No one knew how long the bomb blasts would last. Never knowing if the next bomb blast would be the one to kill you, the men waited and waited for what seemed forever. As soon as one bomb blast faded away, another bomb cooked off. Seven major explosions followed—all from the older thousand-pound bombs. At the same time, rockets and missiles were detonating in the heat. After five minutes, the blasts stopped, and the men started to come out onto the open deck again. The fire was out of control and had to be stopped.

The fire had grown into a massive blaze, enveloping the entire rear portion of the flight deck, and the forty thousand gallons of jet fuel on board the burning aircraft was feeding the fire. The JP5 jet fuel, something akin to kerosene, was not all that easy to ignite, but it would burn furiously. The burning fuel created a shallow sea of fire that was flowing over the sides of the ship. The burning jet fuel poured off the deck and down onto the structures below, setting fires on the sponsons jutting out from the side, the fantail at the very rear of the ship, and Hangar Bay 3 one deck below.

After the initial explosions subsided, Merv Rowland's voice boomed across the 1MC public-address system to tell the crew that they should come out from their cover on the flight deck and go back to work fighting the fire.

"Repair parties, this is control. Re-man your stations! All repair-fleet personnel, this is control. You can now re-man your stations. Stay on the job!"

Men rushed back toward the fire, getting as close as they could to the searing heat and grabbing what remained of the fire hoses that lay sputtering on the deck, most of them ripped to shreds, a frightful suggestion of what must have happened to the men who had been holding them.

As the crew men moved forward again to fight the fire, Beling looked down from the bridge and saw something that gave him a sinking feeling of fear and despair.

Oh my God . . . The deck is open . . .

The burning jet fuel wasn't just flowing over the sides of the ship. It was flowing down through huge holes that had been blasted in the flight deck by the exploding bombs. Beling knew what lay just beneath the surface of the flight deck—berthing quarters where men were sleeping. All over the flight deck, men were thinking the same thing.

There are men down there!

The first bomb had blasted a hole that was ten feet across, with the heavy metal curled down at the edges as if a fist had punched through tinfoil. And the bombs had opened similar holes in other areas on the deck. Beling could only imagine the devastation that the exploding bombs must have caused belowdecks. Now liquid fire was pouring down into the heart of the *Forrestal*.

The men berthing in the area directly underneath the fire scene had been up on their regular shift all night; the morning was their normal rest period, so they were in their bunks when most of the crew were well into their workday. Others sleeping in the same general vicinity had been given permission to sleep late to compensate for the previous night's operations. These men were used to resting in conditions that most people would find impossible; they had become accustomed to sleeping just feet below the deck of an aircraft carrier, with almost no noise insulation. The sound of aircraft taking off and landing was as normal to them as the creaking of an old bed or the snoring of a sibling.

You got used to it after a while, or else you never got any sleep. In this particular berthing area, the men had to get used to the sounds of aircraft slamming down hard on the deck directly above them because they were aft, near the arresting gear where the planes landed. These were men who had learned to sleep through anything, and that would cost many of them their lives.

Just to the rear of the fire area at McCain's plane, Gary Pritchard was asleep in his bunk after a twelve-hour shift. He and his division crewmates had been in a compartment farther back earlier in the trip, not so directly under the arresting gear, but they had been displaced by an air squadron that came aboard and pulled rank to get the choicer spot. Pritchard and his buddies had been forced to move to a compartment directly under the arresting gear and closer to the fire site.

Pritchard considered it the worst place in the world to try to sleep. But they managed, drifting off and ignoring most of the noise, but usually waking with a jolt when a plane slammed down and the arresting cable dragged across the deck.

When the first alarms sounded for fire on the flight deck, many of those sleeping in that area did not even hear it. Those who heard the fire call probably did nothing more than roll over and perhaps listen halfheartedly for further announcements. The fire call did not involve any orders for them to act, and there was no indication that they were in danger. They could not have known that the initial fire call would be their only warning. The men never got a chance to save themselves because the general-quarters alarm came at about 10:53 A.M., just seconds before the first bomb blast hit.

When the bomb from McCain's plane blew up, it smashed through the deck and into the compartment where the sailors were sleeping. Many were killed instantly, never knowing, while others were awakened by the blast and seriously injured. Those who survived the initial blast found themselves under a rain of burning fuel pouring down from the flight deck.

Fifty men sleeping in that berthing area were killed by the explosions and burning fuel, and another forty-one died in nearby areas directly beneath the flight deck. Nine berthing compartments in the aft area were destroyed.

Pritchard's area was just far enough aft of the first explosion that he and his bunkmates survived. But they were close enough to know that they had only *barely* survived.

The bombs were sending concussions through the compartment that were just unbelievable, an incredible, invisible force that rippled through the berthing area, tossing men out of bed and slamming them against walls. The shock waves were so violent that Pritchard was completely disoriented when he woke up. The first thing he knew, he was standing by his bunk with his pants and his shoes in his hands.

The shock waves from the exploding bombs started to come in quick succession as Pritchard and the other crew members in the berthing area responded by donning a bit of clothing and rushing out. Even without any information, they could tell that this area was way too close to whatever was going on outside and they wanted out fast.

Pritchard's buddy Frenchie (not the same "French" who was sunbathing with Frank Eurice) had the bunk right alongside of him and when the two men found each other, Frenchie's eyes were as big as moons. They were temporarily deafened after each explosion, watching the commotion in an eerie silence until the hearing returned, the panicked noise of their buddies swelling to a crescendo again. Pritchard and his buddy tried to stay together as they made their way out into the passageway leading from their compartment, but the area was jammed shoulder to shoulder with men. Some men were wounded already.

"Clear a path! We've got wounded here! Make a hole!"

With general quarters already sounded, Pritchard and Frenchie tried to make it to their GQ stations up on the flight deck, where they could man a fuel-pumping station. The scene was so chaotic on their deck level, however, that they had trouble making any forward progress. People were scared and confused, and no one knew exactly what they should be doing. And no one had any idea what was going on. With all the bombs going off, only one thing made sense.

"We're being attacked! They're bombing us! We gotta get outta here!" The men were shocked to find themselves under attack, but they struggled to make sense of what little they knew. "They're going for the steering! The bombs are all aft. They're trying to knock out our steering!"

Pritchard agreed with most of those around him that somehow the Vietnamese must have gotten close enough to bomb the carrier. He instantly pictured in his head a scene straight out of World War II and countless old movies—a Japanese pilot with a leather helmet diving down on the back of the ship. With adrenaline surging and scared to death, Pritchard clearly pictured a Japanese pilot muttering "Yankee motherfucker!" as he bore down on the *Forrestal*. Pritchard and every other man in that passageway feared they would be trapped belowdecks if the attackers sunk the carrier.

In another berthing compartment a few decks down and farther toward the rear of the ship, Paul Friedman was sound asleep in his upper bunk right up until the first explosion. He had spent a long twelve hours working in the mess hall, and he never even heard the alarms that followed the start of the fire. He had gone to sleep about 6 A.M. and managed to sleep deeply in all the usual noise.

Friedman awoke to the sound of a blast, and when he opened his eyes, the bulkhead to his right was missing. There was some sort of powdery stuff in the air all around him. He was stunned from the explosion and as he lay there, he looked around without moving. He could see fire where another bulkhead was cracked, and he could see other shipmates just lying there motionless, staring back at him. He was stunned, deafened, and was wondering what was real and what was a dream. It was surreal: men awakened from a deep sleep to find themselves in the midst of disaster.

After a few seconds, Friedman looked down toward the foot of his bunk. He could see that his foot was bloody, the red ooze beginning to soak the sheets on his bunk. A piece of shrapnel had gone through the bottom of his foot as he lay sleeping, but he had not yet felt the pain. Then, very quickly, Friedman realized he was not dreaming. His hearing returned and suddenly chaos was all around him. As the explosions continued, he realized the ship was under attack.

Oh shit, we're being attacked by MiGs, Friedman thought, referring to the Soviet-built fighter plane. *God, the five-inch guns are pounding! Why are they firing the five-inch guns? We must really be under attack!*

Friedman sprang out of his bunk, joining the dozens of other sailors rushing to evacuate the compartment. Some already were helping the wounded, carrying injured sailors through the crowd, cradling a head wound, dragging men out of their bunks. Everyone was running to the port passageway to get out, and Friedman was hobbling along on his injured foot, the pain setting in so that it made running difficult. He faltered at one point and fell down in the rushing crowd, but almost immediately, a buddy he knew as Alabama picked him up. A big guy, Alabama picked up Friedman like a twig and eventually helped him get to the sick bay.

Out on the starboard-side gun-mount area where Frank Eurice and his buddy French were sunbathing, the first explosion shook them out of their bewilderment about the black smoke on the far end of the ship. When the explosion occurred, they felt it even where they were, far forward of the fire.

The huge explosion shook them hard and then they could see a sheet of flame, smoke, and pieces of confetti going skyward.

Eurice and French were both momentarily stunned, their jaws dropping open in disbelief. Then Eurice turned to his buddy and yelled, "I think it's time for general quarters!" and took off.

Eurice hustled through the hatch that led off the sponson and back into the ship, with French close behind him. By that time, burning jet fuel was beginning to come off the edge of the flight deck and French was burned on his shoulder as he made it through the hatch.

With the general-quarters alarm sounding throughout the ship, Eurice bolted down to his station, which was the "2 main stern tube" to the rear of the port steering compartment. He made it there in record speed. *We're in deep shit! This is for real, man. We got some kind of real nasty break and we are really in deep shit!*

His duty during general quarters was to "maintain a good leak" on the propeller shaft at the ship's very rear where it enters the water, keeping just enough seawater on the bearing mechanism so that it was cooled but not so much that the compartment would flood. Failure in either direction would mean that the propeller shaft would become inoperable, crippling the ship's propulsion. Despite its importance, this work was normally extremely boring. That's why there was always a tall stack of *Playboy* magazines in the little compartment, no bigger than your average car interior. On this day, Eurice arrived at his station just as the bombs were cooking off far above him on the flight deck.

Eurice was on a little catwalk trying to get to his workstation when one of the thousand-pound bombs went off far overhead. The noise was deafening and the explosions kicked him over a railing and into the bilges, a pit at the very bottom of the ship filled with seawater and various filth.

Throughout the ship, men were rushing to their GQ stations. Ken Killmeyer was running aft to his GQ station, the magazine-handling room for the five-inch port gun aft and below on the fourth deck. The narrow passageways, cramped even when two sailors were calmly passing each other, became tight thoroughfares as everyone tried to get to their appointed stations and started sealing hatches and making other emergency preparations. As he ran down a passageway, Killmeyer felt the first explosion rock the ship and send the waffle-like fluorescent light covers swinging down toward his face. Dust shook off the hatches, lights, and pipe work overhead, creating an unsettling scene for someone who knew what it took to shake such a big ship so violently.

All along the way, "repair parties" were breaking out emergency equipment from repair lockers and manning their own GQ stations. When Killmeyer got to a hatch he would need to access a ladder taking him down to his GQ station, a repair party was there already and one member was plugging his headset into a communications outlet. Bombs were still going off overhead, and Killmeyer followed another crew member through the hatch and started down the ladder to the magazine-handling area.

As he was halfway through the hatch in the floor, one of the repair-party members stopped him.

"Wait, come here!" he called out. "Don't go down there any more!"

Killmeyer saw that the man was talking to someone on the phone, and he stopped on the ladder. Scared but pumped full of adrenaline, Killmeyer wanted to keep going. *I don't know what's going on, but I have to get to my GQ station. Now!*

Killmeyer yelled to the repair party that his GQ station was down that hatch and he *had* to go, but the repair party kept telling him to wait.

"They're talking about flooding the magazines!" the guy from the repair party shouted back over the noise of the explosions and the ship rattling. This was not good news. It meant that Killmeyer could not go to his GQ station, even though others already had gone down, but more important, it suggested that things were very bad. The magazines holding ammunition for the ship's guns and aircraft could be flooded with seawater in an emergency to eliminate the risk of a fire setting off the explosives, but that would always be a last-ditch measure. Flooding the magazines put all of that ammunition and ordnance out of commission, and it was generally something you avoided if at all possible. The only reason to flood the magazines was that you needed to save the ship. That decision, if it ever came, would be made in damage control.

Merv Rowland had joined the mass of men running through the ship, shouting questions and orders, everyone wondering what the hell was going on. He made his way to a ladder that would take him down to the deck housing damage control, and that's when he felt the first bomb go off up on the flight deck. The blast almost knocked him off the ladder.

Awwww shit. They've snuck out there with a goddamn gunboat or something and set off our ammunition.

As Rowland continued making his way, he started thinking about what ammunition was vulnerable to the attack.

Christ, the next strike's ammunition is on the flight deck! That's a big damn strike too. And the next strike's ammunition is on the mess deck, and then another strike is being readied down in the magazines to go up. Son of a bitch, they could blow this whole ship out of the water!

Rowland was scared by what he thought was going on. He counted three more explosions overhead before he got to the damage-control hatch, and then he stopped counting. When he got to central control, Rowland found the room already crowded with sailors assuming their duties for the emergency. A number of men already were manning the phones to get damage reports, and information started flying toward Rowland as soon as his crew saw him dash in.

The first thing he did was to look at the fire-main pressure, the water system that would be used throughout the ship for fighting fires. He told the sailor at that station, "You better make damn sure that fire-main pressure doesn't go below a hundred and fifty pounds." Next, he checked how many generators were on line, knowing all four main plants should be on line because of the scheduled plane launches.

Rowland then took his position in the big chair, assuming control of almost all of the ship's response to the fire. Everything would flow through Rowland's position in damage control. He immediately

ordered another generator put on line, in case one of the present generators was put out of commission. Then he turned his attention to the
tall Plexiglas plotting boards where sailors were already posting information. Many of the young men were wearing headsets and receiving
constant reports from throughout the ship, then posting them on the
plotting boards in grease pencil. With that information, Rowland could
monitor where the fire was, what systems had been damaged, and the
current readiness of vital operations like the ship's propulsion system.

Rowland could visualize the entire ship's operations on the boards,
and if he saw something that interested him, he would call the phone
talker over and get the information straight from him. Information was
key in an emergency, and that put Rowland in a unique position. He
was far belowdecks with no direct sight of any fires, damage, or emergency response, but if anyone on the ship knew what was going on, it
was Rowland.

He realized he was the only man on the *Forrestal* who knew what was
going on throughout the ship. Not even the captain had more information. It was hard to absorb so much, but when he found a hot spot, he
would concentrate on that problem and trust his crew to handle the rest.

Rowland was in close contact with the bridge, so it wasn't long before
Rowland realized that there was no attack and that the crisis had begun
with a flight-deck fire. He couldn't believe a fire on the top deck had
gotten so bad.

*I know goddamn well we'll get this fire out, but I can't believe we just shot
ourselves in the foot. At least some goddamn gook's not going to end my
career.*

Damage control kept the captain and the bridge fully informed, with
Rowland frequently on the phone to Captain Beling, updating him on
the fire damage and the emergency response. Years later, Beling would
modestly claim that all he did was "steer the ship" while others did the
real work in putting out the fires, a vast oversimplification that says
more about the captain's respect for his crew than what he actually did
during the fire. But still, it is true that Rowland was the man responsible, more than any other individual, for saving the *Forrestal*. He was
experienced and capable, and he had no intention of letting his ship
and his boys succumb to this fire.

Much of Rowland's attention was directed to the ammunition magazines throughout the ship. No matter how bad things were elsewhere, Rowland knew that the ship could be destroyed in one devastating blast if the fire got to the ammunition. The question of flooding the magazines had arisen very soon in the crisis, once the bombs started going off and burning jet fuel poured down into the lower decks.

Rowland was watching an array of gauges and indicators that gave him a good idea of what was going on anywhere in the ship. His attention was largely focused on the temperature gauges for the ammunition magazines. Each one's temperature was indicated separately, and this was important enough that he wanted *two* sailors standing in front of each gauge, staring at the numbers, ready to scream out if the magazines started heating up even a little.

With the fires spreading, it did not take long for some of the temperature gauges to start rising. Rowland had to be careful with his decision. If he waited too long, the ammunition could ignite in one split second. He called Clark Chisum, the *Forrestal's* weapons officer, to find out exactly what was in the weapons magazines that were heating up. Chisum told him he thought those magazines held only inert material at the moment, nothing explosive, but he wasn't absolutely sure yet.

"Okay, but the magazines are pretty close to all that hot stuff," Rowland said. "Clark, I think we ought to flood those magazines and make sure we don't have this whole damn ship go up at once."

Chisum didn't argue with him, so Rowland called the bridge to get permission to flood the magazine. Beling couldn't speak to Rowland immediately because he had stepped off the bridge momentarily to get a better view of the fire on the rear of the deck. Though Rowland had authority to do almost anything else he deemed necessary, flooding the magazines was such a serious, irreversible action that protocol required permission from the captain himself.

The navigator on the bridge took the call and told Rowland he could not flood the magazines without the captain personally giving the order.

"The hell I can't!" Rowland screamed back over the phone. "If he doesn't get back and that thing gets any hotter, I'll flood! I'll flood the goddamn thing with or without permission!"

Rowland slammed the phone down and continued to watch the temperature gauges. Beling would most likely have deferred to Rowland's judgment, but fortunately, he soon got word that the magazines in question were devoid of any explosive material, so there was no need to flood. Though damage control constantly produced tense moments like that, full knowledge of the situation made Rowland confident and a damn sight less scared than if he had to wonder about what was going on.

Rowland's confidence stemmed directly from being so well informed, and that put him in a very different position from thousands of other men on the ship. Soon into the fire, Rowland knew that he would save his ship. But others had little or no information to work with, and they were not nearly as sure.

With so many men on the ship, a chaotic situation like a major fire can create vastly different experiences for individuals. Just as Rowland and Beling's experience was far different from those of sailors in the middle of the fire and explosions, so were some sailors' experiences different from other crew members' simply because of where they happened to be stationed for GQ or where they happened to be when the fire broke out. Many men died because they were directly in the vicinity of the fire and the exploding bombs, while many others survived because some quirk of fate or a lucky change in their routine took them out of harm's way. Many survivors would marvel, years later, at how a simple change in their routine had kept them from a place where they almost certainly would have been killed.

Some sailors found themselves isolated from the worst of the danger on board the ship, never truly out of harm's way as the fire and explosions tore through the ship, but far enough away that they didn't immediately fear for their lives. But being that far away also meant that they had little or no information about what was going on, and that could, in its own way, create a different kind of hell. Nineteen-year-old Robert Whelply, an aviation-supply runner, received exactly that kind of mixed blessing when the fire broke out.

Whelply's job was to run for aviation parts needed by the aviation squadrons. The mechanics working on the planes would request a part, and Whelply would be dispatched to the appropriate storeroom to fetch it. It was a fairly simple job that required a lot of running around the ship from one storeroom to another, collecting parts on his list, and then making his way back to the hangar-bay deck to deliver them. On this particular morning, Whelply had made his way to a supply room that was about midship and three decks down. He had another stop to make at a supply room farther aft, and normally he would have gone to that area first so that he had fewer items to carry on the rest of the trip. But on this morning, Whelply had decided to stop at the midship storeroom first and have a cigarette with a friend who worked there. He knew the aft storeroom was a busy place that morning, so the midship stop was a better place to take a breather.

Whelply was shooting the breeze with his friend when the fire alarm sounded, but neither man paid much attention. He was just getting ready to leave and finish his delivery rounds when the general-quarters alarm sounded.

Oh no, not again, Whelply thought, weary of the many GQ drills and the disruption they always caused. But he immediately put out his cigarette, dropped the parts he had obtained at the storeroom, and called out, "See you later!" to his friend. Then he started racing to his GQ station. Because he happened to be at that particular supply room when the GQ alarm sounded, Whelply didn't have far to go. His GQ station was directly above him on the hangar-deck level, requiring only a short run through a couple of bulkheads and then up a ladder.

Whelply's GQ station was a small, nondescript passageway on the port side of the ship. At several spots along the wall, there were portals with ladders leading down to the second deck, a quick way to get down into the bowels of the ship from the hangar-deck level. As was the case for a great many men, Whelply's GQ assignment was nothing exciting or glamorous. He was to report to this passageway area and just wait for further instructions. In an emergency, he might be told to monitor who went down the ladders or to prevent people from going down the ladders into a dangerous area. Or he might be pulled away from the passageway for duties elsewhere.

On the way to his station, Whelply realized that this was not just another drill. The bombs started rocking the ship and Whelply could tell that the ship was in big trouble. He knew how many bombs were scattered throughout the ship for the air strikes.

When Whelply got to his GQ station, no one else was there. He waited, expecting other men to come rushing in right behind him, but they never came. In every GQ drill, there had been dozens of men who reported to that area, all standing around with nothing to do, just waiting for orders or the end of the drill. Now that there was a real emergency, Whelply was the only one to show up.

It was an odd feeling to be alone at the height of a GQ alarm. Whelply was out of breath from his sprint, bent over and trying to recover himself, expecting at any moment to see a crowd of men rush into the area. But he waited, and waited, and no one came.

What's going on? Where is everybody? Geez, did I get something wrong here? No, that was GQ, no doubt about that. So where the hell is everybody? This is really weird.

Whelply remembered all the GQ drills in which the men had put on oxygen-breathing apparatus and sat down next to the bulkhead to wait. There were guys lined up the whole length of the hallway. As Whelply stood there all alone this time, he began to worry that something was desperately wrong with the ship. *Something's got to be really wrong if all those guys didn't come to GQ.* He could hear the explosions overhead, some of them nearly knocking him off his feet as they rattled through the ship. The longer he stood there, the more uncomfortable he became.

Maybe I oughta go see what's happening out there. I'm sure not doing any good here . . . Hell, there's not even anyone here to give me orders.

But the navy trains sailors to understand one very important point about general quarters: you go where you have been assigned to go, and then you wait for further orders or act on whatever emergency you find there. You do *not* just go looking for something to do. The whole idea of general quarters is to have people stationed at important points throughout the ship, ready to respond in whatever way might be needed. The idea of standing in an empty passageway while others fight a fire might be difficult to understand for those without military training, but the entire system of military discipline is based on young men and women doing what they are told, even if the reason is not apparent. Whelply understood that, but his resolve was being tested.

Whelply stood there for a long while, knowing that there was some sort of serious problem nearby but not knowing exactly what. He kept hoping the phone in the passageway would ring and someone would give him orders. Orders to do something, to go somewhere. Anything. He stared at the phone but it never made a sound.

The only thing he could think to do was to start closing hatches in that area. They had done that on a GQ drill once. Seemed to make sense now.

Finally, he heard another voice. Another sailor stuck his head out of an electronics room down the hall and yelled at him.

"Hey! I'm down here!" Whelply shouted down the passageway. *Finally, someone else!*

"Well, I guess it's you and me, kid," the other sailor replied. "Just sit tight. This is where you're supposed to be. If somebody needs you, they should come and get you."

And that's exactly what Whelply did. For hours. He stood his watch in that empty passageway, doing exactly as he had been instructed. He waited for orders that would never come, all the time wondering what was going on on the flight deck and elsewhere. He could tell from the sounds, the rumbling explosions, and the cryptic messages on the public-address system that there was a bad fire and severe damage to the ship. He imagined the worst possible scenario.

God, whatever is going on out there isn't too far away. It sounds like the whole damn ship is blowing up! There's fire everywhere, I can tell that at least. It's not just a normal fire, that's for sure. They never said anything in training about explosions during a fire.

Must have been something really terrible to start all these fires. Could we be under attack? No way! How could the Vietnamese get out here to attack us?

His mind raced with possible outcomes, none of them good. *I hope that fire doesn't come any closer to me. I don't want to be trapped here. I wonder if the smoke will kill me before I burn. I sure hope so.*

The young sailor's mind was filled with images from World War II movies in which the sailors had to abandon ship, scrambling over the side to face their fate in the sea. He wondered if the *Forrestal* would go down. And if it did, would he know in time?

Oh God, what if the ship sinks? Will I hear the abandon-ship call? I don't want to be left behind!

Where do I get a life vest? I haven't seen any around here! Where do I get a life vest???

Whelply spent hours by himself, getting more and more scared, before he finally couldn't stand it any longer and left his post at midday. He had spent about five hours standing there by himself, just waiting to see how he would die.

Chapter **9**

STAY ON THE JOB!

Nine major explosions occurred on the flight deck, all of them from the old composition B bombs. The big fat bombs that had looked so unstable when they were delivered the night before were cooking off in rapid succession. With each blast, the ship vibrated so badly that the men's lower legs became numb.

When all the bombs had exploded, the scene became less hellish, but only slightly. The massive explosions had stopped blowing men and equipment all over the deck, but the fire itself was out of control and spreading. Other materials—fuel tanks, smaller ammunition, various volatile materials on the planes—continued to explode without warning. The fire had spread both forward and starboard, engulfing more planes and equipment, exposing more ordnance to the heat that had caused the other explosions. The fire was getting worse—much worse.

Explosions from the flight deck had spread shrapnel, burning jet fuel, and flaming debris throughout the ship, ripping holes in armor-plated decking and steel bulkheads. With the violent explosions penetrating far beneath the fire scene, the ship was like a crate of fireworks with a bonfire on top, just waiting for one explosion to send one piece of hot shrapnel to the wrong place.

One of the most sensitive spots was the liquid-oxygen-generating plant. In order to supply the pilots' breathing systems in the planes, the ship generated and stored large amounts of oxygen, the quintessential fuel for any fire. The liquid-oxygen plant was located near Hangar Bay 3, on the left side not far below where the fire was raging on the flight deck. On this morning, the tank held 750 gallons of liquid-oxygen stored in the tank there—making it a highly volatile target, far more flammable and explosive than the JP5 jet fuel up on the flight deck. The liquid-oxygen tank was virtually unprotected, with no special armor or protective barriers; an explosion on the flight deck easily could penetrate it and ignite its contents.

The two sailors working there knew how dangerous the liquid oxygen was. John Dickerson and Robert Clark often thought that their workstation was a scary place to be in case of a fire, but like every other *Forrestal* sailor with a dangerous job, they got used to it. The first fire alarm, however, had sparked every latent fear and Dickerson rushed over to the big door leading from the oxygen plant to one of the big hangar bays. He was straining to pull the heavy, watertight door closed when the first bomb exploded. Dickerson kept his grip on the door and went flying with it as the blast flung it wide open. He was left hanging off the door in the hangar bay outside, and when the initial shock wore off, he realized that general quarters had sounded.

I've gotta go, but I have to close this hatch first . . .

Dickerson's general-quarters station was a repair locker some distance away, but he could see that Clark was shaken by the bomb blast and wouldn't be able to secure the hatch right away. He had to get that hatch closed to protect the oxygen plant as much as possible, and to protect his friend Clark, who would stay there for general quarters. Dickerson shoved on the heavy door and threw his body against it, then he started "dogging" the hatch closed by locking all the handles that surrounded the door frame.

Satisfied that the door was secure, he pounded on it a couple times and yelled, "Be careful, man!" before leaving Clark. Dickerson raced off to his general-quarters station.

Back in damage control, Merv Rowland knew what would happen if the liquid oxygen ignited. When a crew member in damage control asked about the vulnerability of the oxygen tank, he made no bones about the result.

"If that thing blows, we're gonna be the biggest damn blowtorch you've ever seen," he said. "It'll blow this ship out of the water, no doubt about it."

In the oxygen-generating plant, Clark recovered from the initial shock of the bomb blast and saw that the fire must be very close. He could feel the heat building to a nearly unbearable level within minutes, and then the bulkheads separating the liquid-oxygen plant from the rest of the ship started to glow red. Clark watched as the paint first bubbled and then burned off. Every time something exploded, red-hot shrapnel would come flying into the compartment. Clark tried to take cover, but he knew that wouldn't help if the shrapnel hit the liquid oxygen. And there was no telling how many more explosions were coming. Clark picked up the phone and called damage control for help.

Rowland had been monitoring the reports from that area closely and personally took Clark's call. The lone sailor sounded scared as he reported that the fire was all around him.

"It's getting hotter than hell out here!" the man yelled over the phone to Rowland. "What do I do, sir? The fire's getting close!"

"Dump it, son!" Rowland yelled back. "Dump it all!"

Rowland wanted the sailor to get rid of the liquid oxygen to eliminate the explosion hazard, but there was just one problem. The *Forrestal* had no emergency dump capability for the liquid oxygen. There was no way to just flip a few switches and send all the liquid oxygen whooshing overboard in a hurry.

Instead, Clark had to hook up a one-inch diameter, sixteen-foot-long hose—no bigger than a typical garden hose—to the liquid-oxygen tank and run out to the platform jutting out from the edge of the ship. There he stood with the hose in his hand, pointing it out to the sea and trying not to spill the super-cold liquid on his flesh. And while he was doing this, the fire raged directly overhead, explosions blowing debris onto the sponson and sending burning material directly down on top of him. A bad stroke of luck could ignite the oxygen venting from the hose, leading directly back to the storage tank.

After a moment standing there under the flaming debris, Clark decided to leave the end of the hose dangling off the edge of the platform and retreat back into the oxygen-generating plant. The fires had not let up and the sailor was still scared, with good reason. While he had been venting the liquid oxygen, the fire and the blast damage had spread to the compartments all around him, trapping him there with the big oxygen tank. He had no way out. He called Merv Rowland again in damage control.

"It's still real bad here, sir!" the sailor said, sweat pouring off his face from the heat. "What do I do if it gets worse?"

"Put on your life jacket and go swimming!" Rowland replied. "That's the only goddamn way you can get away from it!"

Clark considered taking Rowland's advice, but he didn't want to. He looked over the side of the ship and thought about how dangerous it would be to jump overboard, trying to weigh that against the fire. Going overboard was a tempting prospect as he watched the oxygen vent and imagined it igniting. It took more than an hour for the liquid oxygen to slowly pour through the hose. He never jumped over, and later, Clark would find out that the bomb shrapnel blew holes in the deck on opposite sides of the oxygen tank, just missing it by twenty feet on one side and fifteen feet on the other. If fate had thrown either piece of shrapnel just a little closer, the liquid oxygen would have been ignited.

A similar situation involved an eight-inch pipe that ran along the side of the ship and pumped jet fuel from the storage tanks belowdecks up to the flight deck, where it could be pumped directly into the planes. The pipe was blown apart early in the disaster, and if the fuel crew belowdecks had not responded quickly, they would have been pumping six hundred gallons of jet fuel directly into the fire scene every minute. When they got word of the fire on the flight deck, the crew immediately initiated a drain-back procedure to stop the flow of fuel to the flight deck and also drain out the fuel already in the pipes.

When Gary Shaver finally landed after being blown through the air by the first blast, he found himself lying far forward on the flight deck. He had witnessed the death of Gerald Farrier, the head of the crash crew who tried to wave off other firefighters when he saw that McCain's first bomb was about to explode. After what seemed a long journey through the air, Shaver tried to get up, but he couldn't. He couldn't hear anything. The cast on his right hand was gone. He felt a burning pain throughout his body, and when he looked down, he could see why. Blood was everywhere, and his clothes were singed and smoking. And his left arm was gone.

Wait a minute, it's not gone. It's over here.

There was a moment of calm and clarity as Shaver realized his left arm was still attached, barely, but it was draped behind his neck and hanging down the front of his right shoulder, the hand resting on his chest. Shaver reached up and grabbed his left hand with the right, hanging on to it to secure the mangled arm. As he looked over to where his left arm should be attached, he could see bones and bright red flesh. He had a tiny second to marvel that no blood was coming from the wound, and then it started spurting out in great jets.

Just then, Shaver was hit by another explosion and went tumbling across the deck. Then the pain hit him. He had been too stunned to feel it at first, but then it came on like a red-hot poker throughout his body. It was unlike anything he had experienced before, so bad that it went beyond anything he could even conceive of as pain. He was in absolute agony.

Screaming, Shaver tried to crawl away from the fire. His mind was totally out of control, certain he was about to die, consumed by the terrible pain and fear that grew worse with every breath.

As he flopped along the deck, someone grabbed him by the neck and pulled him toward the island. The area behind the island was crowded with injured and dying men, some seeking aid on their own, dragging themselves to the only place on the flight deck that seemed safe, while others were carried there by buddies and strangers. Men were tending to others in the crash-crew shack at the island, on the open deck amid the bombs stacked there, and in the battle-dressing station forward in the island structure. The battle-dressing station was the designated first-aid station, but it was quickly overwhelmed by the dozens of injured men.

Men did what they could for the fallen sailors, but in the early moments of the fire, there was not enough help to go around. The injured were being taken to the sick bay belowdecks as fast as possible, and medical corpsmen were rushing up top to help, but the sheer numbers overwhelmed the first-aid efforts. There were horrible sights all over the flight deck—men with their faces or entire heads blown off by the explosions, limbs missing, bones protruding, severely burned, covered in blood. The victims often were not recognizable even to the men they worked with every day; sometimes only the stenciled name or rank on a man's clothing would give a clue. Some, like Shaver, screamed out in agony, utterly unable to control themselves as they endured the waves of pain and looked at their mangled bodies. Others were too stricken to even speak, and the lucky ones were unconscious.

Shaver was one of the first to be scooped up and carried down to the sick bay. Sailors and aviators did what they could for their fallen friends, using anything handy to try to stanch the bleeding wounds. In lieu of bandages, some were grabbing big fistfuls of coarse brown paper towels and trying to stop some of the worst bleeding. Another ripped off his T-shirt and placed it over a man's exposed intestines, pouring a jug of water over the shirt to keep the wound moist. Their efforts sometimes had little effect on the terrible wounds from the explosions. The deck in that area was covered with a half-inch of blood.

This was the scene that awaited Gary Pritchard and his buddy Frenchie as they made their way out of their berthing area just beneath the flight deck and were fighting the crowds of sailors to get to their GQ stations topside. They still had no idea what was going on, other than that it seemed the ship was under attack. If planes were to be launched in response to the attack, they thought, it was important for them to get to that fuel station on the flight deck and do their jobs. None of the usual paths to the flight deck were passable, so Pritchard decided they should make their way to the island structure on the right side of the ship and go up to the flight deck there.

When they came up into the daylight, they were staring at a small piece of hell. Fire everywhere, smoke, blood, wounded men, screams, alarms. They thought they were looking at how they would die.

"Jesus, goddamn," Pritchard muttered, transfixed by the scene in front of him. "Christ, it's all over. Man, is it all over."

Pritchard's thoughts immediately went to his young wife of only two years, and how she would fare without him. In that split second of thought, he comforted himself with the knowledge that they had no children yet and he had kept up the payments on his life insurance.

Well, at least she'll be all right with the life insurance.

Quickly, though, Pritchard's attention was diverted to the many injured and dying men who had gathered behind the island structure. Men with serious injuries were lying all over, and Pritchard didn't know what to do first. One glance at the flight deck told him that he was not needed at his usual GQ station because they sure as hell wouldn't be pumping any fuel to the flight deck. As he looked around and tried to decide what to do, Pritchard's eyes fell upon a young sailor sitting on the deck and holding a gravely wounded buddy in his arms. Pritchard still recalls the youthful look of the "kid" holding his bloodied and burned friend in his arms, cradling the man's head in his lap. The kid was crying.

"Help me! Help me!" the kid shouted at Pritchard, his teary eyes looking directly up into Pritchard's. So Pritchard turned to Frenchie and said, "Shit, we gotta help this guy!" The two buddies snapped out of their initial shock and swung into action.

As Pritchard bent down to help lift the wounded man off his sobbing friend, Frenchie ran for a wire stretcher. They lifted the man onto the stretcher, and as they did, Pritchard could see that the man was bleeding profusely. Most likely, the man was dead, but he and Frenchie took him anyway.

"It's all right, we got him," Pritchard told the sobbing sailor. "We'll take care of him."

Pritchard and Frenchie took the dead man down to the sick bay, which was already crowded and filling with the sickening smells of blood, burned flesh, and jet fuel. Then they hustled back up to the flight deck.

There, they could see that the injured men who had made it to the island structure were starting to get more help. But all across the flight deck, more men had not made it that far and many were still fending for themselves amid the fire. That's what happened to Airman Charles Price, the fellow who had climbed up the ladder to the flight deck just as the fire initially broke out. After helping in the first minute of the fire, Price found himself among those seriously injured in the big explosions.

He had been knocked unconscious during the first, and when he came to, he was lying facedown. He tried to get up and run, but he could not lift himself off the deck. When he looked down at his legs, he could see that the remains of his left pant leg were lying flat on the deck from the knee down. The left boot was still there, attached by something, but there was almost nothing left between the knee and the foot. He managed to crawl on his hands and one leg a little farther up the deck away from the fire, where he threw himself into the catwalk on the edge of the ship, just below the edge of the flight deck. Hoping this would be a safe place to take cover until help arrived, Price looked around and realized that it wasn't. He was right next to a fuel-pumping station. The catwalk already had been hit hard by the explosions, the metal railings twisted and torn. Fuel and fog-foam solution were pouring off the flight deck onto the catwalk.

Price tried to pull himself back up the ladder, but he didn't have the strength. The pain was terrible, and he had already lost a great deal of blood, making him weak and light-headed. In addition, he had a number of other shrapnel wounds all over his body that he was only beginning to notice. Realizing that he was very badly injured, Price fell back onto the catwalk and started yelling for help. He soon understood that no one would hear him. Shouting took too much effort anyway, he thought, so he just lay back on the catwalk and breathed heavily. He was worried about the blood loss from his shredded left leg, so he found the strength to pull off what was left of his belt and tried to apply it as a tourniquet. Price was becoming too dizzy to fumble with the pieces of the belt, so he pulled off his T-shirt, which was torn and bloodied already. He managed to wrap it around the remains of his left thigh but was unable to cinch it tightly enough to cut off the blood flow.

Price lay there on the mangled catwalk, rapidly losing strength and unable to do much more for himself. He could see through the perforated surface of the catwalk to the ocean below, and as he began to lose consciousness, he could see a big destroyer maneuvering in close to the ship. He slipped closer to sleep as he lay there looking down through the catwalk, the destroyer slipping in underneath him in a hazy image that might as well have been a dream. The last thing he saw before fading out was his own blood pouring beneath him and dropping into the ocean.

Suddenly, Price heard someone else jump onto the catwalk. He managed to yell for help and look up. As he did, he locked eyes with the other sailor approaching through the smoke. The other man was so startled by what he saw that he immediately turned and ran away, yelling for help. Price's torn body was that much of a shock.

Before long, the man returned with a medical corpsman and a wire basket stretcher. They tried to get the stretcher down to Price, but the catwalk was too mangled, so they decided to lift Price back up to the flight deck first. That was difficult without Price able to help himself, so they improvised by using a two-by-four board underneath Price. The two men lifted Price with the board underneath, hoisting him up to the flight deck and onto the stretcher.

Belowdecks, Ken Killmeyer still was trying to get to his GQ station, but with the warning from the repair crew, he realized he could not make it. He looked back toward the rear of the ship, into a crew berthing compartment, and saw smoke for the first time. It wasn't thick black smoke like what was pouring off the flight deck, but a gray smoke making its way through the berthing area and to the passageway where he stood with the repair crew. Someone closed a hatch to the berthing area, sealing off the smoke, at about the time the explosions stopped overhead.

Soon after the pause in the overhead noise, Killmeyer heard an announcement on the 1MC that anyone not trapped by smoke or assigned to a repair party should move to a forward portion of the ship, away from the danger in the rear of the ship. With about ten other men, Killmeyer made his way forward on the starboard side of the ship and as he approached the sick-bay area, he could see blood on the deck. As he got closer, he saw a buzz of activity with people bringing injured men down from the flight deck and in from other portions of the ship.

He continued to move forward, making slow progress because he and the sailors accompanying him had to stop and open hatches that had been sealed for the GQ alarm.

At one point, Killmeyer stepped aside to let a sailor emerge from the sick-bay area. As the sailor climbed a ladder ahead, Killmeyer noticed that he was carrying a bucket full of blood.

My God, how bad is this thing?

Killmeyer and the other sailors making their way to safety continued forward and up to the second deck, one deck directly above his own berthing compartment where he'd started. At that point, they encountered an officer who ordered them to stay in that area.

At 10:59 A.M., bosun's mate W. T. Burgess came back on the 1MC and called for the ship to set condition Zebra, the most extreme of status conditions for a carrier. Even for those who had no idea what was going on topside, which was most of the thousands of men on board, that was another signal of something very serious.

With condition Zebra, the ship was to be secured as tightly as possible to combat fires and other damage. Hatches were sealed all over the ship and that meant that passing from one area to another was not easy, and in some cases impossible. Crew members would allow others to pass in an emergency, and certainly to allow someone out of harm's way, but otherwise the ship was to be kept tightly compartmentalized. Setting the ship at Zebra made it more difficult for latecomers to access their general-quarters station because, once the ship was locked down, an officer or leading petty officer had to approve opening the hatch to allow a sailor to pass. If an officer wasn't around to approve, the sailor might not make it to his station. That was one reason the crew hauled ass when the general-quarters alarm sounded.

Killmeyer found himself with about forty other men waiting where the officer had told them to stay. They talked about what they had seen already and what they thought might be going on, all of them excited and trying not to look scared. At one point, they heard tapping on a nearby hatch that led up to the hangar deck.

Killmeyer went over to the hatch and he could hear men yelling. The hatch had been sealed from Killmeyer's side as part of the Condition Zebra lockdown. He yelled back to ask if the men were okay up there. They said they were, and asked how Killmeyer and the others were doing in that compartment.

"We're fine. We're not doing anything down here, though. We want to help!" someone yelled. "Let us up!"

"Yeah, hey, let us up!" someone else yelled. "Open the damn hatch!"

Someone waiting with Killmeyer realized he could open the hatch and talk to the men above. Killmeyer could hear the reply.

"I can't let you guys up here," someone from the hangar-deck group yelled. "I'll get my ass in trouble by letting you up. I'm not allowed to. You're going to have to just wait. That's all we're doing up here too."

The hatch was closed again. Soon someone new came into the crowd and told them he had heard the gun mounts were gone and the fantail was seriously damaged. Soon after that, the group of men was allowed into the hangar deck above. What they found was a real mess.

The hangar bays were huge open areas running the width of the entire ship and very nearly the entire length. They were almost directly underneath the flight deck, with only one level between—the level where so many men had been sleeping when the fire started. When the bombs blasted through that level, the inferno poured right down into the hangar bays packed with aircraft, various other equipment, and pallets stacked with bombs. When the fire started, Ronald Williams was at his station in Conflag 3, one of several small control rooms overlooking the hangar bays. His duty was to watch for any fire hazards in the hangar bay and react quickly to prevent or stop the fire, as well as to keep an eye on things in the hangar bay. If you were playing football with some buddies in the big hangar bay, Williams was the booming voice that came over the loudspeakers, warning you to keep your long passes away from that helicopter. Someone was always in the conflag centers, twenty-four hours a day, keeping watch over the hangar bays.

When the fire alarms had first sounded, Williams perked up and prepared for any signs of fire in the hangar bays. He didn't have to wait long for the first explosion to send shrapnel firing down, and that's when he called damage control to report blast damage in the hangar bays. He asked for orders, and damage control told him to activate the sprinkler system and close all hangar-bay doors. The doors were a primary safety feature on the *Forrestal:* mammoth sliding steel slabs more than a foot thick that could be closed to divide the large, open hangar bay into three smaller compartments.

With just a few buttons and switches, Williams initiated emergency measures that would prove vital to saving the *Forrestal.* Within seconds, a heavy rain was falling in the hangar bays, suppressing any fires that had already started and preventing any new fires from taking hold. At the same time, the huge hangar-bay doors started sliding shut, sealing off the different hangar bays from one another so that any fires, smoke, or blast damage could be isolated. The massive doors slid out quickly, accompanied by a loud alarm warning people to clear the way. In less than fifteen seconds the doors had sealed off the hangar bays.

By the time Killmeyer and the other men entered Hangar Bay 1, there was no fire. Others already on the scene, however, told the men that Hangar Bay 2 was full of smoke and Hangar Bay 3, closer to the origin of the fire, was ablaze. The sprinkler system probably had extinguished the fire in Hangar Bay 3 by that time, but nevertheless, Killmeyer could tell that he was now in the middle of the ship's crisis. The hangar bay was filled with the acrid odor of smoke mixed with fog-foam solution, explosives, and burning fuel, plastics, and wiring. An officer soon started yelling for the men to start moving planes out of the hangar bay to get them out of harm's way. Oddly enough, the planes were to be moved onto the elevators and then up to the flight deck. Though the rear of the flight deck was the site of the original fire, the blaze was moving downward at this point, to the hangar bay. The forward end of the flight deck was a safer spot to stow the planes.

Killmeyer joined with a number of other sailors moving planes by hand because there was only one tractor available and operable in the hangar bay. The planes normally would have been very carefully towed by a small tractor attached to the front wheel, but it was necessary to move them quickly and however possible. So Killmeyer and the others grabbed whatever part of the plane they could reach, and started pushing. There was plenty of help, so the planes started moving fairly easily. They found that stopping them was harder, and many planes were damaged when they ran into one another. At that moment, however, minor damage to a plane did not concern anyone.

Indeed, damage to planes and loss of aircraft was becoming an increasingly minor concern. Up on the flight deck, the firefighting effort had resumed with a new vigor, the sailors charging back into the inferno now that the worst of the explosions seemed to have subsided. As crews gathered up the remains of shredded fire hoses and others strung up new ones, the fire finally was being hit with substantial volumes of seawater and fog-foam solution. One of the first priorities was to lay a thick blanket of foam between the island and the fire line, creating a buffer that would protect the all-important command structure and leaving the men a safe zone from which to attack the fire. The deck became a slippery mess as the soaplike fog foam built up in shallow pools. In some areas, the fog foam reached nearly knee-high.

The overall firefighting effort was directed by Merv Rowland in damage control, but on the flight deck, it sometimes seemed like every man for himself. Officers on the deck were trying to organize repair parties and direct a controlled response to the fire, but in the fog of battle, many sailors never saw an officer give orders to anyone. The damage-control and repair-party personnel were not easily identified by appearance, so they had difficulty getting the attention of other crew when giving orders and trying to organize a response. This was particularly true in the hangar bays, where men were working feverishly to control fires and prevent further explosions. In the hangar bays and up on the flight deck, men acted on their own to do the best they could in fighting the fire, manning a hose whenever possible and doing whatever seemed like a good response. Some of those self-directed efforts would turn out to be the best response possible, and others would not.

In the effort to fight the fire, for instance, sailors made the mistake of using both water hoses and fog-foam hoses on the same fire site. In retrospect, many would see this as a major failing of the ship's crew, because the combination greatly impeded the effort to extinguish the blaze. Though the crew thought they were doing their best by pouring as much water and foam on the fire as possible, they were actually making a serious mistake that the *Forrestal*'s trained crash-crew firefighters would not have made if they had survived the first bomb blast. The fog foam is intended to create a blanket over the fire and spilled fuel, smothering it and preventing further combustion. When used by itself, the fog foam can be an extremely effective response to aircraft fires.

But when one firefighting team sprays foam and another sprays water on the same fire, the water simply washes away the foam, leaving only the far less effective water to extinguish the jet fuel. The crew would be criticized harshly for this firefighting mistake, but Frank Eurice understood the sailors' dilemma. Unlike him, many of the sailors had no firefighting training and could not resist when they found themselves standing in front of a huge fire with a water hose. He knew they were trying to do their best.

And besides, the firefighting foam alone does nothing to cool the weapons that heated up in the fire. Some of the crew looked at the devastation wrought by the initial bomb blasts and decided that water had to be applied to the other bombs and rockets to cool them off, no matter what effect it had on the foam.

Eurice had stayed at his station until smoke started coming into the tiny compartment, forced in through the ventilation system that normally pumped fresh air into the otherwise stuffy room. When the smoke started, Eurice called damage control and asked what he should do. It took fifteen minutes for them to get back to him and say he could leave his post. By then, Eurice had breathed a lot of smoke and was glad to get out, to go anywhere else.

Damage control had also given orders to abandon the ammunition magazines directly above Eurice's station for fear they would explode. He did not know at the time that that was the reason so many men were running like hell, just ahead of him, as he abandoned his own station. As he brought up the rear, Eurice sealed every hatch behind him.

When Eurice and the others got to the mess decks, they found the ship was shut down tight for Condition Zebra, and they were not sure where they should go next. Because Eurice had firefighting training, he decided to organize the men into an impromptu repair party and go looking for some work to do. He found a stash of oxygen-breathing apparatus, known as OBAs, and passed them out. He gave the men a quick lesson in how to use the devices: The mask fits over your face and you pull the straps to create a snug fit. A canister hangs around your neck and sits on your chest. When you insert the activator cartridge, you've got thirty minutes of air. When the bell goes off, *get out,* because you've only got three minutes left.

Eurice led two of the men—he never learned their names—on a path toward the flight deck. When he got to the level just beneath the flight deck, and in the rear portion of the ship, they could see fire damage and feel the heat coming off of the flight deck above. Smoke was everywhere, so Eurice looked for a way out of that compartment and up to the open air. He opened a hatch that he knew led to a walkway that could take them to the flight deck.

But when he opened the door, all he found was a hole where an entire working space was supposed to be. Eurice was looking out at the ocean and a beautiful blue sky instead of the ship interior he expected. Dazzled by the sudden sight of a beautiful Tonkin Gulf morning, Eurice stood for a moment and just stared. Then he slammed the door and moved on.

They were very close to the fire at that point, so Eurice told the other two men to energize their OBAs and he did the same. They found a fire hose on the wall nearby and unrolled it, and the three men started moving forward into the blackness. Breathing heavily in their OBAs, they crept forward with the hose and could feel the heat growing more intense as their sight grew blacker and blacker. Their faces covered by the black masks with the big round eyepieces, rubber hoses dangling from the bottom and attached to the oxygen generators hanging on their chests, they looked like a trio of slow-moving insects merging with the darkness. Finally, they were feeling their way along the passageway, totally blinded by the smoke.

Suddenly they saw a big red glow ahead of them. *Oh boy, looks like we found it,* Eurice thought. *Welcome to Hell: Population 3.*

Eurice opened the nozzle on the fire hose and hit the red glow with a spray of water that immediately turned to steam and rushed back toward the men, searing their skin. Shouting through his OBA mask, he urged the men to keep low, to stay under the heat and steam as much as possible. Before long, Eurice heard the bell go off on one of the other men's OBA, and almost immediately after, Eurice heard his own bell go off and then the other man's. They had to abandon their fight and back out of the fire area, leaving the red glow almost as red as they had found it.

The three of them headed back down to where they had left the rest of the men, showing up drenched with sweat and water, and with black soot all over. After getting a new canister for his OBA, Eurice decided to go off by himself to find a fire to fight. Rather than go back to the fire they had just fought, which seemed too big for a small crew, Eurice decided to head aft, to the rear of the ship, an area he knew well because he worked and lived there. After passing through compartments already blackened by fire, he found himself on the port quarter, the rear corner of the ship on the left side. This was directly beneath some of the worst fires and explosions, and Eurice could see that he'd found the fire. He looked for firefighting gear to use, but all he found was a hose that had been blown apart by the explosions. Ammunition and planes were still exploding just overhead on the flight deck, and a combination of fuel, water, and foam was pouring off the deck right where he stood. With all sorts of debris and God-knows-what raining down on his head, this was not a good place to be. He could see a destroyer coming in close alongside to render aid, but he was not sure what he should do. The hatch he had just come through now had smoke pouring from it, so going back was not really an option. He had backed himself into a corner.

Eurice started thinking about what was around him. He knew that the ship's post office was on one side overhead and on the other side was a magnesium-flare locker. Magnesium flares—the same thing that had caused the devastating fire on the carrier *Oriskany.* Once they're ignited, they burn white hot and can't be extinguished. Desperate to do something, Eurice picked up the shredded fire hose and bent it over itself so that some of the water sprayed out one of the biggest holes. He pointed the spray up at the overhead, toward the magnesium flare locker.

Well, this is a waste of time. I'm not accomplishing a goddamn thing.

Eurice dropped the shredded hose and looked over at the hatch again, trying to calculate his chances if he forced his way back into the smoke. He had used part of another OBA coming to that area, so he figured he had maybe a good seven minutes left on that thing.

I don't know how far I'll get in seven minutes. That's not long.

He had to do *something*. He definitely couldn't stay where he was. Eurice looked up at one of the gun mounts on the side of the ship and saw some sailors working there. *That's not too far a trek from here, so maybe I can make it on this OBA.* He wasn't at all sure, though. Feeling trapped and knowing the danger of running into a smoke-filled passageway without a full OBA, Eurice considered jumping overboard. But he looked over at the destroyer pulling alongside and realized they would not be able to pick him up; the destroyer was keeping pace with the carrier and both would be long gone after Eurice hit the water. He looked aft and could not see any other ships in the carrier's wake. Eurice was trapped between water and fire.

Okay, if I jump over here and nobody sees me, who's going to know? I don't want to just drown out there by myself. He stared at the water for a minute and tried to make a rational decision. *Water or fire?*

Eurice didn't like his choices, but he figured he had a slightly better chance with the fire. He put on his oxygen mask again and knelt down in front of the hatch with black smoke pouring out. After taking one last glance at the bright blue sky, he plunged into the pitch-black hatch and started feeling his way along.

Chapter 10

Keep up your very good work

The horror continued on the flight deck, but the men were beginning to make progress in fighting the fire. Sailors were manning hoses as best they could, pouring seawater and fog foam onto the burning jet fuel and the wreckage of the planes. It often took a dozen men to man a fog-foam hose, with several holding the hose on the fire and another group manning a water wand, a pipe several feet long with a diffuser on the end to create a fine water spray. The water team held the wand over the heads of the fog-foam team, soaking them as they worked and protecting them from the searing heat of the fire just ahead. (This combination of foam and water was proper firefighting technique because the water did not wash away the foam.)

With the *Forrestal*'s firefighting team wiped out in the first moments of the fire, the sailors had to take over and learn on the job. Some of them had been trained in firefighting techniques but had no real experience, while others had no training whatsoever. As the blazes roared so close it made them flinch from the heat, the men with a little training tried to take the lead. They provided impromptu lessons on how to use the fog foam and the water wands, and they showed the others how to use the oxygen breathing apparatus, the OBAs that allowed the men to get close to the deck fire and some of the burning compartments below. The OBAs were a crucial tool if the men were going to fight the fires anywhere belowdecks, and more was involved than just pulling the mask over your face. Some actually had to sit down and read the instructions that came with the device, while the fires roared nearby and their buddies needed help.

Everywhere they looked on the rear portion of the flight deck, planes were burning furiously and churning heavy black smoke into the air. The entire rear of the flight deck was ablaze, and their first goal was to stop the blaze from moving any farther forward on the deck.

The big explosions during the fire's first moments had spread the fire far beyond its original site at McCain's plane, and smaller blasts of ammunition, fuel tanks, and other items continued for a long time. Ejection seats in the burning planes were firing, sending the remains of a pilot's seat skyward in a weak imitation of their real purpose. Missiles and rockets cooked off periodically, exploding where they lay or their propellant igniting and sending the projectile across the deck at low level, a lightning-fast killer that took out anyone in the way. The warhead on the rocket or missile might then explode with all the explosive power that was intended for ground targets in Vietnam. Every time a bit of red-hot shrapnel made its way to another plane, there was the chance of setting off a whole new fuel spill, fire, and major explosions from the ordnance. Every plane sitting on the deck represented a target for the willy-nilly ways of flying debris. At any moment, the tiniest bit of metal could find a target that could spread the fire much, much farther forward on the flight deck.

There were dozens of vulnerable planes, but none posed more danger than the KA-3B Skywarrior parked on the elevator just behind the island. The Skywarrior was a tanker plane, already loaded with twenty-eight thousand pounds of jet fuel. It was unmanned, having just recently been brought up from the hangar bay below. The plane was to be part of the scheduled air strike, flying off with the attack planes to provide midair refueling. Now it sat on the starboard side of the deck, only yards away from the critical island structure on one side and the roaring fire. If the tanker's fuel exploded, it would probably wipe out everyone on the deck and pour hundreds of gallons of burning fuel down onto the men working in the hangar bays directly below. The fuel tanker was a huge hazard, just sitting there with no protection.

On the bridge, Captain Beling realized the danger posed by all the remaining planes on the deck—and in particular by the Skywarrior and the A-6 Intruders parked just aft of the fuel tanker behind the island.

"Damn it, they're parked right near the uptakes from the boiler rooms," Beling commented, thinking out loud about the dangers to the chimneylike structures that provided ventilation for the ship's vital engine room. "Those planes are armed and loaded, aren't they? If one of those bombs goes, it's going to ruin the draft of the fires"— meaning the boiler fires in the engine room. "We won't have any power."

Losing power would be a major downturn in the ship's effort to survive, preventing it from continuing forward to keep the fire blown back aft and making it impossible to maneuver in cooperation with other ships coming to her aid. Clearly the planes on deck had to be moved, so orders started going out to get them moved in any way possible. Normally the aircraft would be moved either under their own power or by small, low-profile tractors that would attach a tow bar to the front wheel, but that wasn't possible in this critical state.

They had to move the planes by hand, with the sheer muscle power of young men pumped full of adrenaline. All over the deck, they joined together to wrestle planes out of danger and take them much farther forward on the flight-deck, a more frantic and improvised version of the carefully choreographed ballet that was the usual flight-deck scene. The Skywarrior was one of the first concerns, but it could not be moved until a lot of other equipment was first moved out of the way. The tanker plane was parked on the elevator, on the very edge of the deck starboard, and in front of it were two helicopters, a big stack of heavy tow bars, and various other equipment. This area was referred to as "the junkyard" for good reason. Dozens of men set about moving all of this equipment first so they could get to the dangerous fuel tanker. Every minute mattered.

After a while, the path was clear and the men could begin to push the tanker forward. Even with dozens of men pushing hard, they had to find a tractor to take most of the weight. They managed to push the tanker to the center of the flight deck and then turn it right so it could be forced up toward Catapult 1 on the right side of the deck far forward. There they parked the plane as far away from the blaze as they could.

Some planes could not be moved forward, however, no matter how much muscle was applied. Either they were damaged in some way from the blasts, or they already were on fire or were leaking fuel. There was no way to stop a fuel leak in a plane, and they certainly didn't want to move it into the relatively safe area. Some planes ignited from the wheels up, as the magnesium in their brake systems heated from the surrounding flames and the hot deck. Once the magnesium began to burn with its unique ferocity, the plane was a goner no matter what you did. And when the magnesium heated up sufficiently, it could explode like a bomb.

The bombs and missiles loaded on the planes posed their own explosive hazard, of course, and it was not feasible to remove the ordnance in such a crisis. The hazardous planes had to be dealt with, and there was neither the time nor the means to do it delicately. The solution was a fairly universal one on an aircraft carrier: if there's something you don't want on an aircraft carrier anymore, you throw it overboard.

Word of this spread across the deck, from officers trying to organize the men and from orders given by the bridge and by damage control over radio headsets. But mostly the men came to the decision themselves, and it was reinforced when they saw the first plane pushed overboard. Ed Roberts jumped right into the effort to move planes because this was his main job anyway. He joined others who had started forming work parties around individual aircraft, bunching up around the big machines and grabbing whatever they could find to start pushing and pulling. Most of the aircraft were already parked on the rim of the carrier deck, so getting them overboard was just a matter of giving them a good push to get some momentum and then watching the huge aircraft slip over the side of the ship. But others made Roberts curse and scream while he pushed with all his might. The catwalks and various other structures off the ship's edge sometimes made it hard to get the planes overboard in one easy swoop because they got caught, leaving the plane dangling over the edge. Once that happened, it was a tricky proposition to keep pushing it manually because you never knew when the plane or the catwalk would give way and suddenly plummet into the ocean.

Roberts saw that planes and wreckage were being pushed overboard all over the flight deck, but especially at the rear closest to the main fire. That's where the planes were most at risk, and where most of them were already damaged and leaking fuel. While some sailors faced the fire directly with water hoses and fog foam, others worked nearby to man-handle the planes toward the deck edge and over into the sea. Roberts and the other sailors improvised whatever means they could to get the planes overboard quickly, and without taking anyone with them. Much of the deck equipment was burning already or damaged from the explosions, but the men found a few small tractors, a forklift, and, most luckily, the big apparatus known as the "Tillie."

The Tillie, also known as the crash crane, was a big four-wheeled monster that could lift just about any plane, or anything else you stuck in its claws. The Tillie was used to clear out crash wreckage, damaged aircraft, or anything else too big and heavy to be moved easily. Though the Tillie was normally used to lift and carry a load, sometimes without even damaging an airplane, it was also very effective at brutish work. This was a day for getting things done quick and dirty, so the Tillie just ran up to big planes on the deck and forced them right over the side.

But most of the planes were jettisoned with nothing more than muscles and determination. At one point, Clark Chisum, the *Forrestal's* weapons officer, was on deck helping coordinate some of the plane movement, including throwing some overboard. He was with a group of men pushing a plane toward the edge of the deck, straining to move the heavy machine, when he noticed that one of the men was just walking alongside and making no effort to push.

Chisum was about to ask him why the hell he wasn't pushing when he saw the reason. The man was walking alongside the plane with his index finger jammed into a hole in the fuel tank, stopping a fuel leak that could cause the plane to burst into flames at any moment. Chisum decided the young man was doing a pretty good job.

At one point, Ed Roberts spotted serious trouble with a plane being moved by one of the small tractors on board. The driver of the cart had backed the plane up to the edge of the deck, intending to release it at the right moment and let the plane continue off the edge. But the tow bar did not release, and the plane's weight was pulling the cart and driver back with it. The driver was frantically pushing on the brakes, but the

cart was sliding backward in the fog-foam solution. The plane was getting close to the edge, and from the look on the cart driver's face,
Roberts wasn't at all certain that the guy would have the presence of
mind to jump off in time. He knew from his experience in moving planes
that the tractor brakes weren't enough to stop the plane once it got
momentum, but he suspected the guy on the tractor didn't. Roberts
grabbed a wheel chock and walked alongside the plane as it moved backward, just as he normally would, and tossed the chock into place behind
the wheel. The plane was moving too fast and the deck was too slippery;
the wheel just spit the chock back out. He kicked it back into place and
it came out again.

Roberts kicked it back into place again, and this time he jammed his
foot against the chock to hold it in. He had to lean back on his arms and
crab-walk backward as the plane continued to move, the chock skipping
along as he tried to hold it in. He could see the deck edge getting closer
and closer, and then finally the plane stopped six feet from the edge.
The tractor driver gunned the engine to get traction as Roberts eased
his foot off the chock, and then when it seemed it would hold, Roberts
ran up and released the tow bar from the plane. With the tractor freed,
he ran back and yanked the chock away from the wheel. With the deck
tilted slightly and slippery, the plane began to move on its own and soon
crashed over the side, flopping onto its back in the water. Roberts lay
panting on the deck from the effort.

One plane aft of the island, a big Vigilante, which was much larger
than the Skyhawks and Phantoms, was parked right on the edge of the
starboard side when the fire started, just to the rear of where the big
tanker plane had been parked and between the two elevators there. The
plane clearly was in danger of igniting because of its proximity to the
fire; the crew could see that flying debris had already opened the plane's
skin in a lot of places. More than a dozen men pushed on the plane and
got it rolling backward off the flight deck, but then the wheels got hung
up in the catwalk just below the deck. The plane sat there, firmly stuck
with its nose pointing up at a forty-five-degree angle, still posing the
same explosive hazard but now in a position that made it very difficult
for the men to push it. And even if they could, the wheels were caught
up in a tangle of metal that would be hard to break.

Quickly, a sailor came rushing up to the big plane in a heavy-duty forklift normally used to move around pallets of bombs and other materials on the flight deck. Wasting no time, he drove the big forklift up to the plane and raised the forks slightly, shoving them hard up under the fuselage. Then he raised the forks higher, forcing the plane into even more of a vertical position, and gunned the engine on the forklift, pushing forward on the plane as hard as he could. The other sailors stood back for the most part and tried to stay out of the way as the determined sailor pushed hard on the plane, the forklift's wheels slipping in the slippery fog-foam solution on the deck. With the forks raised as high as they would go, the sailor kept pushing hard on the plane, the slipping of the truck causing it to rock back and forth into the plane. The sailors nearby were doing all they could to help by pushing wherever they could grab it, but the fight had really come down to one guy in a forklift trying to shove this damn plane off the ship. In doing so, the sailor was risking his own life, because the forks easily could become jammed in the plane's fuselage and be pulled overboard as well.

At one point, another sailor drove up in one of the squat little tow tractors and rammed it up against the rear of the forklift, trying to keep the bigger truck from slipping so much on the soapy deck. After a long struggle, about fifteen minutes of pushing and wiggling, something finally gave way. Whatever parts of the ship and the plane had commingled on the edge of the deck came loose and the Vigilante finally fell into the ocean. The big plane slipped over the side and hit the water hard, floating for just a minute or so as the ship moved on, then sank out of sight in the ship's wake. The crew eventually pushed over three intact RA-5C Vigilantes and one A-4E Skyhawk, not counting other plane wreckage that had been burned and eventually was pushed overboard.

Those planes posed a major risk to the crew, but not nearly as much as all the ordnance stowed on the ship for that morning's aborted air strike. Tons of bombs were sitting all over, some stacked neatly on pallets in the bomb farm on the flight deck, behind the island where everyone was gathering, and others sitting where they were left on the deck as the fire broke out. Below, more bombs were in the hangar bays, and still more in the magazines belowdecks. In addition, there were hundreds of missiles and rockets on the flight deck and in the hangar bay, each one loaded with fuel and something nasty in the nose that was intended to knock out ground installations, blow planes out of the sky, or wipe out ground troops by the dozens. The rockets and missiles already loaded on the planes were going off as they burned in the big fire, and the crew was worried that the blaze would spread to the others.

And the bombs, of course, had proven to be very sensitive to the heat. Plenty of the old thousand-pound bombs were still left on the ship, not to mention the comparatively smaller ones, and just a handful of explosions from those fat boys had nearly crippled the *Forrestal*. If the crew didn't get rid of the bombs, the fire could set off even more massive explosions, taking more men and threatening the ship's survival.

Beling considered just ordering that the bombs be put on the big elevators and lowered to a safer area of the ship, but the elevators couldn't rapidly handle enormous quantities of ordnance like what was stored on deck. It would be a slow process to get all the bombs belowdecks, and they couldn't risk that delay.

So just as it had with the planes, word spread that the bombs and other ordnance were to be jettisoned as quickly as possible. There was no time to make careful, measured decisions about which bomb was at risk of exploding and which ones could safely be left alone. Officers on the flight deck and in the hangar bays started giving orders to shove it all overboard, *now*, and the crew got the idea fast. Everywhere, men started wrestling the big bombs to the edge of the carrier, sometimes rolling them along the deck, sometimes joining together and straining to lift the heavy weapons. Missiles and rockets were picked up by impromptu teams, sometimes of as many as ten men, drenched from the torrent of seawater falling in the hangar bays, and carried to the big open elevator doors. There they were heaved overboard and lost to the ocean.

This stuff was killing the men, and everybody wanted it *off* the damn ship. They were willing to do whatever it took to get it off.

John McCain had hustled off the flight deck and, after determining that his injuries were not serious, he headed down to the hangar-bay level. There he saw some sailors heaving bombs off of one of the elevators and over the side of the ship. He pitched in.

On the bridge, Captain Beling was concerned that his men would be beaten down by the ongoing fight against the fire and the everyday heat of the Tonkin Gulf. More than an hour had passed and he still didn't have a reliable count of the injured and wounded, but the initial reports indicated the toll would be high. And he could see that men were dropping all over the flight deck from exhaustion. They had to keep fighting, and Beling thought maybe a pep talk would help. He picked up the mike for the 1MC, the public-address system that reached all parts of the ship.

"Men of *Forrestal,* this is the captain. The forward progress of the fire on the flight deck has been stopped. We've got some good confidence in our ability to get these under control. Keep up your very good work."

Beling's words were welcomed. Ed Roberts just wanted some information—any information—and he liked hearing Beling's calm voice.

Well, okay then. At least he didn't tell us to find life jackets. I guess we're beating this thing.

Beling's encouraging words spurred the men in the hangar bay to get rid of more of the bombs. McCain worked with the group of men on the elevator, two or three of them at a time grabbing a bomb and lugging it over to the deck edge. Some sailors found "bomb carts," resembling a hand truck, to move the heavy bombs, but most of the work was done by energetic, highly motivated young men putting their hands on the bombs. McCain saw that the crew was doing their best to use the equipment at hand, whatever they could find, but sometimes throwing things off a ship isn't as easy as it sounds.

One sailor in the hangar bay, for instance, was using a forklift to pick up a big pallet of bombs and carry them to the open elevator door. With the forklift, he was able to move a lot more bombs at once than the sailors could move by hand, but then he had the problem of actually throwing them off when he got close enough. A forklift isn't designed to actually toss something off it, so the sailor couldn't figure out how to dump the bombs off. He could get close to the edge, but then the big stack of bombs just sat there on his forks. He considered dropping them on the deck and pushing the whole stack off, but there was no clean edge on the deck; the pallet would just get hung up.

But like so many other men on the *Forrestal* that day, the sailor decided to do whatever it took. He drove the forklift, with the bomb pallet still raised high overhead, as close to the edge as he could and stopped. Then he put the forklift in gear, let go of the clutch, and jumped off the truck as fast as he could. As the sailor tumbled to the deck, not far from falling overboard himself, the forklift and its danger-ous load flew forward and into the sea.

Extraordinary effort was becoming commonplace on the carrier. Men like Otis Kight stepped up and did whatever they had to do. He was one of the older guys on board, and the day of the fire was, in fact, his forty-third birthday. Kight had been on the carrier USS *Yorktown* when it was sunk during the Battle of Midway, and he had been shot down in a bomber over the Philippine Sea. In 1954, he survived an explosion aboard the carrier USS *Bennington,* which killed more than one hun-dred sailors. So when fire broke out on the *Forrestal,* Kight knew that dogged determination could mean the difference between living and dying. Joining in the effort with men less than half his age, Kight wres-tled and heaved the big heavy bombs overboard with a ferocity that amazed those who saw him. Kight weighed only 140 pounds, but he single-handedly lifted 250-pound bombs, carried them to the elevator doors, and threw them overboard.

Those responsible for the ordnance were doing their best to prevent more explosions, but often that just meant directing the effort to throw bombs overboard and lending their own muscle to the effort. In the hangar bays, however, Chief Ordnanceman Thomas Lawler was trying to put his skills to work on some missiles he knew were dangerous. Lawler had been in his maintenance shop nearby when the fire first started. He had thought the ship was under attack, and when the ceil-ing of his shop started to glow red in a matter of minutes, he and his assistant fled into the hangar bays. Then he remembered that there were some F4 Phantom jets parked in Hangar Bay 3, already loaded with missiles. Plenty of men were running around already trying to jet-tison bombs and other ordnance, but missiles loaded on a plane can't just be yanked off by unfamiliar hands. So Lawler ran to Hangar Bay 3 and found the Phantoms parked in the darkness and under a torrent of water. The lights were out and a thick smoke was gathering, so Lawler couldn't see a thing except for the shadows and familiar forms of the planes. With his assistant at his side, he groped from one plane to another, feeling for the missiles and disengaging them from memory alone, unable to see anything they were doing. They felt for the various attachments, and once the missile was free from the plane, they would lower it to the deck and carry it to the edge of the ship.

Like Beling, Merv Rowland was starting to worry that the long fight might get the best of his men. The crew in damage control was performing well, but he knew that the initial adrenaline rush would wear off and then a man's attention could wander. He couldn't have any of that.

"This damn thing's not over yet!" Rowland called out in damage control. "Stay focused on your job and don't get slack on me. We've still got a lot of work to do."

Rowland also used the 1MC system to update the crew and give orders, his gravelly voice tinged with a sense of urgency that contrasted with Captain Beling's ever-calm tone. Rowland sometimes hesitated as he gave instructions to the crew, and in the background, his damage-control crew could be heard feeding him information to pass on, such as where to find needed equipment and electrical controls.

"Repair parties two, three, and four report to your repair party if not needed elsewhere. Do not, I repeat, do not flood out the magazines until directed by the captain!

"All repair parties, this is control. There are two major fires on the fantail, port and starboard one, two, and three levels.

"Order: Make every effort to jettison the fuel drums on the port quarter. On the starboard fantail. I repeat, repair parties fighting the fire on the port quarter, make every effort to jettison the gasoline drums on the starboard fantail! A quick-release will run through the bulkhead, right by the access going to the carpenter shop."

After helping throw bombs overboard in the hangar bay, John McCain made his way to the pilots' "ready room," where they often gathered for briefings and other meetings. Several other pilots were there already, and McCain joined them in watching the flight-deck action on a television monitor. The stationary camera was still transmitting the scene from above, though the operator had long since fled from the danger.

The pilots were impressed with the *Forrestal*'s crew.

"We're professional military men, and I suppose it's our war," McCain said after the fire. "And yet, here were enlisted men who earn a hundred and fifty dollars a month and work eighteen to twenty hours a day—and I mean manual labor—and they certainly would have survived had they not stayed to help the pilots and fight the fire."

The crew was mobilizing to do whatever they could, but they needed help. Fortunately, the ships nearby had sensed the urgency of the situation immediately and sprang into action. Some of the other ships on Yankee Station were within sight of the *Forrestal*, and the moment the fire first started, the sailors standing watch on those ships called in the emergency to their commanding officers. From miles away, the sailors on the other ships could see that something terrible was happening to the *Forrestal*. The ship in the distance suddenly sprouted an ugly black smoke plume that rose high into the morning sun, and they could see debris blown into the air and the splashes made by planes, debris, and people hitting the water.

Even without knowing what was going on, they radioed for help from any U.S. vessels in the area. Soon, messages from the *Forrestal* itself made it clear that the ship was in a desperate fight to survive. The USS *Oriskany* and the USS *Bon Homme Richard*, two aircraft carriers, immediately ceased their own flight-deck preparations and turned their attention to the *Forrestal*. With a fellow flattop in such dire trouble, the crews of the nearby carriers knew that their resources could make the difference in the ship's surviving the fire. At 10:56 A.M., the destroyers *Mackenzie, Rupertus,* and *Tucker* also turned toward the *Forrestal* and awaited orders for coordinating a rescue effort with the other ships. Less than five minutes after the fire started, help was on the way.

Unlike the carriers, the destroyers would be able to maneuver in close and directly aid in fighting the fire. All three ships sounded general quarters and turned toward the *Forrestal*. They poured on the engines to nearly full throttle, rushing to close the distance. By 11:02 A.M., eleven minutes after the fire started, the *Rupertus* was close enough to drop its relatively small "motor whale boat" in the water and start assisting in the rescue of men in the water. The *Rupertus* started maneuvering in close to the *Forrestal*'s left rear, all the time watching closely for men and debris in the water, dodging left and right to avoid them.

The aircraft carriers were launching all of their helicopters to aid in the rescue, and the men already in the water were a primary concern. Some had been blown into the water by the first bomb explosions, and others were still jumping into the sea to escape the fires. A total of forty-seven men went overboard. Up above, Angel 20, the helicopter crew that had been on plane-guard duty and saw the fire start, was the first helicopter on the scene, approaching the *Forrestal* from the right side and crossing in front of the bridge before curving around to the rear of the ship on the left side. As David Clement positioned the helicopter to follow the carrier's wake and look for men overboard, one of the big bomb explosions rocked his craft violently. Clement righted the helicopter and looked in awe at how bad the fire was, then he repeatedly radioed for assistance. His calls for help broke up as his helicopter was buffeted by the shock waves from explosions on the deck, shaking the craft hard and causing it to bounce wildly through the air with Clement struggling to maintain control.

"We have multiple men in the water, repeat, multiple men in the water!" Clement radioed. "Angel twenty requesting assistance!"

The pilot considered pulling away from the stricken carrier because of the danger from the concussions and flying debris, any one bit of shrapnel capable of hitting a soft spot in the fuselage or shearing off a rotor blade. But almost immediately, Leonard Eiland spotted one of several men in the water. He pointed him out and Clement headed in that direction.

Though they had trained extensively for picking up downed pilots and the occasional man overboard, Clement and one of the rescue swimmers, Albert Barrows, had never participated in a real rescue. Eiland and the other swimmer, James O. James, each had one rescue under their belts. Clement dumped seven hundred pounds of fuel in the ocean to make the helicopter lighter and more maneuverable during the rescue. Then he put Angel 20 right over the man in the water and Barrows jumped in with a "fish pole" used to reach the rescue sling lowered from the helicopter and push it toward the victim, who could be panicky. James, the other swimmer, stayed aboard to direct the pilots and operate the winch that would haul the man in once he was in the sling. Barrows used the fish pole to help the first man get in the sling, making the first water rescue only four minutes after the fire started.

James helped the burned man into the helicopter and then the pilots maneuvered over to another man in the water. They picked up two more men in the next ten minutes, both of them badly burned. But after the first rescue, Barrows realized the victims were nearly helpless and stopped using the fish pole, instead swimming directly to the injured men so he could put the rescue sling around them. The swimmer had a hard time hanging on to the victims because their burned skin kept coming off in his hands. The helicopter crews weren't used to seeing so much trauma on the men they pulled out of the water. The men coming off the ship were badly wounded and a great many of them were severely burned over most of their bodies. Many were in shock, unable to help in their rescue, and their clothes had been blown off in the explosions.

As on all the other helicopters working to rescue men from the sea, the crew of Angel 20 was working at a feverish pace, pushing their aircraft to the limit. The helicopters flew at top speed back to the carriers once they had wounded men on board and hovered for long periods while the swimmers tried to save the injured. The prolonged hovering put a strain on the aircraft. As Angel 20 approached a fourth victim in the water, Clement saw that the engine was seriously overheating.

Clement reported back to his flight controllers on the *Oriskany* that he was redlining the engine, and they ordered him back to the carrier. He acknowledged the order, but then he couldn't bring himself to pull away from the men in the water. He kept looking at the instrument gauges and then back at the men in the water. He couldn't do it.

I can't leave them. We've got to get those men.

Clement ordered his swimmer back in the water and he hovered for another long while, watching the temperature gauge creep a little higher every minute. Clement knew he was risking his own life and that of his crew, but he knew they didn't want to leave either.

The fourth man was brought aboard, burned like the others, and then Angel 20 hustled back to the *Oriskany.* They off-loaded the injured men while undergoing a "hot fuel," in which the craft is refueled with the engine running and the rotors turning, ready to jump off the deck as soon as the fuel hose is pulled back. By 11:12 A.M., Angel 20 was in the air again and heading back to the *Forrestal.* Clement was relieved to see the engine temp drop once they stopped hovering so much.

Clement and his crew made one more rescue and then landed on the *Forrestal's* deck to unload the man, using a spot far forward of the fire. With more helicopters on site for water rescues, they headed back to the *Oriskany* to start shuttling supplies between the carriers.

All around the *Forrestal,* surface and air ships were closing in like friends and family eager to help in a crisis. On the other carriers, sailors were hauling their own firefighting gear to the flight deck for transfer, filling big cargo nets with fire hoses, fog-foam solution, and air masks, as well as medical equipment. The air swarmed with helicopters, and a half-dozen ships and smaller boats were coming into sight.

The destroyers were the hard-charging friends rushing in to help the stricken carrier as directly as possible, able to move in remarkably close to the big carrier. The other aircraft carriers nearby could provide much-needed assistance in the way of helicopters and supplies, but they could not maneuver closely enough to actually aid in the firefighting. The destroyers, though not small ships at all, were highly maneuverable and so they were able to rush right to the *Forrestal*'s side.

Captain Beling radioed from the *Forrestal* bridge that the destroyers had permission to move in as close as possible, but he also emphasized that he was *not* ordering the destroyers to do so. Realizing how dangerous such maneuvering would be to the destroyers, he made it clear that the destroyers should move in only at their own discretion.

The skippers of the destroyers did not hesitate to move in close. They steered close in to the big carrier, carefully matching the big ship's speed and diligently keeping a steady course in the uneven water so they could get close enough to direct their own firefighting hoses on the carrier's fires. The destroyers had men stationed on their decks with charged fire hoses, ready to fight the fires visible on the carrier, and when they got within range, the sailors opened the hoses and started pouring water on hot spots that were inaccessible to the carrier's crew. The destroyer crews also stood on the deck tossing life jackets and inflatable life rafts overboard to the men in the water.

In an extreme exaggeration of the supply-ship maneuvering that the carrier experienced all the time, the destroyers maneuvered to within twenty feet of the huge carrier for long stretches, hugging her heaving bulk in a delicate operation that required the very best of the destroyer's crews. At one point, the *Mackenzie*'s upper mast was only five feet away from the *Forrestal*'s elevator deck. Impressive ships in their own right, the destroyers nonetheless were dwarfed by the huge carrier, their tall masts barely reaching the level of the flight deck. With the destroyers at general quarters, the best of the best were manning the bridges, but still, the operation was a tense, extremely demanding exercise in close-quarter steering and propulsion. The young men on the bridges of the destroyers could see nothing but the looming hull of the carrier as they looked out the windows, and at times the clouds of thick black smoke from the *Forrestal* blinded everyone on the destroyers. It took all the concentration they could muster to maintain a steady course without crashing into the side of the bigger ship. Sailors on the bridge and on watch on the bow kept an eye out for men and debris in the water, and periodically they called out for a sudden course change. And as the *Forrestal* crew worked to jettison burning planes and bombs, the destroyers had to zig in and out to avoid them. The crews watched for items being pushed over the carrier's flight deck, and suddenly the destroyer would heave out to avoid the falling debris and move around the plane as it slowly sank in the carrier's wake. Then the destroyer moved back in close again, once again carefully calculating its speed and course to match the carrier's. The destroyers needed to be as close as possible, but all the while, the destroyer crews knew they could be crushed almost instantly by a sudden movement of the carrier. And at the same time, the destroyers had to counter the bigger ship's natural tendency to suck in anything nearby as its huge hulk cut through the water. Steering a straight course with the carrier wasn't enough; the destroyers had to constantly pull away from the carrier just enough to counter the pull toward the carrier. With only twenty feet between the ships, there was absolutely no room for error. Any lurch to the left or right by the carrier could be devastating to the destroyers alongside. Such maneuvering is delicate enough when both ships are in good shape, but it became even more risky when the huge carrier's control was compromised. They had no idea whether the *Forrestal*'s steering and propulsion were damaged, praying only that the carrier could maintain a steady course as they cruised alongside. This tense scene would continue for three hours.

The *Forrestal* was surrounded by friendly ships, but there also were a few that weren't necessarily interested in helping the stricken ship. The big black cloud pouring off the *Forrestal*'s deck had attracted the attention of everyone on the water for miles around, and that included a number of Vietnamese or Chinese boats in the area. It had not been unusual for the *Forrestal*'s crew to see local boats in the water, often the wooden junks or sampans with big sails that were common to the waters off Vietnam. The officers knew that many of them were enemy boats watching the American ships and sending reports back to the mainland by radio. Normally, the boats stayed a fair distance away, even though the open water allowed them a clear view of the carrier's operations. The crew noticed a couple of boats in the area that morning before the fire, but nobody cared much. They were tiny and far away.

But with the *Forrestal* on fire, some of those junks started moving in closer. By 11:10 A.M., about twenty minutes into the fire, crews on several ships reported seeing the local boats as close as two thousand yards away. With men in the water awaiting rescue, and with the carrier clearly in a vulnerable state, the appearance of the junks was not a welcome sight.

While he was on the flight deck helping with the firefighting, Ed Roberts looked out and noticed that suddenly boats were everywhere. He hadn't noticed any local boats at all before the fire, and now suddenly there were dozens.

"What the hell is that all about?" Roberts asked someone nearby. "They just out here to gawk at us?"

"It's more than that," the other man said. "They get thirty-five dollars if they bring in an American body or an American ID card."

"Motherfuckers . . ." Roberts muttered, shaking his head. The two men forgot about the boats until they heard a thunderous boom from the water nearby. They turned to look and saw that one of the destroyers had fired its big guns on a local boat. The boat disintegrated, bits of wood raining down like confetti. Within minutes, the swarm of boats disappeared as quickly as it had arrived.

As the other ships in the area closed in to help, the *Diamond Head* could only hang back and watch the fire from afar. Still in the area after supplying the *Forrestal* with the faulty ordnance the night before, it could not maneuver close to provide any hands-on help because no one wants an ammunition ship anywhere near a fire. The best it could do was to follow behind at a distance of several miles, the last in a long line of ships following in the carrier's wake. The *Diamond Head* sailors scanned for any men left in the water, but they found only debris. The crew eventually transferred some firefighting gear to the *Forrestal* later in the day.

Not knowing much about what was going on except a fire on a carrier, the *Diamond Head* crew were left to wonder how bad the situation was. The black smoke and the buzz of activity around the ship told them it was serious. Even at a distance, they could see explosions on the flight deck. When word first spread that the *Forrestal* was on fire, the *Diamond Head* crew dropped whatever they were doing and went to the upper deck to see. There they stood, men who had grown accustomed to the daily fear that their own ship might blow up underneath them. They were watching a navy carrier fight for its life, and the explosions on the flight deck were coming from the ordnance they had provided just hours earlier.

As they stood in the bright sun of the Tonkin Gulf, the crew of the *Diamond Head* felt they were watching their own worst nightmare befall someone else, and there was nothing they could do to help. The men were completely silent as they watched the *Forrestal* burn, imagining the horrors that must be happening there, and more than a few cried.

Chapter 11

THEY WERE SAILORS TO THE END

This was Shelton's nightmare. The fires, the explosions, the flashes of light. The men torn down by explosions and screaming in pain. Shelton was watching his nightmare of the past two nights unfold.

Throughout the *Forrestal,* thousands of men were experiencing their own personal tragedies and crises amid the bigger chaos surrounding them. In different parts of the ship, men found themselves trapped, wounded, and uncertain as to what they should do to help themselves and their ship. Many responded with the kind of fortitude that leads others to call them heroes, none more so than the three men trapped in port aft steering. One of those men was James Blaskis, Robert Shelton's buddy who had traded work shifts so he could work in port aft steering instead of on the bridge.

When general quarters sounded, Shelton had been relieved from his station on the bridge. He was supposed to go to his station in the secondary conn, but he quickly realized that he couldn't get there with the ship sealed for general quarters—not to mention the fires. With no assignment, he stayed in the bridge area for a while, watching in disbelief as the fires raged and the bombs exploded on the flight deck below.

As he looked back toward the rear of the ship and realized how bad the explosions had been, he had a stomach-churning realization.

Oh my God. Blaskis.

Shelton realized that Blaskis could be trapped in the steering compartment. He raced down from the bridge area and headed toward that area. He didn't get far before he reached the infernos of the berthing areas below the flight deck. The smoke and flames were too bad, the fires still at their worst, and there was no hope that Shelton could get to his friend. He reluctantly made his way back to the bridge, thinking maybe he should see if they needed his assistance there.

Maybe Blaskis is okay. The steering compartment is pretty far down. Maybe he'll be fine.

The port aft steering compartment was a small room in the very rear of the ship, on the left side, several decks down from the flight deck and close to the port rudder that steers the ship. The rudder, of course, was a basic but vitally important part of the ship's steering control; turn the rudder and you turn the ship. Each side of the rear of the ship had a steering-control compartment that was about eight feet by eight feet and spanned two deck levels. A massive rudder shaft ran right down the middle of the compartment, disappearing through the floor and eventually going through the hull of the ship and connecting to the rudder itself. There were mechanisms attached to the rudder shaft that turned it in reaction to commands from the bridge.

In normal operations, the rudder was controlled electronically from the bridge without any manual assistance in the steering-control room. But as a precaution, each steering-control room always was manned by two electricians and a machinist who were ready to take over steering control if the bridge was not able to do so. They could receive orders from the bridge and then manually make the adjustments to control the rudder in the steering-control room, bypassing most or all of the electronics that normally made the rudder move.

When the fire broke out, Blaskis and the other two men in port steering control were directly underneath it. The big bomb blasts were powerful enough to penetrate layer after layer of steel down to steering control, blasting holes in the compartment and mangling the only access routes in and out of the compartment. The blasts went all the way through the steering compartment and opened the hull of the ship, the very bottom, and seawater was flooding the compartment below the men. Within minutes, Blaskis, Ronald Ogring, and Kenneth Fasth were trapped at their station. By the time general quarters sounded, there was no way for them to leave and no way for anyone else to get in. And within the first few minutes, before the three men even knew what was going on, they were all seriously wounded.

The explosions tore through all the spaces above the port steering compartment, inflicting grave injuries on all three men. They were missing limbs and suffering a number of other injuries, but they still remained conscious and did their best to protect themselves from the jet fuel that rained down into their compartment from above. With little room in which to hide, they tried to avoid the pyrotechnics—flares and similar devices—that fell down from the storage compartments ripped open above them.

Walls of burning jet fuel were pouring right down over them, by them, above them, and around them. The jet fuel was coming down like a waterfall on fire.

Blaskis managed to call damage control on the phone system and report that they were badly injured and trapped. In the identical steering compartment on the starboard side of the ship, the three men working there listened as their counterparts in port steering explained their situation.

"Central Control! Central Control! This is port steering . . ." Blaskis called. The twenty-one-year-old was in charge of the other two young men.

Soon, a phone talker in Central Control responded and asked for a damage report.

"We got hit bad! The machinist's mate was hit in the hatch, and the electrician's mate's arm is severed. It's bleeding badly! We need medical help bad!"

The phone talker in Central Control assured Blaskis that a repair team was on the way, but reports from that area had already made it clear that the port steering area was a mess. The officers in Central Control studied the situation for any solution, but the repair parties in that area kept saying there was no way they could get to Blaskis's steering

When the USS *Forrestal* sailed for Vietnam in 1967, she was the world's largest and most powerful aircraft carrier. The 5,000 sailors and airmen aboard joined 400,000 ground troops already fighting in the jungles, plus the sailors aboard other ships. The bombers who flew off the aircraft carriers played a key role in the ongoing war against the North Vietnamese.

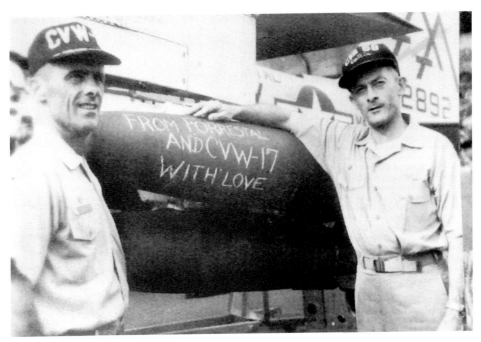

Captain John K. Beling (right), with an unidentified officer, was at the pinnacle of his career when he took command of the *Forrestal*. A World War II pilot who narrowly survived being shot down in the Pacific, Beling was proud to command the carrier and eager to show what his crew could do.

Eighteen-year-old Gary Shaver joined the navy partly as a way to cope when his girlfriend broke up with him. He left his hometown of Carpentersville, Illinois, and thought he might make a lifelong career of the navy. Shaver was assigned a job on the flight deck, directing planes as they moved about the crowded work space.

Nineteen-year-old Ken Killmeyer couldn't find a job back home in Pittsburgh because employers feared he would be drafted soon. After talking it over with his dad, they decided that Ken should join the navy. "You'll be coming home, Ken," his dad said. "We don't know that for sure if you get drafted."

Back home in White Marsh, Maryland, eighteen-year-old Frank Eurice spent his days drilling holes in bowling balls at the local Montgomery Ward. The day he was laid off, Eurice took it all in stride until he got home and found out he had been drafted. Like boys all over the country, he had a scale model of the *Forrestal* in his bedroom.

Paul Friedman was not eager to leave his home in Rockaway Beach, an ocean community outside of New York City. He spent his days riding his surfboard and finding girls to romance, but like many young men in the late sixties, Friedman worried about being drafted. By joining the navy when he was eighteen years old, at least he could be sure to avoid the infantry.

Robert Shelton was twenty-one years old by the time he started thinking about enlisting in the military, and his first choice was the air force. But when the navy recruiter found Shelton waiting in the Texas heat because the air force office was closed, he welcomed the young man inside and pretty soon, Shelton was in the navy.

Gary Pritchard (center) joined the navy right after graduating from high school in Fort Lee, New Jersey, just before his eighteenth birthday. He saw the navy as an opportunity for an education and a career, neither of which was likely if he stayed home. On the *Forrestal*, Pritchard's bunk was right under the noisy flight deck.

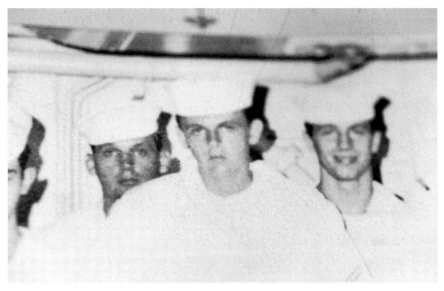

In 1966, Ed Roberts (center) was living every teenage boy's dream. His rock and roll band, the Fugitives, was hitting it big in Atlanta and was on the verge of even bigger success. When he was drafted, Roberts kept it a secret from his bandmates for as long as he could.

Milt Crutchley (center) joined the Navy in 1964 right out of high school, when he was only seventeen years old. His older brother had joined already, and his cousin was a navy chief stationed in Norfolk. Crutchley saw the navy as a career opportunity and was glad to be assigned to the *Forrestal*.

The Zwerlein family ran the local Tastee-Freez in Port Washington, New York, and Robert was the second of three boys. All of the sons joined the volunteer fire department just like their dad, who also had served in the navy. Robert's parents hoped his firefighting training would keep him safe on the *Forrestal*.

Dr. G. Gary Kirchner had just finished his residency in Rochester, New York, when he was drafted and assigned to the *Forrestal*. He was overwhelmed at first by the size of the job, caring for 5,000 crewmen along with only a few other doctors.

Merv Rowland, an experienced sailor and engineer at forty-eight years old, was one of the old salts on the *Forrestal*. He had survived many scrapes in World War II, and he would prove vital to the carrier's survival in her worst moment. As chief engineer, Rowland was in charge of damage control and the firefighting response, making him the one individual most responsible for saving the ship.

When a rocket accidentally fired across the flight deck while planes were being prepared for launch, it went right through John McCain's plane. Hundreds of gallons of fuel poured onto the deck and ignited immediately. In an instant, the entire rear portion of the flight deck was on fire.

The accidental rocket firing immediately caused a fire, but the situation grew much worse when one of the thousand-pound bombs caught in the fire exploded after only one minute and thirty-four seconds, much sooner than anyone expected.

A huge black cloud rolled off the ship as the fire spread quickly and sailors scrambled to fight it. The flight deck was crowded with planes that had been prepared for launch, loaded with fuel, rockets, and bombs. The fire quickly got out of control.

Sailors did whatever they could to fight the fire, forced to improvise after firefighting equipment and the ship's trained firefighters were killed in the first bomb explosion. The deck became so hot from the fires burning below that the sailors had to hoist the fire hoses up on their shoulders to keep them from burning through.

As smoke cleared on the flight deck after the initial explosions, the sailors could see that the bomb blasts had opened huge holes in the armor-plated steel deck. Once the deck was open, burning jet fuel poured through the holes into the decks below, spreading the fire far throughout the ship.

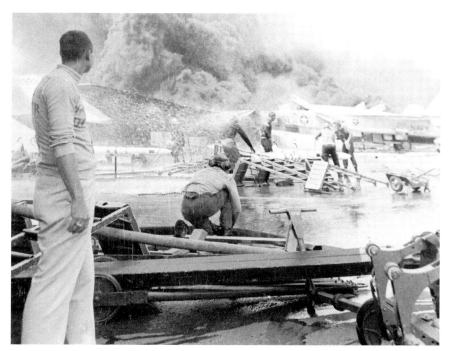

The sailors on the flight deck pitched in to move equipment and planes away from the fire, desperately trying to prevent further explosions on the flight deck. With some planes already damaged and loaded with explosives, the only option was to push them overboard as quickly as possible.

Captain Beling supervised the crew's response from the bridge, where he had a view of everything happening on the flight deck. He witnessed the terrible blasts that blew men overboard and struck down dozens at a time.

One of the main concerns was extinguishing the fires burning inside the ship. Many of the burning sections were cut off by blast damage, so the crew tried to pour water on them through the holes in the flight deck.

As the fires raged for hours, rumors spread that the captain had called for the crew to abandon ship, even though he never did. As the young sailors fought for their lives, some (like this unidentified sailor) donned life vests just in case.

It soon became clear that the bombs were exploding in the fires and word spread that the crew should dump overboard any ordnance that could not be moved safely out of the way. Using brute strength, they moved bombs weighing as much as 1,000 pounds to the deck edge and tossed them over.

In the hangar decks, crew members were concerned that rockets and missiles there could explode in the fire, so they formed impromptu teams to carry the weapons to the open edge and throw them over.

As soon as the scope of the fire on the *Forrestal* became apparent, other navy ships on Yankee Station ceased their own operations and came to the carrier's aid. The carrier crews also loaded helicopters with nearly all of their own firefighting gear for delivery to the stricken ship.

The destroyers nearby could rush in close to the burning ship because, though they were not small, they were highly maneuverable. The destroyers *Rupertus* and *MacKenzie* hugged the carrier close as they glided through the sea, pointing fire hoses at spots the carrier's crew could not reach.

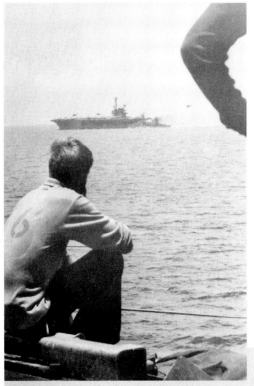

On the *Oriskany*, another aircraft carrier in the area, sailors watched the *Forrestal* burn in the distance. The carrier sent as much help as she could, and many of the injured sailors were transferred to the *Oriskany* for medical aid. The sailors on both ships knew the risks of working on a carrier, but the smoke coming off the *Forrestal* was still shocking.

The *Forrestal* suffered $72.2 million in damage, including the loss of twenty-one aircraft and damage to forty more. Some of the planes pushed overboard that day cost more than $5 million apiece, others $2 million each. The ordnance destroyed or jettisoned during the fire was valued at just less than $2 million.

Once the fires were extinguished, sailors faced the grim task of recovering the bodies of their friends. Some of the compartments could only be reached from above because of blast damage, so sailors were lowered in through the holes on the flight deck to retrieve bodies. For weeks after the fire, crew were still finding bodies.

One hundred thirty-four men died on the *Forrestal* on July 29, 1967. The bodies were first taken to the hangar deck and assembled for identification. Many sailors were stunned by the loss of their friends and tried to find them among the bodies.

Captain John K. Beling returned home from Vietnam much sooner than expected, much to the delight of his children. He was terribly saddened by the loss of his men and the early end to his mission, and he knew the navy would hold someone accountable.

DIED IN FIRE AND EXPLOSIONS ✝ USS FORRESTAL JULY 29 1967

PR2 MARVIN J ADKINS
WEST VIRGINIA
JULY 28 1934

ADJ3 EDWARD R DORSEY
CONNECTICUT
JUNE 30 1947

AMS3 RUSSELL L FIKE
PENNSYLVANIA
NOVEMBER 27 1947

AE3 LEROY MOSER
SOUTH DAKOTA
AUGUST 27 1944

ATR3 JOHN M PRUNER
MICHIGAN
MAY 14 1948

SN NELSON F SPITLER
OHIO
JULY 2 1946

LT DENNIS M BARTON
IOWA
JANUARY 19 1935

AE1 WALTER T EADS
NEW ZEALAND
AUGUST 24 1937

AN JOHNNIE L FRAZIER
TEXAS
JULY 3 1947

AMHC RICHARD L OWENS
CALIFORNIA
MAY 11 1929

AME2 DALE R ROSS
MISSOURI
APRIL 23 1947

LCDR GERRY L STARK
NEBRASKA
DECEMBER 23 1929
GULF OF TONKIN VIETNAM
U S NAVY

AEAN ROBERT J DAVIES
ILLINOIS
NOVEMBER 21 1947

AME1 JOHN J FIEDLER
WISCONSIN
AUGUST 24 1934

ADRAN RALPH E MANNING
ALABAMA
SEPTEMBER 12 1947

AMH2 ERNEST E POLSTON
SOUTH CAROLINA
MARCH 10 1936

AMS2 JOHN F SNOW
NEW YORK
SEPTEMBER 10 1938

AN HAROLD D WATKINS
KENTUCKY
JULY 16 1945

Of the 134 men killed on the *Forrestal*, 18 were never recovered or identified. A monument at Arlington National Cemetery, just behind the Tomb of the Unknowns, marks the resting place of 12 to 14 bodies that could not be identified and memorializes those never recovered.

compartment. The fire was too intense, and the blast damage was too severe.

"Central Control!" Blaskis called again after a few minutes. "The smoke is getting really thick in here! We can't breathe! Where is the repair party, Control?"

The phone talkers in damage control kept Blaskis on the line, assuring him that help would reach the men soon, urging him to hang on. The dire situation had captured the attention of everyone in the busy room, and several enlisted men took turns on the phone to offer words of encouragement to a sailor they had never met. Just hang in there, they urged, we'll get to you. Every single person who talked to Blaskis that day was left with one impression—the image of a twenty-one-year-old sailor barely hanging on through his own injuries, but concerned only with getting help for his buddies, the men for whom he was responsible. He never mentioned his own injuries to those in damage control, even though they were quite severe.

As the situation in port aft was becoming clear to those in damage control and on the bridge, Shelton was making his way back topside. When Shelton returned to the bridge, everyone noticed when he walked in. He looked like he'd been through hell, his white uniform covered in black soot and grease, his hair matted, and his face filthy from trying to make it to Blaskis.

"Shelton! How did you get out of port steering?" someone called to him. In the confusion, no one seemed to remember that Shelton had been on the bridge when the fire started. When Rowland had notified the captain that the men were trapped and that nothing could be done, the crew on the bridge had looked at the duty roster to see who was trapped in the steering compartment. It said Shelton.

"I wasn't there," Shelton replied, hesitating. "I didn't go there this morning. Why?"

Shelton understood the answer before they explained. Just as he had feared, his buddy was trapped.

He's working my shift. That should have been me.

Shelton volunteered to help out on the bridge, and before long a call came in from damage control with an update on the situation. Someone on the bridge asked Shelton if he wanted to talk to Blaskis. His heart raced as he took the phone.

"How you doing there, buddy?" he asked. There was no immediate answer. "Just hang on, okay? We're going to get you out of there."

Everyone on the bridge watched, knowing that Shelton was talking to a good friend he might never see again. The men maintained a respectful quiet as much as they could, averting their gaze when Shelton looked up.

There was little communication from Blaskis, and Shelton could tell that his friend was in bad shape. He was near tears when he hung up the phone.

Blaskis stayed on the phone with damage control for almost half an hour, occasionally dropping the phone to administer aid to one of the other men. He applied tourniquets to both of Fasth's arms, but the bleeding continued. The enlisted men in damage control continued to encourage Blaskis, but then it became clear that there was no way to rescue the men. The repair parties had tried over and over, but the fire and continuing explosions in that area of the ship were just too great. Someone had to tell the men in port steering the truth, so one of the damage-control crew asked Merv Rowland if he wanted to speak to the men.

He did. The old man got on the line with Blaskis, and his paternal instinct kicked in hard. Rowland always looked at the young crew serving under him as surrogate sons, and they looked up to him as a gruff but reassuring authority figure. Rowland's gravelly voice was uneven as he tried to tell Blaskis that he couldn't help the men.

"Son, I understand you've got a bad situation there."

"Yes sir, it's real bad down here," Blaskis said, coughing through the smoke. "We need some help right away, sir."

"I understand, but the fire and the damage are too bad right now," Rowland said, trying hard to encourage the young man without lying to him. "We keep trying, but it doesn't look like our repair parties are going to make it to you. I'm afraid you're going to be on your own, son. You're going to have to do the best you can."

There was a pause that seemed to last forever for Rowland.

Silence.

And then a quiet, softly spoken response.

. . . "Sir, we're dying."

Rowland stopped for a minute, desperately trying to think of anything he could do. He looked at the plotting board again, even though he knew what was there. Fire was everywhere around the trapped men. Damaged compartments. No way in and no way out. He already knew the truth. These men would die where they lay right now.

"Just hang in there, son. We'll get to you if we can, but it looks real bad right now. I don't think there's anything I can do for you."

Blaskis acknowledged Rowland with a quiet "Yes sir" and then put the phone down. Rowland put down his phone and looked up at the rest of the crew in damage control; they had all been staring at him silently as he talked to the men. Rowland barked an order for the men to get back to work.

Before long, though, Rowland realized that the men's story might not be finished. Though the men were in terrible shape, Rowland started thinking they might have to play an important role in saving the ship. He started to consider giving important orders to the dying men. As the fire progressed and the magnitude of the damage became clear, Rowland began to worry that the ship could lose steering control. All the worst damage was right back on the fantail, and the blasts had penetrated far down to the hull. The damage to port steering control alone was enough reason to worry.

"If anything happens to the steering engines, the ship will be out of control," Rowland explained to one of his crew nearby. The crew member understood already, but Rowland had to say it out loud. He had to remind himself why he was going to give those poor dying men their last orders. "If something happens to the hydraulic steering to move the rudders, the only way to move the ship will be two engines on the port head and two engines starboard back, stuff like that. We can't let it get like that."

And as Captain Beling reminded Rowland, the steering was especially vital at the moment because the two destroyers were so close alongside. If the carrier lost steering control, a destroyer could be crushed. So Rowland made the decision to have the men in port aft steering transfer their steering control to the starboard aft steering compartment. That way, the undamaged steering compartment on the starboard side could control both rudders if the normal control mechanisms were lost.

In most circumstances, this would not be an extraordinary request. But Rowland already knew that the men in port steering were barely hanging on. They were dying and there was nothing he could do about it, and now he had to order them to perform an important task. And Rowland knew, though it pained him to acknowledge it, that he had to give the order soon if they were to live long enough to carry it out. Rowland picked up the phone and instructed the young men to transfer the steering control.

Blaskis was fading fast by that point, but he acknowledged Rowland's orders and set about making the necessary changes to the steering control. Despite their terrible wounds and knowing that they would die where they lay, the three sailors responded well when Rowland ordered them to transfer the steering control. The process was slow, partly because they were so severely wounded, but the men did their jobs. Rowland was on the phone with them the entire time, and then soon after completing the task, he listened as each of the three men died from their wounds. Blaskis told him when the other two died, and then Blaskis fell silent.

Rowland put the phone down and couldn't hold back the tears any longer. They streamed down his face, partly from sheer frustration. There was not a goddamn thing he could do. Not a goddamn thing.

And he cried because he admired the men's determination. The old man had seen some real bravery in his day, but those three young men struck him as the epitome of navy service.

They were sailors to the end. They never begged for mercy. They never whined. They never whimpered.

Chapter *12*

I DON'T WANT TO SCREW UP

The ship had become an inescapable scene of drama and desperation, the fire now having spread throughout much of the rear portion of the ship and down many levels. The explosions had ripped open the ship's hull down past the waterline, causing compartments to flood with seawater. That flooding, combined with the seawater being pumped throughout the ship to fight the fires, was beginning to upset the ship's balance and she started leaning to the left. That list was dangerous because it could cause equipment to shift suddenly and slide off the flight deck or across the hangar bay, and, if not controlled, could eventually lead to the ship capsizing.

The list scared the hell out of some of the crew. When they felt the big ship leaning to one side, some worried for the first time that they were going to sink. They were accustomed to the carrier being nearly as stable under their feet as the ground back home, but then they felt the huge ship tipping enough to make them lean hard for balance, and causing water and fog foam, plus any remaining jet fuel, to slosh over the side. They had no way of knowing if this was a temporary problem or the beginning of the end. One thing was certain—they didn't have to be engineers to know that, if it continued, the list would cause the *Forres-tal* to fall over on its side, and from there it wouldn't be long before it sank to the bottom. Up on the flight deck, Ed Roberts wondered if the crew would have to abandon ship, and he started planning his own survival. He could see the Vietnamese coastline in the distance, and his mind raced with scenarios that involved him swimming to shore and having to fend for himself. With this in mind, he raced down to his bunk and got the big knife he had just recently bought. He strapped that onto his belt, thinking it would come in handy on shore, and then he grabbed a carton of cigarettes and headed back up to the flight deck. Somehow, in the terror of the moment, it all made sense to him.

But down in engineering, Merv Rowland was on top of the problem. Once the list began, he ordered his men to shift fuel oil from one storage tank to another, compensating for the seawater entering the ship on the other side. Before long, the ship righted itself.

The efforts to fight the fire were taking hold, but all over the ship men found themselves locked in their own individual struggles. Frank Eurice had plunged into the darkness of the smoky passageway to make his way off the fantail, where he had found himself trapped in the worst of the fire, groping his way through the darkness and hoping that the seven minutes of air on his breathing apparatus would be enough to get him out. He wasn't at all sure it would be, and he was relieved to finally see sunlight breaking through the dark smoke. As he threw himself through the hatch and onto the gun mount on the side of the ship, Eurice realized that he had made small progress in saving himself. The gun-mount platform, a small deck jutting out from the side of the ship and holding one of the carrier's big five-inch guns, was only a slightly better place to be than the fantail where he had been trapped. But now he had used most of his oxygen mask in getting here, which meant he was stuck.

Eurice found a few other men already on the gun mount, the ones he had seen from below on the fantail, but they barely acknowledged him as he threw himself out of the smoking passageway and onto the wet, slippery deck. Then one of them came over to help Eurice to his feet and he realized it was a friend from his same division. The other men were manning a hose, so Eurice and his buddy took positions in the rear, helping control the heavy, lurching fire hose. When some of the smoke cleared a bit, Eurice could see that they were cooling down the ammunition-loading assembly for one of the five-inch guns. One of the gun assemblies had exploded already or been torn apart by the explosions above, but the other one was intact. They aimed the hose at the gun to keep it cool, and also because they didn't have much else to do until they could find a way off of the gun mount.

Over on the other side of the ship, the sailors on the identical gun-mount platform were in far more danger. Located directly under the place where the flight-deck fire originated, the gun-mount deck jutting out from the side of the ship was being drenched in flaming jet fuel and debris, and the situation was no better inside. When the fire first started, twenty-year-old Milt Crutchley was at his usual station in the control room that targeted the five-inch guns. The job usually didn't promise much excitement because the carrier, by its very nature, rarely got close enough to a vessel or plane for its guns to be used in defense. Crutchley's job mostly consisted of maintaining the systems and occasionally honing the crew's tracking skills by using a friendly plane as a target for the radar systems.

Crutchley heard the first alarm for a fire on the flight deck, and as with most of the crew, it only piqued his curiosity. Not expecting much, he started to make his way from the gun-control room to the gun-mount structure nearby so he could take a look at the flight deck. But as he went through the hatch that led to the exposed gun mount, Crutchley heard the general-quarters alarm and turned back inside to man his gun-control station. At nearly the same moment, the first bomb blast rattled the ship and sent flaming debris all over the gun-mount structure.

Two of Crutchley's crew stumbled into the compartment as the explosions continued just overhead, knocking them off their feet. The three of them were shouting and questioning one another about what was happening, but no one really knew. From the force of the explosions that continued, Crutchley assumed the worst.

Damn it, somebody's snuck in and attacked us! We're going to be the first aircraft carrier to take damage from the North Vietnamese!

The explosions were deafening and kept knocking the three men around the control room, making them work hard just to stay on their feet. Before long, the men could smell smoke nearby. And soon after that, they could see it entering their control room.

The other two crew members were about Crutchley's age, but he was in charge of that control room, so they were his responsibility. He soon got on the phone and called the department that would direct the gun use during combat, but the sound-powered phones designed for combat use had gone dead. The regular phones, expected to go dead in combat, were still operational. Once he got through, the news was discouraging.

"There's a major fire on the flight deck. The bombs are going off," someone told Crutchley. "You might as well abandon your GQ station because we don't have any gun mounts for you to control anyway. They're in the fire."

Crutchley hung up the phone and told the other men they were all going to abandon the space, a relief to the men until they started looking for a way out. In just minutes, they had become trapped by the fire all around them. The smoke was still coming in the room, even though they had closed the door and turned off the ventilation system. They had to get out somehow. They wouldn't live long in this room.

They looked out onto the gun mount and decided that was a lousy place to be, already covered with flaming debris and right under some of the worst fires on the flight deck. The only other option, no matter how bad, was to try to make their way through the ship to a safer area. That meant leaving the smoke-filled room and venturing into the even smokier passageways. Crutchley thought about it for a minute and decided they had to go. But still, he was scared to death. The worst part was that he had to take responsibility for these other two men. At twenty years old, he had to save their lives.

Oh God, I hope this works. I don't want to screw up and get somebody killed.

The men had no oxygen masks, so they had to just rush into the smoky passageway and hope to find clear air before long. They headed out and found that the passage was getting darker and smokier, until finally they reached Hangar Bay 3, the huge open area directly under the flight-deck fire at the rear of the ship. Unbeknownst to Crutchley, the big bay doors had been closed already to seal off the burning hangar space. Once they got to the hangar, the air was even heavier with smoke and there was no light at all. The fire-deluge system was pouring water down from the ceiling, but the water pipes were directly under the flight-deck fires, so the water was scalding hot. Crutchley told the other two men to link arms with him so that they could stay together in the pitch-black darkness, and they struggled along slowly trying to find something by touch, anything they might recognize and that would lead them to safety. They struggled along slowly, choking and hunched over to withstand the hot water pouring on them. Before long, Crutchley decided that this trek was futile.

We're just going to stumble around here in the dark until we suffocate. We have to get out of here!

Still linked arm in arm, the three men snaked back the same way they came and eventually made it back to their starting point. They fell into the control room and slammed the door shut, but the room was filling with smoke nearly as bad as in the hangar bay. The three men were exhausted from their escape attempt, covered in soot and soaked from the water deluge in the hangar bay, choking and coughing up black phlegm. They lay there on the floor trying to breathe and wondering what the hell they were going to do next. Crutchley was starting to think they might die right there on the floor.

He tried calling combat control again, and surprisingly the phone still worked. Breathing heavily, he told them that their escape attempt had not worked and they were trapped. Combat control said they would send help if they could, but made it clear that Crutchley should not wait for rescue.

The three men lay there, feeling the heat seep in with the smoke, trying to stay as low as possible to find the little bit of air still in the room. They could hear the explosions and the fire all around them. Their sense of panic had been left behind in the hangar bay, but the fear stayed with them. Now they were just completely fatigued and concentrating on every breath. They lay there on the floor for an hour, terrified, holding wet rags across their faces and praying that the compartment would have just a little bit more air for them to breathe.

Crutchley's responsibility to save the men in his charge kept him motivated to find a solution. He thought about the hatch that led to the gun-mount structure outside, but he was reluctant to open the armored, watertight door and let in everything that was coming off of the flight deck. Desperate for a way out, he called combat control once more to ask what they knew of the gun mount outside. The gun mount's on fire, they told Crutchley, but we don't know for sure how close it is to that hatch. You can take your chances if you want to.

Crutchley thought about the risk of opening that hatch and stepping right into the fire. He discussed the option with the other two men and they agreed they had to try. Things weren't getting any better in that damn control room.

"We're either going to die in here or we're going out on that sponson," Crutchley said to the other men. "It can't be any worse out there. And even if it is, maybe it'll be quick."

The three men dragged themselves over toward the hatch leading to the gun-mount structure, and with a mixture of dread and hope, Crutchley slowly opened it. He peered out as he opened the hatch just a couple of inches, and the sunlight flooded into the dark compartment. Without opening the hatch too much, he tried to see what awaited them on the other side.

Fresh air!

Crutchley opened the hatch wider and saw that the gun mount was indeed a mess, but the fire was on the other end, away from the hatch. All three men scrambled over the lip of the hatch and fell onto the gun-mount platform, breathing heavily and coughing as they took in the clean sea air. The gun mount was far from a safe place to be, but it was a damned sight better than dying in that smoke-filled control room.

After getting their breath again, the men realized they still could not rest. The gun mount was right under the flight-deck fires, and periodically they had to dodge flaming fuel, debris, and molten metal. There was no other way off the gun-mount platform except the hatch they had just come through, so their only other option was jumping overboard. They started talking about that, but no one liked the idea much. The only good point was that they'd found a bunch of life jackets lying around. The gun-mount platform had a life-jacket-storage bin and one of the explosions had blown it open. Jackets were floating around in the water-and-foam swill that covered the platform, so they started looking for one that hadn't been damaged.

They found three good jackets and put them over their heads, strapping the waist belts around. Then they went to the railing farthest from the fire and debated whether to jump. Nobody wanted to, but it didn't take long for them to decide they had to go overboard, because the gun-mount structure was getting worse every minute. They were scared to death of going in the water, knowing how risky that would be, but Crutchley decided they had to.

The three men climbed over the railing and held on to the ship as they looked down at the sixty feet they would fall before hitting the water. From the railing, there was nothing between them and the water far below. They felt the wind on their faces and turned away as a gust of smoke choked them. They kept looking down at the sea and back at the fire, holding on tight to the railing. A destroyer was approaching from the rear, giving them some hope that they would be rescued after they hit the water. But they also worried that the destroyer would run over them.

All they had to do was let go. But they hesitated. And in that second, one of the men spoke.

"Milt, I'm not jumping."

"Whaddya mean you're not jumping? We have to!" he replied.

"I can't swim. This vest isn't going to be enough. I can't swim."

Crutchley realized that the man had come to the *Forrestal* through the navy reserve, which didn't require its recruits to prove they could swim as the regular navy did. Crutchley didn't feel like he could force the man to go overboard if he couldn't swim, and they certainly weren't going to leave him behind. Besides, Crutchley and the third man weren't eager to jump overboard either.

So the three men climbed back over the railing and tried to think of another plan. They were arguing about whether there really could be any other plan, and still considering the idea of jumping, when the flaming tail section of an airplane came tumbling down from the flight deck and crashed onto the gun mount right near them.

The men crouched down to avoid the debris as much as possible, and then Crutchley spoke up. They could work their way underneath the railing of the gun-mount platform and then leap down to a little platform that jutted out underneath. It wouldn't be easy, and it was quite a leap to the platform below. There still wouldn't be anywhere to go once they got down there. But at least they'd be farther away from the fire, he told them.

The other men agreed, and they climbed over the railing again, this time close to the ship. They gingerly worked their way down the out-side of the gun-mount platform, and when they could climb no lower, they let go and fell about fifteen feet to the other platform. They all made it safely and looked around for the next step. As they looked out, they saw that they were close to the big crane that was used to move air-planes and other large cargo on and off the ship. Its long arm was tucked alongside the ship's body when not in use. Surveying the scene, they could not believe what they saw on the crane.

A man was hanging from the crane's hook. He was in a safety harness but hanging limp as a rag doll. Crutchley supposed the man must have been doing some sort of maintenance work when the fire started, and then he was left hanging there, subject to every one of the explosions going off only thirty yards away. He must have had assistants with him when he was doing the work, but they had left him there, hanging out directly over the water and unable to bring himself back in. He seemed to be barely conscious, probably in shock, and unable to hold his head up.

Crutchley and his crew called to the man to wake him up, to see if he could be helped. After a moment, the man roused and looked over to them but he could not do much more than that. They had to shout encouragement to him for several minutes before he awoke enough to really respond, and then Crutchley took off his own life vest and tossed it to the man. Surprisingly, the man was able to catch it and put it on. Then he seemed to wake up more and, with the encouragement of the guys on the platform, was able to hoist himself up on the crane arm. He got himself on the arm of the crane and then just rested, clutching the steel supports until he could move further.

After helping that man, Crutchley and his crew returned to their own plight. They couldn't stay on the platform because fuel, molten metal, and other material were still raining down on them. The more they thought about it, the more they realized the airplane crane was their best bet. The crane was roughly the shape of a triangle, with a vertical column attached to the side of the ship and a lifting arm that jutted out over the water. From the tip of the crane arm, a third support with cables ran back to the vertical column against the ship. That meant the upper support led right up to the flight-deck level, but it was an awk-ward path angled up at about forty-five degrees. Luckily, the crane was moved in close to the ship, rather than extended all the way over the water.

If they could get up on that crane support, Crutchley thought they would at least have more options for how to escape. But the crane was not close enough to jump to, and there was no easy way to get to it. Once they did get to it, it would still be a dicey operation. The crane had no walkway that went up the length of the support arm, so they would have to just inch their way along its round pipes.

It all seemed pretty iffy, but they realized that they had to get out on the crane to help the man who was trapped. He didn't look like he was going to hold on much longer.

But how to get there?

There was one way, but no one was eager to suggest it. In all the mess that had been blown off the flight deck, one of the arresting cables, the big cables that snag the plane's tail hook on landing, had been severed and one end was blown their way. The big heavy cable was hanging down off the flight deck and draped near their platform, out over the crane arm. It was strong enough to hold the men if it didn't shift from their weight. They discussed it and decided once again that they had no better choice. They had to use the cable to get out on the crane.

Reluctantly, Crutchley and the other two men climbed up on the platform railing and grabbed the cable. One by one, they pulled themselves hand over hand along the cable until they could reach the platform. If their strength gave out or the cable dislodged, they would go right into the water, maybe after bouncing off some structure on the ship. Crutchley didn't even have a life vest anymore, having given it to the injured man on the crane.

After a tense while, all four men were hugging the crane arm and looking down at the sea sixty feet below. They stayed there for a while, just trying to hang on and not to move too much for fear of falling off. They were about to start inching their way up when they saw the destroyer *Rupertus* moving in close to the ship, almost right underneath them. As the ship drew closer, they could see that the crewmen were on the deck with fire hoses aimed at the *Forrestal*. When they noticed Crutchley and his crew up above, they shouted at them to offer help.

"Are you going to jump?" they yelled from the destroyer.

The men looked at one another and considered the idea again, not sure if they would safely make it all the way up the crane arm. But then they realized that the prospect of going overboard was worse now than it was before. In addition to the long fall, the possibility of drowning, and being pulled into the carrier's big propellers, now they might also be sucked under by the destroyer or even crushed between the two ships.

"Hell no! We're not jumping!"

After waiting a while longer on the crane, just wondering what to do next, Crutchley decided they had to move. The longer they stayed there, the higher the risk that something would come flying off the deck and knock them off. So he and his crew decided that they had to make their way up the crane arm, inching along the little service walkway and then onto the round arm that led the rest of the way up to the flight-deck level. Crutchley's crew climbed up the arm first, balancing on the piping and holding on to the control cables that ran down the arm. The climb was tricky, up a steep incline on a round pipe covered in slippery foam solution. Near the bottom, the control cables were too high for the men to grab for support, and then as they got closer to the top, the cable converged on the upper end of the piping and was too low to hang on to. After the first two made it most of the way up, Crutchley reached the man who had been hanging there, and helped him up. The guy was remaining conscious, but that was about all. Crutchley wasn't at all sure the guy was going to be able to get up the crane arm and all the way to the flight deck, so he followed along close behind, ready to grab him if he slipped.

As they neared the top, Crutchley could see for the first time just what a mess the flight deck had become. Fires were still out of control, but Crutchley had no doubt that the flight deck still was their only escape. Just then, a fuel tank exploded on one of the planes, showering flaming fuel in Crutchley's direction. The burning fuel and other debris flew past Crutchley, enough of it landing on him and the dazed man to make them wince with pain, the thunder of the explosion already making them duck down as much as they could without losing their grip on the crane.

Crutchley saw that his companions had reached the flight deck already, but the last steps seemed to take forever for him and the injured man. After pausing to shake off the hot debris that landed on them, burning through their uniforms, they inched their way along, slowly getting all the way up to the flight-deck level, where Crutchley's two crew members were waiting, urging them on. They grabbed the injured man and pulled him up on the flight deck as he got close, and then they helped Crutchley up. The injured man collapsed as soon as he was safe, and crew members who had been fighting the fires rushed over to help the obviously exhausted group.

The men had come up on the flight deck near the spot where Jim Bangert's plane had fired the rocket, now in the worst of the fire zone after the fire had spread. Even nearly two hours after the fire started, this still was not a good place to be. But it was a hell of a lot better than where they had been. Crutchley felt a huge sense of relief.

Thank God. I didn't get anybody killed.

On the other side of the ship, Eurice and his friend started heaving overboard anything else on the sponson that could be moved. Crates used to store ammunition, as well as various other debris that had been blown off the flight deck, were burning all around them, so they cleared out the area as much as they could. Periodically, Eurice looked over toward the fantail where he had been trapped, and knew he had made the right decision. That area was now covered in flaming jet fuel and other material.

After about half an hour out on the gun-mount structure, Eurice noticed that the smoke billowing from the hatch was diminishing and turning from black to white, a sure sign that the fire was being extinguished. The smoke eventually diminished to nearly nothing, and the men on the gun-mount structure started thinking it might be safe to venture inside. As they were standing there debating whether to trek through the passageway without a breathing apparatus, a miraculous sight appeared. Out of the sooty, still-steaming hatch came a sailor carrying a tray of orange sodas. He had raided a nearby refrigerator and was passing out drinks to everyone fighting the fire.

It was a small delight that took on massive importance for the men. For the first time in the ordeal, Eurice and the other men on the gun-mount platform got the idea that maybe everything would turn out okay. They still didn't know much about what was going on outside their line of sight, but nobody takes the time to pass out orange sodas when a ship is sinking.

After guzzling several orange sodas, the best he'd ever tasted, Eurice decided to leave the gun-mount platform in search of more fire hose. If they could get their hands on more fire hose to attach to the one they were using already, they might be able to do more firefighting than just cooling down the gun mount. A catwalk had been blown down onto the gun mount in such a way that it provided access to the flight deck, so the men searched for enough hose to go up and help out with the fires still raging topside.

Eurice made his way to Hangar Bay 3, by now a water-soaked mess, and started looking for fire hoses to scavenge. As he searched, he noticed that some of the men were gesturing in one direction, and turned around to see Captain Beling slogging through the hangar with his two marine orderlies close behind. True to his nature, Beling was taking a walk through the ship to see the damage for himself. He had already been to pri-fly and seen the shattered windows, the debris left when the staff there made a hasty retreat. Beling had access to more information than anyone else on the ship, but that wasn't good enough. If his boys were fighting and dying nearby, he had to see it.

Eurice and many other sailors were shocked to see the captain off the bridge in the middle of such a crisis, astonished that he would put himself in harm's way as the fires continued to burn and small explosions continued on the flight deck. His marine escorts were not at all happy to see the captain on the front line of the fire, and they were doing their best to dissuade him from entering some of the more dangerous areas.

Beling strolled through the hangar bay and assessed the damage from that vantage point, stopping to talk to several sailors about what they had seen. From there, he made his way through much of the ship not actively involved in the fires, reaching the conclusion that things weren't nearly as bad as he expected from what he had seen on the flight deck. As he went through one of the big dining halls for the enlisted men, he could see that a meal had been under way when the general-quarters alarm sounded, with trays of food left on tables everywhere. Beling grabbed a couple of carrots as he walked by, and munched on them while he continued his tour.

One thing in particular reassured him that the ship was surviving the damage. Throughout the parts of the ship not actually burning or damaged by explosions, the air-conditioning was working just fine. The *Forrestal* was one of the first warships to have air-conditioning throughout most of the ship, and the cool air was always seen as a luxurious symbol of the ship's bragging rights. Now, Beling found the system's durability comforting in the midst of this disaster.

After Beling's appearance, Eurice went back to searching for fire hose and eventually found enough to lug back to the gun mount. A few other men had brought some back also, so they coupled all the sections together and then headed to the flight deck by way of the catwalk hanging down on the gun mount. When they reached the flight deck, they were stunned. They knew that the situation was bad, but they were not prepared to see the flight deck covered in burning plane wreckage, fires still burning, injured men and bodies still lying where they had fallen. The entire flight deck was a steaming, hazy mess. The smell of burned plastic and explosives hung in the air, along with the stink of the jet fuel and fog foam.

Eurice and the other men surveyed the situation for a moment, brought to a halt by the shock of it all, and then started pulling their fire hose over to the rear portion of the flight deck where they could see that most of the work was being done. When they got closer, they could see that men were aiming fire hoses down into horrendous craters blown in the deck, and nearby, other teams were using an acetylene torch to cut holes in the deck. Compartments below the flight deck were still burning furiously, and the only way to get water in them was to make new holes in the flight deck and fight the fires from above. Black smoke burst out as soon as the torch broke through the armored deck, and a team poured water down the hole. Luckily, Rowland and Beling had authorized the purchase of a special acetylene torch just before departing for Vietnam. The *Forrestal* didn't normally carry one capable of cutting through armored steel, and without it, the crew would have found it nearly impossible to get through the armor-plated flight deck.

As Eurice and his hose team started to pour water down a hole made from a bomb blast, one that didn't have a hose team on it yet, they could see that the other men were yelling and gesturing to them.

"Pick up the hose! You gotta pick up your hose! The deck's too hot!"

That's when they first noticed that the other hose teams were hoisting the heavy hoses onto their shoulders and holding them there as they fought the fires. And that's also when Eurice first noticed that he could feel the hot deck through his shoes, way too much actually. The fires in the compartments below were so hot that the flight deck was becoming unbearably hot to the touch, and several fire hoses had actually burned through as they lay on the deck.

Eurice and his hose team assumed the same position with the hose on their shoulders and fired water down into the hole, standing there for a while before the smoke cleared enough to reveal what they were soaking. As Eurice peered over the edge and into the hole, he could see an unexploded five-hundred-pound bomb about ten feet below.

Chapter 13

I'M READY TO GO

The men battled the fires and their own fears for the entire morning and much of the afternoon. The flight deck had become a terrible mess, a remarkable contrast to its usually pristine order. After the fire spread across most of the flight deck to the rear of the island structure, it consumed everything that could not be tossed overboard. The sailors made slow but steady progress in extinguishing the blaze. They were encouraged by the white smoke that signaled a fire under control, and then alarmed when the smoke turned black again and roiled into the sky with a new ferocity.

Every few minutes, the 1MC address system crackled to life, sometimes with a whistle tone to alert the crew and then orders from Merv Rowland or someone else directing the firefighting effort.

"You are reminded that the emergency is not over," Rowland's gravelly voice boomed throughout the ship. "There are still fires. Re-man your GQ stations and stand fast until you are directed to do something! Do not go wandering about the ship! Re-man your GQ stations and stand fast until directed to secure."

The fire played a cat-and-mouse game with the sailors, roaring up in one spot and then another, then hiding in the many compartments belowdecks. Even when the biggest of the infernos died down, sometimes only because they had consumed nearly everything that would burn, there was still smoldering debris everywhere, pockets of intense heat trapped between the many layers of the ship's steel structure. The fire would not die easily or quickly, and it was taking a toll even on those who had survived the explosions, the searing flames, the deadly gases, and the sea below.

Exhaustion was hitting the men hard. In the initial hours, men had been fueled by adrenaline and the instinct to survive. But by early afternoon, they were losing steam. They had been working feverishly for hours, some with injuries they'd ignored or hadn't even noticed until there was a pause in the action. The combined heat of the fires and the Tonkin Gulf afternoon was wearing them down. All over the ship, men were collapsing in heaps, soaked with sweat, seawater, fog-foam solution, fuel oil, and God knows what else. They were a mess from head to toe, black from the smoke or seared a bright red, their clothes ripped or blown off. Often, they had no idea if the rest of the ship was being saved or not. They knew only that their area, the one problem they were fighting at the moment, wouldn't kill them right away and so they could take a minute to rest. For most of the men, the best they could hope for was a moment to sit down and catch their breath while someone else took a turn on the hose. Maybe they would even find a soft drink to choke down.

A few of the key officers found another way to keep going. As the day wore on and Rowland began to feel fatigued, he could see that more coffee wouldn't be enough to keep him going. He could not leave his post, and he probably wouldn't be able to do so for more than a day. Rowland had to be alert and capable if he were going to help keep the ship alive, so he sent word to the sick bay that he needed some Benzedrine. Known to the rest of the world in 1967 as "uppers" or "speed," Benzedrine was pure energy in a pill. It could keep a man alert and active for days, but eventually at a cost.

When Dr. G. Gary Kirchner got Rowland's request, he didn't even think about it before agreeing. Military doctors often had Benzedrine on hand and it was not extraordinary to administer it in such an emergency situation. Kirchner didn't hand the stuff out like candy, but for someone like Rowland, he knew it was necessary and that Rowland could be trusted with it. Rowland wasn't the only officer who used speed to stay alert for a long period during the fire and its aftermath.

Kirchner dispatched a runner to damage control with enough Benzedrine to keep Rowland alert for a while.

Kirchner's post in the sick bay was the center of the *Forrestal's* pain. The fire had not reached that portion of the ship, but all of the wounded were being funneled to the small medical department and immediately the magnitude of the disaster had overwhelmed the medical staff. Kirchner was one of four doctors on board, in addition to a couple of "flight surgeons" who worked specifically with the aviators and were attached to their squadrons. There also were sixty-five corpsmen who provided first aid throughout the ship and helped get the wounded to sick bay.

Kirchner had been working on a patient that morning. The young man had been on one of the nearby destroyers when he crushed his hand, so he had been transferred by helicopter to the *Forrestal* for medical care. The injury was serious, more than the usual stomachache and lacerations that the doctor saw on a typical morning. Kirchner had just finished injecting the man's hand with Xylocaine, an anesthetic, in preparation for reducing and casting the hand. That's when they heard the first fire-alarm calls; Kirchner paused, but he was not concerned until he heard the call for general quarters, almost instantly followed by the first explosion. They were two decks below the flight deck and about in the middle lengthwise, but even so, the explosion rattled the tray of instruments at his side and the cabinets full of medicine and gear.

"Damn, that's gotta be a plane striking the deck," Kirchner said to his patient. Both of them were staring up at the sick bay's ceiling as if it would somehow explain the tremendous shaking. Kirchner was already starting to think ahead, realizing that if a plane had crashed he should prepare to receive serious trauma patients.

As he paused and thought about what to do, more explosions caused the lights to flicker and knocked items off the walls all around Kirchner and the patient, both of them reaching out to steady themselves on a nearby counter. The kid with the broken hand looked at Kirchner expectantly, and the doctor realized he couldn't continue treating him.

"Get the hell out of here!" Kirchner yelled at the young man. "Come back when this thing settles down and we're no longer at general quarters! Your hand won't hurt for a while because of the medicine. Just don't do anything with it."

The kid took off running with his injured hand cradled against his chest, and Kirchner headed out of the operating room toward the sick bay's central receiving area. They called it the emergency room, but it was just a small compartment with two beds and some equipment for treating trauma. He had been there for less than a minute, preparing to receive patients, when he felt another huge explosion. Before the noise died down, Kirchner caught sight of his first patient, the first of many.

Several men were dragging a limp body down the corridor, screaming for help. As they carried him through the door, Kirchner's heart sank at the sight but he quickly shifted into the high gear of a trauma surgeon. The young sailor had taken a hit directly in the face and wasn't breathing. His face and neck were a bloody mess, ripped apart by an explosion. Kirchner started an emergency tracheotomy, cutting a hole through the man's neck directly into his windpipe so he could breathe again. Hunched over the patient and working quickly, he inserted a breathing tube through the hole. Only then did he pause to talk to the men who had brought in the patient.

"What the hell is going on out there? What crashed?"

The men started talking over one another, screaming because everyone's ears were ringing from the explosions. All Kirchner could understand was that a fire had broken out on the flight deck and bombs were exploding. That's all he would know for a long time, because within minutes, he was faced with so many patients that he barely had time to think of anything at all.

Patients were pouring into the sick bay, almost all of them gravely wounded, and more help was coming to sick bay too. Explosions still were going off overhead and he was surrounded by bloody, dying men. The sick bay was becoming crowded with the injured, their buddies, and the medical corpsmen who would help Kirchner. Everyone was screaming "Doc!" and "Medic!" and for the moment, that meant Kirchner. The scene in the sick bay was completely chaotic. Dozens of men were dragged in, bleeding profusely, their clothes still smoldering from their flames, charred flesh hanging off their bodies, mangled and fleshy stumps waving where limbs had been blown off. Men arrived with parts of airplanes and bomb fragments still jammed in their flesh, and their buddies sometimes followed behind them, carrying the severed limbs they found on the flight deck. Kirchner regretted that most of the men, even those horribly mutilated in the explosions, were still conscious. With young, healthy men like those on the *Forrestal*, even severe trauma doesn't always knock a man unconscious. What a shame, Kirchner thought. It would have been a blessing for most of them.

The smell was overpowering, and something that the men present would not forget for the rest of their lives: the unique stomach-churning stench of burned flesh mixed with the fumes from jet fuel that soaked many of the men, plus the sickly sweet smells of the fog-foam solution and blood—which was everywhere.

And the sounds that filled the sick bay—these were the sounds of young men in terrible pain, young men terrified and afraid to die in that place, alone in a frenzy. Many lay silently despite horrible burns: third-degree burns can destroy the nerve endings that transmit pain. But others, the ones torn apart by the explosions or the ones who felt their bodies continue to burn, screamed in ways that bore into Kirchner's soul. They moaned and begged for help. And when the pain and the fear became too much, when they overcame the men's minds and there was nothing else in their world, they cried, tears running down their bloodied and burned cheeks. In desperate moments, twenty-year-old men screamed out for their mothers when the pain was too much, when they looked down and saw what had happened to their bodies and knew they would die.

Gary Shaver was still out of his mind with pain when he arrived in the sick bay on a wire stretcher. His left arm still was wrapped around his neck; his rescuers had been too scared to touch it, fearing the whole thing might come off his shoulder. Shaver screamed and cried uncontrollably, even though he had been given morphine before being taken to the sick bay. The morphine had made no difference whatsoever to his pain. The men who brought Shaver down put him in one of the bottom bunks and ran back out.

Kirchner was clearly in a triage situation. In mass casualty incidents, the doctors and others on the scene have to prioritize patients according to their need, as well as the likelihood that medical care will actually save the patient. When the number of patients overwhelms the medical care available, it is necessary to avoid spending time and supplies on patients who are likely to die anyway. Those patients must be triaged as such and left to die while the doctors work on patients who might be saved.

Triage is a familiar concept in military medicine, so Kirchner immediately started this system in the sick bay, aided by the corpsmen and the other ship physicians who were arriving. One of the first tasks was to clear the area as much as possible. The small compartment was clogged with people who had brought patients in and were hanging around to comfort them, but Kirchner started ordering out everyone who wasn't seriously injured. The rest were triaged with tags marking them as needing immediate attention, dying and not to be treated unless there was time, or "walking wounded" without life-threatening injuries. Kirchner tried to ensure that the men tagged as too far gone to treat received adequate pain relief. He could not save their lives or even take the time to try, but he could not entirely turn his back on them either. He instructed the corpsmen to start intravenous lines in those men and provide ample doses of morphine. The corpsmen and doctors also were administering morphine to those being treated, and even to the occasional sailor who got hysterical with emotional trauma, which meant that many of the men were doped up on the powerful narcotic.

Robert Zwerlein was dragged to the sick-bay area, and Kirchner went to work on him immediately. The boy was burned severely over most of his body after being caught up in the fuel spill outside McCain's plane. Kirchner made sure Zwerlein got an intravenous line and a good dose of morphine, but the young man from the ice-cream shop in Port Washington, New York, was too far gone for him to do much else. Zwerlein lay quietly on a stretcher in the sick bay, covered with a blanket to keep him from getting too cold and going into shock. The morphine relieved his pain, but he was in very bad shape.

Kirchner soon went to Shaver's side, and even in his pain, Shaver recognized the doctor as the same one who had set his broken hand weeks earlier. Kirchner told Shaver that he was bleeding badly inside and that the pressure had to be relieved. The injured man looked down and watched as Kirchner cut a hole in his side and inserted a tube, leaving the end hanging off the side of the bed. Bright red blood poured out of the tube and onto the floor of the sick bay.

Paul Friedman also made his way there and was shocked by what he saw. When he was carried in and deposited on a couch, he couldn't believe the type of injuries he saw all around him. And instantly he felt he shouldn't be there with his relatively minor foot wound. As he looked around, he realized that he knew the man sitting next to him. They had been to a navy school together.

"Howard, hey buddy. You okay? What the hell is going on?"

Friedman poked the man on the arm to get his attention, but Howard never responded, just staring forward with a dazed look in his eyes. Then Friedman looked down and saw that the man had a compound fracture of the leg, with the bone jutting out of his pants leg at a severe angle. Friedman looked down at his own wound and felt lucky.

A corpsman came over to Friedman and offered him some morphine.

"No, I don't need it. I think all I need is a battle dressing and I can get out of here," Friedman said. "But this guy here can probably use it. Give him the morphine."

The corpsman took a look at Howard, still dazed and unresponsive, and never replied to Friedman. He turned to another patient. Friedman sat on the couch dumbstruck by what was going on around him, watching as victim after victim was carried into the sick bay. On the floor in front of him, he saw one man so horribly burned that Friedman could not tell if he was black or white. The man seemed to be conscious, so Friedman was wondering why he did not seem to be in pain. The man was just lying there quietly, his flesh blackened and the features wiped off his face, his eyes open and looking around. Another man was brought in on a stretcher and looked startlingly clean and uninjured, but he was unconscious. The man lay in the wire stretcher in his neat khaki uniform, with no sign of blood or trauma. Soon, Kirchner came over and declared the man dead.

John McCain also visited the sick bay, when he realized he was still bleeding from his chest wounds after helping the crew jettison bombs from the hangar bay. When he walked in, McCain heard a voice calling him over, and though he could not make out the young man's face because of his burns, he suspected the man was part of his air wing's support crew because he called him "Mr. McCain." The charred man asked McCain about a chief petty officer in their squadron and McCain assured him that the man was fine, he had seen him just recently.

"Thank God he's okay," the man said. And then as McCain stood there and watched, the man died.

Overcome with emotion, McCain quickly left the sick bay without being treated.

Kirchner and his staff were so overwhelmed by the severity of the injuries and the number of injured, more than three hundred before the day was out, that he quickly realized they could do little to help the men in the *Forrestal*'s own sick bay. Though the bridge was sending information to him, it was not at all clear how long the emergency would last and how much damage the ship would take. Only minutes after the patients started flooding his sick bay, Kirchner knew there were too many.

I can't handle the patients I have in here right now, and who knows when they'll stop coming? I've got to get them out of here.

Aside from the need to get them out of harm's way and in the hands of more doctors, space was at a premium. There were forty-eight beds available for patients, but half of those were top bunks. And with the volume of patients coming in, Kirchner and the other doctors only had time to stabilize patients by stopping the flow of blood and helping them breathe. They didn't even have time to suture wounds. Sophisticated first aid was all he could provide. The wounded needed to be taken off the *Forrestal* as fast as possible. Luckily, the other carriers in the area had their own sick bays and physicians, ready to help. Kirchner sent word to the bridge that he wanted to transfer all the severely injured patients to the carriers *Oriskany* and *Bon Homme Richard*, both positioned nearby and already helping out with their helicopters and other equipment. The bridge informed Kirchner that the other carriers were ready to take the wounded, and they passed on another bit of good news. The U.S. hospital ship *Repose* was leaving Da Nang, where it had been stationed to treat soldiers from the jungle war, and would rendezvous with the *Forrestal* the next day.

Soon after the decision to send the *Forrestal*'s wounded to the other carriers, a familiar face appeared to Kirchner in the sick bay. It was a surgeon from the aircraft carrier *Bon Homme Richard* who had trained with Kirchner in the civilian world. He had caught a helicopter ride over to offer his help.

"Gary, what can I do?" the doctor asked as soon as he walked in the sick bay.

Kirchner was glad to have help, but not here.

"Get the hell out of here!" he yelled at his friend. "Go back to your ship! I'll send as many of these people back as I possibly can. You see what this ship is like now. We're on fire and we're at general quarters and this whole situation is just unstable!"

The surgeon followed Kirchner's orders and assisted in transferring some of the most seriously wounded patients back to his ship. By now stressed and unable to waste time with niceties, Kirchner grabbed a corpsman walking by and pulled him close. He put his face close to the corpsman's and talked quietly but firmly.

"What are you doing with a life jacket on?" he asked the scared young man.

"Uh, it looks real bad out there, sir. We're in real bad trouble."

"Take it off. Take it off right now, dammit!" Kirchner ordered. "These men are wounded already and I can't let them see you walking around with a life jacket like the ship's about to sink!"

The fires burned well into the afternoon, but after the crew gained a foothold on the flight deck, Captain Beling decided that the forward portion was safe enough to land helicopters. The rescue helicopters used the free space immediately to return sailors plucked out of the water, and then Beling forwarded Kirchner's request to send all the seriously injured patients to the other two aircraft carriers. They were ready on the other ships. They knew, just from looking at the smoking ship in the distance, that the *Forrestal* could not handle all her injured.

Beling sent word to Kirchner that the transfers could proceed, and from that point, the doctor's main objective was to keep the patients moving. Stabilize them, and then get them off the ship as fast as possible. Before long, the helicopters were landing on the forward portion of the flight deck every few minutes while the fires still burned on the rear, bringing with them as much cargo as they could carry. The helos were stuffed with canisters of firefighting foam, fire hoses, oxygen-breathing apparatus, and first-aid supplies, sometimes with even more carried below the craft in a big cargo net. When the helicopters landed, crew from the *Forrestal* rushed to unload all the supplies and, with the helicopter still idling at high speed, they loaded stretchers with wounded men and a few who could walk. The helicopters sprang off the deck again and made their way to one of the other carriers.

Gary Shaver, Robert Zwerlein, and Paul Friedman were transferred before too long. Zwerlein was still lying quietly in the wire stretcher basket, calmed by the morphine and mercifully relieved of most pain by the extent of his burns. Two men picked up Zwerlein's stretcher and carried him to the hangar bay, where one of the big airplane elevators was being used to carry the injured to the flight deck forward of the island structure. Once they were moved off the elevator, Zwerlein waited with several other badly injured men until the next helicopter arrived and was unloaded. As it came in, the men carrying Zwerlein leaned over him and used their bodies to protect him from the debris blowing in the downdraft of the rotors. They didn't know Zwerlein, and they probably would not have recognized him if they did, and they weren't even medical corpsmen. They were volunteers who had offered to help with transferring the injured. All they knew was that this badly burned man was a fellow crew member, and they were going to protect him until they put him on that helo.

Shaver regained consciousness while he was lying on the flight deck waiting to be loaded onto a helicopter. He opened his eyes and saw the fires still raging on the other end, and then he looked down at his body. All he saw was a sheet covering him, almost completely red from his blood. The sight terrified him. His vision blurred and he felt his eyes closing. He knew he was dying. As he lost consciousness again, he was sure it was the last time.

They landed on the *Oriskany* in a buzz of activity that mirrored what they had just left behind, except without all the imminent danger.

The carrier had ceased its planned operations for the day and was concentrating solely on helping the *Forrestal*. Indeed, all operations on Yankee Station had come to a halt, and even some "in-country" helicopter units were mobilizing to fly out to the stricken carrier if needed. The *Oriskany*'s crew felt a special urge to help, because it had been only nine months since their own onboard fire that killed forty-four men. They knew from firsthand experience the terror of being trapped on a burning ship.

Lenny Julius, the twenty-five-year-old medical administration officer on the *Oriskany,* had been conducting a fairly mundane task when the *Forrestal* fire started. He was touring the ship with a corpsman trained as the sanitation officer, inspecting all the coffee stations because some of the men had gotten sick from curdled milk. They were in the hangar bay when they saw men running over to one of the open elevator doors, dozens of men gathering to look at something. Curiosity surpassing their need to look for spoiled milk, Julius and the corpsman trotted over to see what was causing all the commotion. As soon as they stepped up to the doorway, they could see the *Forrestal* a few miles away, spewing an ugly plume of rich black smoke. They stood with their jaws dropped open as explosions erupted on the *Forrestal*'s deck, sending bright flaming debris in every direction, and then after a second or two, a loud boom arrived at the *Oriskany.*

"Oh my God! The Chinese!" Julius shouted. "The Chinese are hitting the *Forrestal*! We'd better get back to sick bay!"

Julius and the corpsman took off at full speed for the sick bay, both of them anticipating that the *Forrestal* would very shortly send injured their way. As the medical administration officer, Julius was not a doctor but was charged with keeping the clinic operational while the doctors and corpsmen did their work on patients. In addition, he was trained the same as the medical corpsmen to provide advanced first aid. It was not uncommon for him to provide hands-on care in the sick bay in addition to keeping track of paperwork and supplies.

The *Oriskany*'s four doctors soon showed up, alerted by the 1MC announcement that the *Forrestal* was in dire trouble. Dozens of corpsmen were also arriving to wait for assignments, as were the ship's dentists. Everyone was working fast to get the sick bay ready for the wounded, breaking out supplies to have them within reach and quickly organizing a system of on-site triage so that patients could be channeled in the right direction once they arrived. One surgeon went to the operating room and waited for his first patient, eventually staying there for most of the day without a break.

Julius was concerned that his sick bay run smoothly in this time of utmost need, so he was organizing some of the corpsmen to support the others providing actual treatment to patients. He grabbed one corps-man in the sick bay and gave him an assignment.

"Al, look here. I don't want anybody to suffer because we don't have enough of our supplies," he said. "So your job is not to take care of patients. Your job is to go back and forth and make sure we have every-thing we need. The minute the doctor sticks his hand out for some-thing, I want it to be right there."

Julius gave the young man a list of items to retrieve from storage and sent him running off.

It didn't seem like much time passed before the wounded arrived. And once they started coming, there was a flood. The *Oriskany*'s med-ical crew pounced on the first to arrive as soon as they were brought into the sick-bay area, and then the numbers started overwhelming them. With more and more badly injured men arriving every minute, the doc-tors and corpsmen could not immediately tend to each one as they arrived. Dozens of men were lying in stretchers all over the sick-bay area, quickly turning it into a copy of the frenetic, grisly scene in the *Forrestal*'s own sick bay. All over, men lay with a red "M" scrawled on their foreheads in grease pencil, indicating that they had received a dose of morphine. The red "M," often applied after wiping off enough blood to make a clean spot, served as a warning to others not to overdose the patient. Though the *Oriskany* crew later prided themselves on knowing that every patient left their sick bay with a complete medical chart, there was no time for paperwork while the doctors were trying to save so many lives.

For the *Oriskany* crew who had been through this less than a year earlier, the sight of horribly burned men was distressingly familiar. The *Forrestal*'s injured men, however, included a number who had severe trauma from the bomb explosions, upping the ante in terms of gruesomeness.

Julius was making his way through the sick bay, monitoring every-thing that made a difference in caring for the wounded. He came upon two *Forrestal* sailors who had just been plucked out of the ocean by a destroyer, then delivered by helicopter to the *Oriskany*. The two young men had no signs of serious injury, though they were covered head to toe in fuel oil. They had swallowed a lot of seawater when they were blown off the *Forrestal,* but they would live. The *Oriskany* crew had told them to sit out of the way and wait until they could be seen, but they grabbed Julius as he was walking by. Their eyes were wide with excitement.

"We've got to get back to our ship!" one of the men said. "Our ship's on fire! We've got to go back to our ship!"

Julius was impressed with their determination to go back and help after barely surviving themselves, but he couldn't let them go.

"You don't need to go back anywhere," he told the men. "They have enough people to take care of themselves. Just stay here."

The men were frantic and Julius's words did not reassure them. A few minutes later, he looked back in their direction and they were gone. He heard later that they had caught a ride on a helicopter back to the *Forrestal.*

Admiral Lanham jumped on one of the helicopters delivering wounded to the *Oriskany* and visited the sick bay to see the *Forrestal* sailors. He went from bed to bed, speaking with the wounded and unable to hide his own shock and sadness. He could not believe what had happened on his flagship.

Gary Shaver regained consciousness and opened his eyes, but he saw nothing but blackness around him. But then he noted a light above that was getting smaller and smaller and smaller. He felt the pain again as soon as he opened his eyes, and along with whatever medication he had been given, it made his mind fuzzy, almost dreamlike. He remembered the explosion, then lying on the flight deck waiting for the helicopter, and he remembered falling asleep for the last time. That was the last thing he remembered. He remembered dying.

He looked again at the light above him. It kept getting smaller, as if it were moving away. No, *he* was moving away. He became aware of a falling sensation, moving downward steadily, slowly. And he could hear machinery grinding away—gears clacking and chains clink-clink-clinking. He couldn't move. And it was dark. All except for that light, now getting so small above him.

In a flash, Shaver realized what was happening. He was dead and on his descent to hell. And the pain was still with him. *Oh my God.* His mind suddenly became clear. He was dead, he was on his journey to hell, and perhaps the worst part was that he was taking the pain with him. He began to thrash about, screaming in an all-consuming panic.

No! No! Please, no! Oh God, please, please!

The journey continued and Shaver had time to contemplate his eternity in hell—an eternity of pain—before he passed out again.

It would be a long time before he found out that he had woken up on a dark ammunition elevator on the *Oriskany,* which was being used to move the large numbers of wounded down to the sick bay. At that moment, and for quite a while after, Shaver's trip to hell was absolutely real.

Shaver joined a crowd of seriously injured men in the *Oriskany's* sick bay. By then, his world was a fuzzy place that came and went, always overwhelmed by pain. He would pass out for a moment and then wake up screaming in agony. Even when he was given morphine or other painkillers, the powerful drugs took the edge off only for a moment. Then the pain would come roaring back. His nightmare worsened a little more when Shaver lost his sight soon after arriving in the sick bay, a temporary effect from trauma and medications.

Shaver lay there wondering how long it would be before he died, wishing it would come soon but still terrified that he would resume the journey to hell—he had not yet realized he'd been on the ammunition elevator. When a dental technician came by to check on him, Shaver pleaded with him for relief.

"Please shoot me," he begged, barely able to make the words come out. He had been crying nonstop and his mouth was desperately dry. The request was sincere. Shaver preferred dying over spending one more minute with the pain. "Please. Please. Go get a gun and shoot me."

The man assured him he would be okay, that they would get him more pain medication. Shaver cried harder when he realized he had to live, that he would have to endure the pain. He looked at the dental tech and made another request.

"Water."

Once again, the man had to say no. Shaver's internal injuries were too severe for him to have any water, no matter how thirsty he was. Shaver begged for just a tiny bit of water, but the answer had to be no. Trying to help, the corpsman went away and quickly returned with a wet washcloth, wiping it over Shaver's face as it contorted in pain. The wet cloth felt good on his face. As it brushed near his lips, Shaver desperately tried to suck the cloth into his mouth to get water.

As Shaver looked around him, he noticed a man lying in a stretcher on the floor nearby. The man's severed legs had been placed across his chest. It looked like the man was staring right at him. And then Shaver saw Lonnie Hudson, his friend whom he had last seen driving his tractor back so he could switch places with Shaver. Shaver had gone forward of where the fire would be, and Hudson had gone back to where the fire would be the worst. It wasn't Shaver's decision, but switching places with his friend would haunt him forever.

Hudson had been trapped behind the fire at the very rear of the ship, and he was soon manning a fire hose with another sailor. It hadn't taken long for them both to realize the fire was too hot and too close, so they retreated down a ladder on the side of the ship. As they did, Hudson's clothing caught fire from the burning fuel and he had nowhere to go. The other man pushed him off the ship, then jumped in after him.

Shaver stared at his friend's terribly burned and swelling body. Shaver thought that Hudson was dying, and he was right. He turned his face away as the pain surged through him again, and then Shaver finally, mercifully, passed out. Hudson died soon after, along with the man who had jumped overboard with him.

Lenny Julius was aiding patients as much as he could. So many patients were needing attention, and like others in the sick bay, he was working hard to make sure no one suffered without being noticed. As he passed by one of the most seriously injured men awaiting care, Julius wanted to be sure he was not in too much pain. There was no "M" on his forehead or anywhere else because there was nowhere to put it, but Julius assumed that the man had received a dose already. The young man was burned terribly, his flesh charred completely in every visible area. The burns were so extensive, and so deep, that Julius could not tell if the man was white or black. He had no identifying features, the fire's damage having turned him into an everyman for the *Forrestal's* wounded. The man was lying very quietly, his eyes open and looking around, the whites contrasting with the blackened skin so much that they seemed to gleam. Julius knew right away that the man would die, and that was why the doctors were not treating him yet.

Julius leaned over to speak to him, working hard to suppress the horror he felt at seeing, and smelling, the man up close.

"Do you need any morphine?" Julius asked. "I can get you some if you need it."

The man looked up at Julius and said no, he didn't need it. With a startling grace, as if they were discussing something much more banal, he thanked Julius for offering. The words did not come easily, because the man's throat had been seared from inhaling the flames and smoke, and his lips were mostly gone. Julius nodded and turned to walk away, but then the injured man spoke again.

"Doc?"

Julius turned back to the man. He leaned over so the man wouldn't have to work too hard at speaking loud enough.

"Doc, there is something. I . . . I can't urinate."

Julius understood immediately. Because of his injuries, the man was unable to pass urine and his full bladder was becoming painful. That was a common problem among the injured and ill, and the common response was for a physician to insert a catheter to relieve the pressure. The physicians had no time for that task at the moment, but Julius knew he could do it. He had worked on a urology ward at one point in his medical training, so he found a catheter and proceeded to insert it for the injured man.

Julius started to think that maybe the man was southern, maybe black, because his voice had an accent that came through even though the injuries made his speech difficult. Julius offered him some words of encouragement as he completed the catheter setup, but the patient didn't say anything else for a while.

After a few moments, the man's pain was eased. He was very grateful.

"Thanks, Doc. That feels a lot better."

Before leaving him, Julius asked the man if there was anything else he needed.

The man looked up and then looked away, just staring. Julius stayed, sensing that the man wanted to say something. Finally, he did.

"I'm going to die."

Julius swallowed hard and paused before saying anything. Then he tried to come up with something that might cheer the man up.

"Oh, nobody knows when they're going to die," Julius said, trying his best to sound like he meant it. "None of us knows how long we'll live. Hell, I may die before you."

The man lay there listening to Julius, quiet and not moving. Julius couldn't think of anything else to say. He knew the man would die soon, and it weighed heavily on him that he could not help him pass more easily. He wanted to say the right thing, anything that would make the man suffer just a little bit less. But he couldn't, so he stood there looking down at the dying man and, despite all his efforts, his feelings showed.

When the dying man looked up at Julius's face and saw how sad he was, their roles suddenly reversed.

"That's okay, you don't have to feel bad," he murmured. "I haven't done anything that I'm ashamed of. I'm ready to go."

Julius was overwhelmed by the man's generosity, his ability to think of someone else even as he waited for his last moment. There was little Julius could say in return, but he wished the man well and turned to leave, holding himself together until he could make it outside into a hallway. That's where he fell apart.

Chapter **14**

Injuries, multiple, extreme

Gary Shaver, Robert Zwerlein, and Paul Friedman stayed on the *Oriskany* for the rest of the day as Julius and the other medical crew exhausted themselves providing advanced care for the injured and preparing them for transfer to the hospital ship that was rushing to meet them the next morning. As the day wore on and the most immediate needs were met, Julius left the sick bay to take a break. When he passed by one of the machines that generates fog foam and pumps it to firefighters' hoses throughout the ship, he noticed that all the canisters of foam solution were gone. The *Oriskany* crew had sacrificed most of its own protection to aid the *Forrestal*.

He worried that the *Oriskany* was putting itself at risk if even a small fire broke out, and his heart jumped when he heard the fire alarm sound while he was in the shower. Julius raced to the fire site but found the situation was under control. He wearily went back to finish dressing, and then he returned to the sick bay. Plenty of wounded men still needed help.

Back on the *Forrestal*, the crew was winning its own battle with the flames. By midafternoon, the fires on the flight deck were extinguished and teams of impromptu firefighters were making progress with the ones that had wormed their way through the labyrinth of passageways and compartments deep within the ship. Most of the rear portion of the ship, all the way down the hull, had become a miserable mess of charred and smoking debris, seawater, fog foam, oil, and fuel.

After several hours of intense fear and activity, the men realized that they were not going to sink. But that realization did not come for quite a while. Many of the men expected to hear the captain call "Abandon ship!" over the 1MC at any moment and were prepared to go, some with life jackets at the ready. In the confusion and frenzy of the crisis, rumors even spread that the captain had already called for the crew to abandon the *Forrestal,* often leading those hearing it to a panicky fear that they would be left behind as the ship sank. The rumors always turned out to be false, and on the bridge, Captain Beling had no intention of giving up.

As the fires were controlled, but not completely extinguished, late that Saturday afternoon, Beling addressed the crew on the 1MC. While they continued their efforts to combat the fire and help their injured crewmates, Beling and other officers made frequent announcements on the 1MC either to pass on important information or, in the case of the captain, to bolster his crew's morale.

"Men of *Forrestal,* this is the captain," Beling began. "I want to let you know that *Forrestal* is again making twenty-five knots. We are going to rendezvous just before dusk with the USS *Repose* to get our hurt people off. I want to commend the whole crew today for your heroic actions. You certainly saved the ship with your bravery and you saved many, many lives. We will be back fighting very soon."

Already, Beling's mind was focused on how fast he could get his ship past this terrible incident and back to her job in Vietnam. He had no doubt that she could be repaired and back on duty. The damage was severe in portions of the ship, but the *Forrestal* was far from defeated.

Not everyone would share Beling's determination and dogged optimism, however. The captain was looking at the ship as a whole, with the confidence of someone who has every bit of available information at his disposal. Others were looking only at the charred remains of the structures they had just extinguished, still so hot that molten metal dripped and a fire hose would just create a backlash of scalding steam. And the crisis was far from over. Even as the worst seemed past, fires continued to flare up again all over the ship. As Beling acknowledged in another address to the crew, one of the priorities at that point was to keep crewmen out of the dangerous areas as much as possible. It could be disastrous to have crewmen wander into an area thought safe and then have the fire flare up again.

"Men of *Forrestal,* this is the captain. I want to tell you that it is not all hunky-dory yet. We have got some uncontrolled fires, which at the moment are getting worse and they are all the way aft on the ship, both port and starboard, on the oh-two and oh-three levels. We need to have all personnel stay clear of that area unless they are actually engaged in fighting fires. Take that to heart, please! We are going to slow the ship so as to not fan these fires and we may be just a little late in meeting the hospital ship. Anyway, we have a very good capability ourselves in taking care of our wounded here. In summary, stay clear of the aft part of the ship."

The fires continued to burn well into the night, though the crew had them under control by then. With the immediate crisis behind them, the leadership of the *Forrestal* had to turn some attention back to maintaining the daily needs of the ship and its crew, no small task when a carrier is in perfect condition and a major challenge when it is heavily damaged. As night began to fall on the *Forrestal,* Commander Ralph Smith, the executive officer a step below the captain, addressed the crew.

"Good evening, men. This is the executive officer. The fires are still stubbornly burning in the after section of the ship, therefore *Forrestal* is remaining at GQ. This is to maintain our fighting posture, to keep the ship sealed, and this gives us the best possibility of combating the fires and organizing our work. We are not out of the woods yet. We have much work to do tonight." He went on with instructions to the crew on how to manage the ongoing crisis. In the forward half of the ship, those persons not physically engaged in firefighting or repair work could "stand easy" but had to remain at their GQ stations. All of the crew were instructed to take turns going to the bathroom and to the forward mess deck for chow. And in perhaps the best sign that life was inching its way back to some sense of normalcy, Smith started complaining that the ship was dirty. On any typical day, sailors spend a lot of their time cleaning the ship, so this was another indication that they were recovering, not floundering.

"I have examined, inspected the ship forward to frame one-fifty-four and I noted the decks are getting sloppy and wet from our tracking in from the firefighting area," Smith said. "Tracking fog foam all over the decks has made them slippery and hazardous. We must clean the ship from frame one-fifty-four and forward. People in GQ stations, clean the decks and the area of the ship of your GQ responsibility. The officer or petty officer in charge of the GQ station will supervise this effort. In the island structure from oh-four and above, oh-four level and up, leave your GQ stations, proceed to the mess deck, and report to Lieutenant Kohler. That is Lieutenant Kohler in front of the engineering log room. He will organize your efforts in assisting to clear the mess deck forward and to restore it to the normal mess deck with tables and chairs for the crew's eating. We want a special effort for the next hour and a half, two hours, to clean the ship. Get the berthing area squared away, and the mess deck in condition for chow. Thank you."

Soon after, Smith came back on the 1MC to announce that trash should be dumped overboard at the number-one elevator. "There will be a marine guard posted there to control traffic, and please go single file to prevent another hazard of anyone falling over the side."

Another inevitable task fell on Ken Killmeyer. Even before all the fires were tamed, the crew began gathering bodies. This task would go on for days, and two bodies were found even weeks later, wedged into inaccessible spots where they had been blown by an explosion. Killmeyer was still in the hangar bay after helping jettison bombs and other materials, and then helping move the wounded up to the helicopters on the flight deck. As he walked through the hangar bay, someone called him over to help.

"There's a dead guy out here on the sponson," he said. "Come here and give me a hand."

Killmeyer could see that the sponson, a platform jutting out from the side of the ship like a veranda and directly under the flight-deck overhang, was still a smoky mess. He wasn't eager to go out there, but he couldn't really say no. Someone handed him an air mask, and he put it on, following the other man out there. Killmeyer stepped through the hatch and waited there, not able to see much, and the other man made his way farther out on the sponson. The smoke was still rolling off the flight deck from above, so Killmeyer could hardly see what they were doing. But as he bent close, he could see that the dead man was burned completely black, his arms outstretched in his last moments of life. Nothing was left on his charred body except his boots.

Two other men showed up with a light and a blanket. Killmeyer was horrified by the body and it took all his willpower to force himself to bend over and help move it. Relieved that the mask kept the others from seeing his terrified expression, Killmeyer helped roll the dead man onto the blanket so they could use it as a stretcher. But as soon as they took a few steps toward the hatch that led back into the hangar bay, he saw a problem. The man's outstretched arms would not fit through the hatch. Already mortified by the task, Killmeyer turned his head as someone else wrapped a blanket around one of the man's forearms and pushed down. Killmeyer flinched as he heard the bone break and the flesh crackle.

They carried the dead man to a spot in the hangar bay where bodies were being collected. Ten were there already, lying on stretchers or just on the hangar floor, a few in body bags. Blankets covered all the bodies except the ones in bags, but the upturned limbs and odd postures gave a clue that many of them had been badly burned. Several of the ship's dentists were already there starting to look for identification on the bodies.

Retrieving the body from the sponson had shaken Killmeyer badly, and he started crying. But somehow he managed to keep from falling apart. Plenty of people were in the hangar bay by then, so he took a break and headed down to his division's berthing area. Soon after he got there, he heard someone call for help with the curtain rigging stored nearby. His division often helped set up for ceremonies on board, so there was a supply of heavy blue curtains and stands. The curtain stands were heavy, so they wouldn't tip over easily, and a petty officer in the division was gathering several men to take them to the hangar bay.

"We've got to rig the curtains around the bodies," he explained.

Killmeyer joined the effort and soon found himself back with the bodies in the hangar bay, setting up the curtains to provide some degree of privacy and decorum as the bodies continued to gather in the makeshift morgue. The dentists worked behind the curtains, uncovering the bodies and gingerly looking for dog tags or any other identifying information. Once the curtains were up, Killmeyer was eager to leave again, but then an officer told him and a few others that they had to stay.

"Just guard the bodies," he told them. "We've got too many guys coming up here and trying to see if their buddies are here. Just keep everybody out."

Uneasily, Killmeyer and his companions took up positions around the rectangular curtained area and tried to keep people out. They weren't very successful. The blue curtains just seemed to get everyone's attention in the open hangar bay, so people were drawn over. Once they realized that the bodies were behind the curtains, some men were eager to see if a friend was back there. Killmeyer was a lanky young kid, not much of a match for an overwrought sailor insistent on finding his buddy. He said no and tried to explain his orders, and he even got in a shoving match when the men tried to push through. But he wasn't much of an obstacle, and his heart wasn't in it.

Then Killmeyer saw six marines walking through the hangar bay. They were part of the marine contingent whose tasks included guarding the nuclear bombs on board. Once it became clear that the nuclear bombs were not threatened by the fire, some of the marines went topside to volunteer their efforts. When they saw the bodies, they headed that way. Killmeyer was relieved to see them.

"We're supposed to be guarding these bodies but we can't stop these guys from going in," Killmeyer called out to them. "I'm glad you guys are here!"

The marines took over and quickly established positions around the curtained area. They assumed "parade rest" positions and just stood there with .45s on their hips, as intimidating as marines always are. Killmeyer and his companions were grateful to be done with the task, and as they left, they saw that no one was fighting to see the bodies anymore.

On the evening of the fire, Beling decided it was time to officially address the loss. He waited until the situation was relatively calm, and then he went to the microphone on the bridge. Beling was burdened by the loss of so many men, and he began the address with a heavy heart.

"Men of *Forrestal*, this is the captain. There are no words that say what comes from our hearts tonight. Yet we must try." Beling spoke slowly, evenly. "I ask you to join with me in this humble effort to express our thanks and our deep, deep debt to almighty God. Let us pray: Our heavenly Father, we see this day as one minute and yet a lifetime for all of us. We thank you for the courage of those that gave their lives in saving their shipmates today. We humbly ask you to grant them peace. And to their loved ones, the conciliation and strength to bear their loss. Help us to renew the faith we have in you. We thank you for our own lives. May we remember you as you have remembered us today. From our hearts we turn to you now, knowing that you have been at our sides in every minute of this day. Heavenly Father, help us to rebuild and re-man our ship so that our brothers who died today may not have made a fruitless sacrifice. Amen."

Some of the crew were released from general quarters that night, though others remained at their stations until noon the next day. There was still much work to do, but release from general quarters meant the men had much more freedom to move about the ship and seek whatever aid and comfort they needed. For most of them, that meant rest. Thousands of men, weary and filthy, emotionally exhausted, had to find places to sleep. Those whose living quarters were undamaged welcomed stragglers to share their spaces, handing out spare changes of clothing and whatever else their crewmates needed.

Ed Roberts and some others from his division found that their berthing area had not been burned, but they didn't want to sleep belowdecks; there was still too much uncertainty about what areas were safe. Instead, they found space out on the catwalks and lay there under the Tonkin Gulf night. Some men fell asleep immediately from exhaustion, but others lay quietly. Someone had found a portable radio and tuned in an American music broadcast from Vietnam.

After the song ended, a Vietnamese woman spoke to the crew in English. She was Hanoi Hannah, the propagandist that American soldiers and sailors had to tolerate if they wanted to hear the music from back home.

"Hello, a special hello to all the men on the American carrier *Forrestal*. What happened to you today, huh? Maybe a little accident? Surely you Americans realize now that even the fates are against you now. Why fight us? This is not your war. You are dying so the rich men in America can get richer."

Nobody liked hearing it. "Listening to her is bullshit," Roberts said, and rolled over.

For many of the crew, just lying down in a safe, almost quiet place was a godsend. But exhausted though they were, many could not sleep. They closed their eyes and waited, but their minds were full of images from their day.

And when sleep did come, it often brought nightmares. For a long time after the fire, the sailors would be awakened by fellow crew members screaming out in terror, pleading for their buddies to come out of the fire, or just crying. Those awakened by the screams might throw a pillow or yell a harsh command to shut up, but inside, they had more sympathy than they could express. They knew what it felt like, even if they managed to keep it inside.

The night overtook the *Forrestal* as the ship steamed on to meet the *Repose* hospital ship, the *Oriskany* and the *Bon Homme Richard* following with many of the *Forrestal*'s wounded. The men still at general quarters were exhausted and emotionally drained, but they muddled on through their chores or just tried to stay awake. For many, it was hours or even days before they realized the extent of the crisis they had just survived, and many marveled at how close they had come to dying. There was little opportunity to talk or pass on scuttlebutt while they were at their stations, but when they took their turns heading to the mess hall for chow or when someone came through their compartment on the way to somewhere else, some crew members eagerly asked about news from other divisions, other parts of the ship.

"How bad was it there? Did you see it? I heard the whole aft portion is gone."

And some men asked about specific crewmen, their buddies who were working near the origin of the fire. Sometimes they would find out the guy was just fine, and sometimes they wouldn't learn anything for a long while. A great many of the *Forrestal* sailors would be reluctant to discuss anything about the fire for a long while after. Those who survived seemed to avoid some of the obvious discussions about how bad it all had been, who had been killed, and the horrors they had witnessed themselves. They just avoided talking about it all, as if talking about it made it real.

The last major fire was extinguished at 4 A.M. on July 30. On the way to meet the hospital ship that day, with smoke still seeping from her burned decks, the *Forrestal* rendezvoused with another carrier, the USS *Intrepid*. The *Intrepid* was taking over the duties scheduled for the *Forrestal* on Yankee Station, but the arrival of the carrier was a sad moment for Beling. His ship was being relieved after only four and a half days of combat, sent home like a rookie who couldn't take the heat. Beling knew that wasn't the case, but he cringed every time he imagined how others were looking at his ship. As the two ships steamed toward each other for a predetermined point where some necessary supplies would be transferred to the *Intrepid*, Beling pushed his ship at a brisk twenty-seven knots. He was proud that the damaged *Forrestal* could produce such speed without having to use more than four of the ship's eight boilers. He waited until the two ships were close enough to see each other. When the *Intrepid* was in range, Beling ordered a visual message flashed to the other ship's captain, John Fair, a friend from way back.

"John, how's this look on four boilers?" was the greeting.

After the transfer, the *Forrestal* steamed on with the *Oriskany* and the *Bon Homme Richard*. The three carriers rendezvoused with the hospital ship *Repose* the next morning at a featureless spot in the waters off of Vietnam. The big white ship had rushed at top speed from its station on the coast, where it had been treating soldiers wounded in the jungle fighting. An ungainly big white box on water, with a prominent red cross painted several stories high on the side, the *Repose* clearly was not a fighting vessel. On board, she had dozens of doctors, some of the most sophisticated medical equipment in the world, and plenty of room for the *Forrestal*'s wounded. She was needed.

The crews of the aircraft carriers had prepared for this moment and were ready to transfer patients almost as soon as the hospital ship came within sight. The helicopters swarmed the carriers again, this time in a more orderly and deliberate fashion than the previous day's rescue efforts. Much of the activity was centered on the *Oriskany*, where the most seriously wounded had already been sent. The *Oriskany* crew had stabilized the men and performed some of the most urgently needed surgery, but the patients still needed much more sophisticated care on the *Repose*. The helicopters touched down on the *Oriskany* deck over and over again, ferrying terribly burned and mutilated young men to the doctors and nurses waiting on the *Repose*. Once more, Gary Shaver, Robert Zwerlein, and Paul Friedman were loaded onto helicopters and taken a step farther from the *Forrestal*.

Several times, Shaver woke up on the *Repose* to find the actor Robert Stack, better known as Eliot Ness of the television show *The Untouchables*, sitting by his bedside, talking to him, soothing him. A popular celebrity, Stack was touring Vietnam to greet the troops and had volunteered to see the wounded on the *Repose*. By then, Shaver's pain was controlled enough that he could briefly speak to Stack before passing out again. Paul Friedman got even luckier. He had his picture taken while Connie Francis was singing to him.

The *Repose* offered advanced care, but for many of the wounded, the long journey had just begun. The terrible wounds they suffered would lead to a series of operations, long and slow recuperations, excruciating physical therapy, and prolonged stays in hospitals.

Transferring the wounded to the *Repose* was a relief to Captain Beling because he could rest easy that his injured men were in the best hands, but also because he could get back to his primary job of running the *Forrestal*. Men were finally getting a breather throughout the ship, but not in damage control. The day after the blaze started, Rowland and his crew still had plenty to do, keeping their eyes on each remaining hot spot in the ship and trying hard to keep anyone else from falling prey to the *Forrestal* fire. The mess left by the previous day's fires was creating all sorts of hazards, and one of the worst was chlorine gas. The millions of gallons of seawater sprayed from fire hoses and pumped into the hangar bays had found its way to a battery-storage compartment, where it mixed with the acid from broken batteries to form deadly chlorine gas.

"There is suspected chlorine gas in compartment 03-217-4Quebec," Rowland cautioned over the 1MC address system. His voice sounded weary, almost exasperated. "All hands are cautioned to stay clear of the area. Cautioned to stay forward of frame two-ten. We don't want to have to carry out any more people that went up to help and passed out. Chlorine gas is *deadly* and it *is* up there!"

Despite the warnings from Rowland and others in the area, three men charged into one of the compartments filled with chlorine gas because they mistakenly thought people were trapped there. They quickly succumbed to the gas and were the last three men to die.

By the time he felt confident enough to leave his post on Sunday, Merv Rowland had been on duty in damage control for seventeen hours, and he had been awake nearly forty-five hours because he had been up the night before working on a machinery repair. The Benzedrine from the sick bay had kept him buzzing along and alert enough to do his job, but now that he could stand down, he felt like hell. Rowland was dog-tired but jittery, his eyes wide open but eager to close. His nerves were shot and his hands trembled.

The drug still had him firmly in its grip, propelling him along despite the weariness he felt in every inch of his body, forcing him to hear and see every little thing around him despite his desire to just stop. Thinking he might be able to rest if he got some food, Rowland made his way to one of the mess halls. A lot of others were there in the early morning, milling around and talking about what had just happened to the ship. The mess hall had become a gathering spot for many of the crew, including some of the aviators, who were nicknamed "Airedales." As Rowland made his way through the line and picked up some chow, a few of the men recognized him and knew he could answer all their questions. They waited until he took his tray over to a table and started to sit down, and then someone from another table asked, "Hey, what's the story? What really happened up there?"

The combination of extreme fatigue, stress, and the drug's effects made Rowland nervous and cranky, not a good combination for an officer already known for his hot temper.

"I'll tell you what happened. Those goddamn Airedales blew up the ship!"

The room fell silent. All of Rowland's frustrations from the previous day were coming out at once, and he couldn't stop them. The aviators in the room, not exactly a shy, retiring lot themselves, took exception to Rowland's comment. One of them started to reply, "You're full of . . . ," but whatever else he said was lost in the noise as Rowland leapt off his seat and lunged for the man. Rowland was ready for a fight; once the man opened his mouth to speak, Rowland considered it a personal affront and disrespectful to the ship he had just fought so hard to save. Rowland's mind was a mess, and that aviator had just volunteered to be the whipping boy for everything the old man was mad about.

Rowland swung wildly and had just gotten his hands around the aviator's throat when a dozen others piled on them and tried to pull Rowland off.

"I'll kill you, you son of a bitch!" Rowland roared, his eyes a frightful indicator that he meant what he said.

It took several men to pull him off—with one grabbing him from behind and pulling hard on his neck—but the aviator survived. The men made Rowland sit down as the aviator's buddies hustled him out of the room, but Rowland was still grumbling and yelling at the man. Rowland was breathing like a racehorse and his eyes were wide with adrenaline. The men who pulled him off the aviator realized that Rowland needed help, so they convinced him to walk with them down to the sick bay.

When he got there, one of the doctors could see what bad shape Rowland was in. He told the other men to leave and got Rowland to sit down for a minute. The doctor went to a locked cabinet and then came back.

"Okay, I've got some medicine for you," he said.

"I don't want your medicine!" Rowland snapped. "I've been taking your goddamn medicine and I'm done with it!"

"This is different, Merv. This is what you need."

Then Rowland could see that the doctor had brought out a big bottle of one-hundred proof brandy, kept in the sick bay strictly for "medicinal purposes." Otherwise, alcohol was forbidden on the ship. He filled a water glass with the brandy and handed it over. The old navy officer didn't need any more prompting. He took the glass and drank it all straight down as if it were water.

"Okay, that ought to help," the doctor said. "Now let's get you back to your quarters."

The doctor walked Rowland back to his quarters and told him to just go to bed. The brandy was taking effect by then and overwhelming the Benzedrine. Rowland didn't bother to undress and just collapsed on his bed. He was asleep as soon as his head hit the pillow.

Rowland slept for twenty hours. When he finally awoke, he was disoriented and didn't know how long he had slept. He reached for the phone by his bed to call damage control and get a report, but when he picked up the receiver, nothing. It was dead. *Awww shit. What's that mean?*

He picked himself up off the bed, every muscle protesting after the long rest, and staggered to the door of his room. His mind was foggy. When he opened it, he was surprised to see an armed marine standing there.

Holy shit . . . Captain's put a guard at my door.

Rowland stood there for a moment trying to figure out what was happening. His mind was still foggy, but there was only one reason a marine would be guarding him.

I must have really screwed up. Wait a minute, something happened in the mess hall. Did I beat the shit out of somebody? . . . What did I do in that mess hall?

The marine just looked at Rowland and said, "Good morning, sir." Rowland wasn't sure what he should say in return, but he spoke anyway.

"Yeah . . . Well, what in the hell are you doing here?" Rowland demanded.

"The captain told me to stand here and not let anybody knock on your door until you open the door yourself and come out happy. They disconnected your phones, too, sir."

Rowland thought about it for a minute and realized he wasn't under arrest.

"Okay, well . . . I'm all done."

"Yes sir," the marine replied, and immediately started down the hall. Rowland stood in the doorway and watched him leave, still trying to remember what happened in the mess hall.

Beling knew exactly what Rowland had done in the mess hall, but he understood why. In the day after the fire, the crew began tallying up the number of dead and wounded, plus the physical damage to the ship. Some of the figures would not be complete until later, when there was time to assess the damage more closely and some of the seriously wounded had passed away, but in the end, the numbers were disturbing: 134 men dead or missing, 161 seriously injured. Of 134 dead or missing, 18 were listed as missing and presumed dead. The crew and the other ships recovered the remains of what appeared to be between twelve and fourteen bodies, so four to six bodies were lost completely.

Most of the death certificates listed the cause of death as "injuries, multiple, extreme." Many of the others died from burns, some from smoke inhalation, a few from chlorine gas, and some drowned as they were trapped in flooded compartments.

The ship had suffered $72.2 million in damage, including the loss of twenty-one aircraft and damage to forty more. Some of the planes pushed overboard that day cost more than five million dollars apiece, others two million dollars each. The ordnance destroyed or jettisoned during the fire was valued at just under two million dollars.

As soon as word reached the United States, the *Forrestal* fire was front-page news. It was no surprise that everyone wanted to know more about what happened on Yankee Station. Even those who didn't follow the war closely or who didn't have a particular interest in the *Forrestal* wanted to know how an American carrier could shoot itself in the foot and lose 134 men. The *New York Times* featured the fire as its lead front-page story on Saturday, July 29, the day the fire started, reporting only the earliest information that a "raging fire" broke out on the carrier and that deaths were expected. "It would have been impossible to avoid deaths," a military spokesman said.

By Sunday, the *Times* had photos of the carrier ablaze and reported that at least seventy crew were killed and the "craft is out of action." Other papers carried similar coverage, and the August issue of *Life* magazine devoted its cover to a photo of flames and smoke billowing from behind planes parked on the *Forrestal*. Many of the early accounts got the details wrong, understandable because the event was chaotic and the information relayed from around the world. In particular, the early accounts attributed the cause of the fire to an auxiliary fuel tank dropping off of John McCain's plane apparently for no reason, the fuel then igniting from either a plane's exhaust or "the superheated steam" of the catapult launching system. Once it became clear that a rocket had fired, the initial theories were that a plane's hot exhaust or the exhaust of a nearby tractor had overheated the rockets on another plane, causing one to fire. One story in the *Times* described the cause as a plane experiencing "an extreme wet start. This malfunction, comparable to what happens when a cigarette lighter has been overfilled, occurs about once a week on attack carriers, but almost never so severely as it did on Saturday."

That theory was soon discarded, but by then the fire was no longer front-page news. Except in the Norfolk area, where so many families had relatives on the ship, the story was quickly shouldered aside by the other major news of 1967. President Johnson held a news conference on July 31 and did not mention the *Forrestal* tragedy. None of the reporters brought it up either. Three days later Johnson announced that he was sending 45,000 more men to Vietnam, bringing the total to 525,000. By August 1, just three days after the fire, the *Times* front page featured "Shots Fired in Washington as Negro Youths Rampage" and "Milwaukee Calm After Negro Riot." Another story on the front that same day, "*Forrestal* Blaze Cuts Down Raids in North Vietnam," related the difficulty in continuing air raids on Vietnam without the *Forrestal.* That was one of the last front-page reports on the fire in the *Times.*

For some on the *Forrestal,* a difficult task was still in front of them. Bob Kohler, the ship's administration officer, was in charge of sending messages to the navy offices back home about who was dead and who was missing. He held shipwide head counts every few hours to see if the missing men could be accounted for; if a man who was previously thought missing was found, Kohler insisted that he personally report to him and verify his identity. Kohler wanted to minimize any chance of sending a family bad information.

Many of the crew were eager to let their families know they were okay, but the communications available to them in 1967 were not of much help. The only way to make contact quickly was by telephone, and patching through a call from a ship off the coast of Vietnam to some little town in Minnesota was a frustrating endeavor. And even when such a call was possible it meant standing in line for hours. For those who got through, the call was usually brief, with a young sailor saying, "Mom, I'm okay. I made it okay," and then, "Don't cry, Mom. I'll be home soon." Some gave their wives a list of people they knew were okay, so they could spread the word among those waiting in Norfolk.

Getting word to the families was complicated because some families were on summer vacations and some wives were living with distant relatives while their husbands were away at sea. The news reports were brief at first, indicating only that the *Forrestal* had suffered some sort of bad fire on board. It would be a few days before details emerged and much longer before the media would get access to a reliable list of the dead and wounded. And then the news coverage would fade quickly as the country turned its attention to race riots and other news from Vietnam.

For many of the families, the news gave them only enough information to make them worry that their son, brother, or husband was among the dead or wounded. The worry could go on for days as they waited. Even Captain Beling's wife knew little from the outset.

On the Saturday of the fire, Eve Beling had been moving the family from one home to another, having just sent the moving van off with the final load of furniture from the house. The Belings' oldest son was going off to college that same day, and he kissed his mother goodbye and drove off in his little MG about the same time as the moving van. Eve Beling was left standing in front of the empty house, about to leave herself, when she caught sight of the last thing a navy wife ever wants to see—a navy car driving up to the house with a stern-faced officer and a chaplain. Her heart pounded as she waited for them to pull up and walk the short distance to where she was waiting.

"Mrs. Beling, may we go inside?" the officer asked.

"Well, no. There's no furniture," she said, trying to keep her composure.

"Yes ma'am, I see. Could we sit down right here, then?"

She sat with the officer and the chaplain on the front steps of the house, and listened quietly as the officer told her about a fire.

"What about John? Is John okay?"

"We actually don't know yet, ma'am. We're still getting information from the *Forrestal,* and all we know right now is that there were some deaths and injuries. Mrs. Beling, we wanted you to know about this as soon as possible."

Beling's son heard about the fire on the car radio on the way to school. It would be days before the navy could confirm that Beling was safe, days in which Eve Beling put on a strong face and appeared confident. She had to, because many of the wives of the *Forrestal* crew looked to her for leadership on the home front, for information and support that helped the wives get through their long stints without a husband at home.

Other families all over the country, but mostly the East Coast, were getting visits from naval officers as officials received confirmations of the dead and wounded sailors. Bill and Ruth Zwerlein, Robert Zwerlein's parents, were in Ohio for a friend's wedding on the day of the fire. Some of the wedding attendees had heard about it on the radio, but no one wanted to mention it to the Zwerleins. They were having such a good time, and no one wanted to be the one to break the news.

Two of their sons were working at the family's Tastee-Freez back home when they heard about the *Forrestal* fire on the radio. That evening, they called their parents in Ohio. Bill and Ruth were concerned, but they thought maybe their Bobby would be fine. After all, he had had all that training as a volunteer firefighter. The news reports sounded bad, but they kept hoping that Bobby had been spared.

"He's a fireman," Ruth said more than once. "He'll know what to do."

They flew home from Ohio immediately, but there was no news about Bobby until Monday. Then a navy car pulled up to the Tastee-Freez and an officer came in, causing the shop to fall silent. Everyone in town knew that Bobby was on the troubled ship.

The officer asked to speak with the Zwerleins privately, and when they sat down, he dashed their hopes.

"Reports from the *Forrestal* indicate that your son has been wounded. He was transferred to a hospital ship and his condition is listed as guarded."

Ruth began to cry and Bill worked hard not to, fidgeting and avoiding the officer's eyes. They asked what happened and the officer explained that there had been a major fire on the flight deck and their son had been caught up in it somehow. The Zwerleins sat for a minute, Ruth crying and Bill trying to console her. After a minute, he had to ask.

"Was he burned?" Bill said quietly.

"Yes sir, the report is that he was badly burned. His condition is listed as guarded."

Their hearts fell. Ruth sobbed. The officer promised that the navy would keep in touch and pass on any more information as it came in. But no more information came for the next couple of days. As they waited and worried, Bill and Ruth realized that their son might be dying, alone. The idea tore at them, with Ruth particularly besieged by the idea that her Bobby was hurting and needed his mother. She was tortured by the image of him lying on the hospital ship with terrible burns, in pain and so alone, craving the kind of comfort that can come only from the gentle touch of a mother.

The Zwerleins decided that they could not just sit and wait. They contacted a family friend who had connections with the navy and started inquiring about how they could go to Vietnam. If their son was dying, they needed to be there. They were ready to get on a plane.

But before they could explore that option very much, the naval officer returned to the Tastee-Freez at 11 A.M. one day. Ruth was next door at the beauty parlor, trying to carry on while she worried about her Bobby. When the naval officer appeared again, everyone on the street noticed. There was a hush as Ruth left the beauty parlor and went next door to their shop, everyone anticipating major news, good or bad.

When Bill and Ruth were together, the officer told them the news. Bobby had died on the hospital ship.

For Ken Killmeyer's parents, the news was much better. He had managed to call them soon after the fire, telling them he was okay. It was clearly a relief to his mother, who broke down in tears when she heard his voice. He promised he would write with more details and then he would be home soon.

In the days after the fire, Killmeyer found time to finish the letter he had been writing when the fire broke out. He retrieved it from where he had stuffed it under his bunk for safekeeping and sat down to complete it.

He had been writing his six-year-old sister, but after the fire the letter turned into something a six-year-old shouldn't read. The page started out with "Dear Patty, Thank you so much for your letter. You don't know how much that letter means out here. Well, we took on bombs last night. Tonight fuel and tomorrow more bombs. I am very tired."

The letter went on to describe the man overboard that interrupted his sleep, and said the man had not been recovered. "They left two destroyers to search for him, but there is no chance. W . . ."

General quarters was called on that last "W." Then Killmeyer resumed writing after the fire. At the very top of the first page, he added "I was writing this letter when it all started. Thank God I am alive."

Halfway down the second page, he picked up the letter again. "Right here is where I stopped writing when fire quarters was called away. I don't have a fire quarters station, so I just sat and was going to keep writing when general quarters stations [sounded]. When I was running aft to my GQ station they said over the 1MC that there was a fire on the flight deck aft. From what I can remember I was about 10 feet away from the hatch I showed you where I go down to the magazine," he wrote, referring to a family day visit when he had shown his parents where he worked on the ship. "When the first bomb went off and then another, everybody froze in their tracks. It was coming from overhead and down the passageway. I was never so scared. I thought we would all be dead soon."

Killmeyer went on for four pages explaining what he did during the fire, including helping to push planes overboard and his grisly assignment to recover the burned body. After the detailed account of his experiences, he told his family how he had escaped injury right up to the end of the day. Finally, an officer had taken a look at the wet, bedraggled kid and told him to take a rest.

"A guy came and gave me a box of K rations and I cut my finger open on the can"— a small irony that would stick with him for years. "I am going to church. Love, Ken."

Ken's father wrote him back to say how grateful he was that Ken had survived and how proud the family was of Ken's work. It was the first time his father had ever written him.

Beling was adamant that his ship was not defeated. He could not stomach the idea that the *Forrestal* had been brought to its knees by an accident on board, the East Coast navy's first carrier in Vietnam sent limping home like a wounded puppy after only four days of combat. This was, at minimum, a matter of pride, and Beling would argue with anyone that it was more than that. From touring the damaged areas and studying the engineers' assessments, he had determined that the ship looked a lot worse off than she actually was, and there was no question in his mind that he could get her back to fighting form. Rowland wasn't so sure, but he agreed that the damage looked worse than it was.

As soon as Washington and Norfolk got word of how serious the accident had been, officials there started suggesting that the ship should just come home for a major overhaul. Beling was still arguing with them when they ordered him to go to Subic Bay for an assessment, making it clear that they expected the *Forrestal* to leave Vietnam and probably never return.

Beling was determined to avoid that indignity, not only for himself but also for his crew, so he kept pleading his case with the navy. The answer was always the same: head to Subic Bay and then probably on home to Norfolk. Beling still didn't give up hope, though.

It sounds bad to them now, but maybe once we get to Subic and clear away some of this mess, they'll see that the damage isn't so bad. Maybe we can do some repairs and get back to work here.

Admiral Lanham admired Beling's determination, but he could see that the *Forrestal* would be tied to a dock for a long while in repairs, either in Norfolk or in Subic Bay. So he made arrangements to return to the States, where he could be of more use. Lanham flew off of the *Forrestal* and on to the United States, not bothering to make the long journey back with the carrier, even though she had been his flagship. Most of the crew also were eager to get home and see their loved ones, but Captain Beling let them know he had other intentions.

On Sunday morning, Rowland was already sound asleep when the 1MC crackled to life with Beling's calm, carefully measured words.

"Men of *Forrestal,* this is the captain. I want to say a few words to you this morning to sum up the situation that exists at this time and where we are going forward in the future. However, before I do so, the first thing I want to do is to read to you a message which I have just received from the president of the United States. I quote, 'The following is a personal message from the president to Captain John K. Beling, commanding officer of the USS *Forrestal.* I want you and the men of your command to know that the thoughts of the American people are with you at this tragic time. We all feel a great sense of personal loss. Your devotion to duty and the courage of your men have not gone unnoticed. The sacrifices that they have made shall not be in vain.' End of quote. I will answer that on your behalf this morning.

"Now, what for the future. The ship is extensively damaged in the upper after portion. We are going to have to rip off the after section of the flight deck, and most of the structural work down to the main deck will have to be renewed. I think that that is very minor damage for what the ship has been through. It now appears that she sustained explosions of six [later determined to be nine] one-thousand-pound bombs, among other things. A very tough ship. And for your information, the two destroyers which started up to escort us to Subic yesterday are now two hundred and fifty miles behind and we are only using half of the ship's boilers. So there is a lot of spirit left in *Forrestal*. Today at thirteen-hundred we will have a memorial service for those of our comrades who gave their lives for their country. After that we will go into Subic with our band playing and our flag flying. Then we will get started getting fixed. We will be met by a team of experts who will help us assess the damage and where it can best and most quickly be fixed. I do not know at this time whether the damage will be fixed in Japan or on the West Coast. Needless to say, we want to do it in the place where it can be fixed fastest so we can get back on the line."

After his talk, Beling realized that he had a golden opportunity to make his case and keep the *Forrestal* in the fight. He had personally received a message from the president of the United States that morning expressing condolences for the tragedy. Wouldn't it be rude not to reply?

Actually, Beling was rationalizing his own misgivings. He knew that it would be a very cheeky move to make such a suggestion directly to the president when it flatly contradicted the navy's position. But he was willing to take that risk to keep the *Forrestal* in the fight. Beling knew that President Johnson and his advisers would welcome a chance to keep the carrier in Vietnam, and he was willing to live with the fallout from the navy. He was willing to take the chance because he felt he owed it to his men of *Forrestal,* and because he was already thinking that his career might have ended when 134 men died on his watch.

But Beling didn't want to use his trump card too early. He would wait and see if he needed it.

As soon as they had time to catch a breath and start asking questions, the crew tried to figure out what had happened on Saturday morning. On the trip to Subic Bay, the ship's ordnance specialists traced the fire back to its first moments. By interviewing surviving crew members who witnessed the rocket fire, and by reviewing the footage from the flight-deck camera, the *Forrestal*'s investigators pieced together the initial series of events and realized that a Zuni had hit one of the planes on the opposite side of the ship, leading to the fire. How and why the rocket could have fired was more of a mystery, but more investigations would follow once the carrier reached Subic Bay and Norfolk.

The carrier's arrival in Subic Bay, two days after the fire, drew everyone's attention. Those working at Subic Bay or there from other ships were eager to get a look at the big ship and see for themselves how bad the accident had been. They crowded the dock to get a look at the burned ship and as the *Forrestal* drew near, they heard a sound that sent chills down their spines.

"Fire! Fire! Fire!"

Ringing out across the water that separated them, the alarms reached those on the dock, signaling that yet another fire had flared up within the ship, two days after the ordeal began. They had to wait while the fire was brought under control, and only then was the *Forrestal* given permission to dock. Soon after, fifty-two canvas bags containing bodies were wrapped in American flags and borne off the carrier with quiet ceremony. Even then, the tragedy was not yet complete. Crew were still cutting through some mangled portions of the ship looking for more bodies, and smoldering materials still flared up.

While the ship was in Subic Bay for the initial repairs, the crew was allowed liberty for the first time in weeks. Free to roam the Subic Bay bars and nightclubs, the men stood out from the other sailors there because they wore their denim work clothes instead of the spotless dress uniforms usually required for liberty calls. The *Forrestal* sailors couldn't put together enough dress uniforms for everyone after the fire, and that was just fine with them. Going on liberty in their casual work clothes was a treat.

Ed Roberts ended up at a bar with a few of his workmates, and they were more than ready to blow off some steam. When they sat down at a table, someone pointed out a big chart hanging over the bar listing dozens of drinks available, all for about forty cents each. As soon as they saw the chart, they agreed: *That's what we're having. We're going to have one of all those drinks.*

And so they started drinking. They made it through only about seven or eight different drinks, but that was plenty. At one point, one of the guys held up a fried chicken leg and said, "Hey, here's Scotty's foot!" before taking a big bite out of it. It was a reference to their buddy who had lost most of his foot in the fire. The joke was tasteless and not even very funny, but the guys laughed hysterically. They needed to.

Beling was not hitting the bars. He oversaw the inspection of his ship by the engineers at Subic, taking every opportunity to show them how well the ship had withstood the damage. As much as he could, he tried to persuade them that *Forrestal* could get back in the fight. Though they sympathized with Beling, it was clear to everyone that the damage was just too extensive. The navy's instructions were just what Beling expected: Bring the ship home to Norfolk.

Well, okay, then. I've got nothing to lose.

So Beling went ahead with his plan and sent his message to the White House. He reported that inspections in Subic Bay show "our damage isn't anywhere near as bad as we had thought, and if we had six weeks in a Japanese shipyard and replacement of our aircraft, we could operate with at least 80 percent of our normal ability." Beling was stretching the truth a bit, putting an extremely optimistic spin on the engineers' assessments.

Beling waited anxiously for a reply, expecting the Pentagon to send a sharp retort about protocol. He only hoped that the scolding would be accompanied by a change in his orders. But Beling never heard back and the navy's orders were not changed. His gambit had not paid off, but there also was no punishment for his cocky maneuver. At least not right away.

With some of its structural mess cleaned up at Subic Bay, the *Forrestal* headed back to its home port in Norfolk—a journey of thirty-four days. Rear Admiral Forsyth Massey, a highly experienced carrier aviation officer, had met the *Forrestal* at Subic Bay and embarked to begin the navy's official investigation of the fire. Beling knew Massey well and respected him as a capable officer. Massey and his aides would spend the ensuing month inspecting the damage, interviewing witnesses, and conducting tests. They also reconstructed much of the scene on the flight deck and conducted a thorough review of the ship's policies, procedures, and overall readiness.

For much of the voyage, Beling received his orders from the Pacific Fleet command, which instructed him to steam at twenty-two knots.

That was a respectable pace for any carrier, and Beling had no trouble keeping up the speed. He pointed out to anyone who would listen that the ship was holding up just fine, not even straining to make the twenty-two knots.

Speed meant power. He was happy to show anyone who was watching that the *Forrestal* was still a fearsome warship. But when they crossed the "chop line" where the Atlantic Fleet command took over, Beling's new orders were to proceed at a more leisurely sixteen knots. He had no choice but to comply, even though it riled him.

First they stopped in Florida to off-load some planes based there and then headed up the coast. When the carrier left the Florida port and headed north, the fleet command was supposed to issue a new order to maintain sixteen knots, but somehow that order never came. With no orders constraining him, Beling immediately kicked the ship's speed to an astonishing thirty knots. By God, he was going to head into the *Forrestal*'s home port with enough speed to dispel any notions that the ship was almost dead in the water.

Soon after leaving for Norfolk, Beling received word that a Soviet spy ship was shadowing them, not an uncommon occurrence even so close to home. Knowing that the sub had been sent to take a look at the damage on the big American warship, the cocky captain couldn't resist sending a message dripping with bravado.

"Let me know if you require assistance," Beling sent by blinking light. He knew the Soviet ship would get his meaning quite clearly.

As the ship neared Norfolk, Beling had one more trick up his sleeve. The *Forrestal* still had six A-6 attack aircraft in pristine condition. Beling was thinking of one more way to help the ship save face, but this he had to clear with Admiral Lanham, who had flown out to rejoin the *Forrestal* as it neared Norfolk. Beling went to the admiral's quarters one evening and asked to speak with him. Lanham was in his pajamas when Beling entered his cabin.

"So what is it, John?"

"I want to launch all six of those aircraft as we're coming up the channel and approaching the dock," Beling explained. He said it as if he was certain it was a fine idea and just needed Lanham's sign-off.

The admiral looked at Beling for a minute and then said, "John, are you crazy?"

"Oh, the forward catapults are *fine,* no damage at all," Beling said. "We can do it. It'll show that the ship's not as bad off as everyone thinks."

The admiral understood Beling's motivation, but he had to be the voice of reason.

"John, if anything goes wrong, *which it could,* just think what they would do to you. And it would be my butt, too. What if the bridle snaps and the plane goes in the water? Wouldn't that be great, with a thousand or so visitors and crew members' family watching."

Beling tried to think of a response, but then reluctantly decided to just let it go. He agreed with the admiral that the plan was too risky. At least he felt like he had done all he could to preserve the ship's honor.

When the ship arrived in Norfolk, a crowd of three thousand people was waiting. A navy band played as crew members' families strained for a look at the sailors lining the rim of the flight deck, forward of the damage. Most of them were in blue denim work clothes instead of the dress whites they normally would wear for such a homecoming.

Those awaiting the *Forrestal* had heard about the damage and most had seen pictures in the newspaper, but the sight of the once mighty carrier pulling up to the dock was still shocking, even after the crew had cleared away the burned wreckage and cleaned up the ship as much as possible. Joyous grins turned to looks of shock and concern as the *Forrestal* came into view.

Eve Beling and her children were the first to come on board after she docked. The captain couldn't leave the ship right away, but his family wanted to see him. When a reporter tried to bound up the gangplank first, a burly marine stepped into his path and told him, in terms probably still ringing in the reporter's ears, that the captain's family was boarding first.

The crew was allowed to disembark and greet their waiting families. The captain spoke to the press soon after returning and praised his crew as a "concrete demonstration of the worth of American youth," an especially meaningful compliment at a time when the country was starting to see some young people as ill-mannered and unpatriotic. Beling went on to say "there were many examples of heroism" and "not one single example of cowardice."

Continuing his effort to lessen the public impact of the disaster, Beling told the press that the *Forrestal* was "in good shape except for the after section." He put on an optimistic face for the world, but when he turned away, Beling's loss threatened to consume him. The return was not what Beling had envisioned months earlier when the *Forrestal* first sailed away to its destiny. Now she was home, but as a sad imitation of her former glory. And more important, she had returned without nearly three hundred of her crew.

Beling knew someone had to be held responsible.

Chapter 15

Investigations

The questions started long before the *Forrestal* returned home and they would continue for a long time afterward. How did the fire start? How did it get so bad? Why did the bombs blow up so quickly? Could more lives have been saved? For days and weeks, the men sorted out who was killed and who survived, who was missing and who was injured but alive. Young men like Ken Killmeyer and Frank Eurice survived relatively unscathed, while others like Paul Friedman and John McCain made it through with minor injuries. Rowland survived another tragedy to cap off his long military career, and Beling survived the fire itself but knew that he faced more heat from the navy.

The *Forrestal* sailors started reflecting on their own experiences soon after the fires were out, after they had a little time to rest and get over the initial shock. There already was talk of heroics and how well the crew had responded, but there also was talk of the errors they had made. Fate has a way of showing itself in the aftermath of such a deadly incident, inviting survivors to praise it or curse it, quite often both. After the men had time to compare notes, they marveled at the small coincidences and twists of fate that spared their lives, as well as the ones that killed their buddies. Quietly, a sailor told of going on a coffee break, during which everyone at his workstation was killed. Others told of being on a hose team, fighting to control a raging fire hose with several other men, when one of the big bombs went off. After the blast, there might be one man left, the rest of the hose team on either side of him obliterated by the explosion. That man forever wondered why.

For the aviators on the flight deck, their location when the fire started played a large role in whether or not they survived. The three pilots who died in the fire were all to the rear of McCain's plane, where the fire started, their planes caught up in the conflagration as burning fuel spread to the rear of the ship. Their planes were equipped with ejection seats that could fire while the plane was sitting still, but apparently none of the trapped pilots tried that escape option. Ejecting from a plane is always a last resort, extremely violent and risky, and the *Forrestal's* situation introduced new hazards that made ejecting even less desirable. The pilot could have floated down right into the fire, and landing out in the water was never a good idea. And why eject if you could just jump out of the plane or wait mere seconds for the firefighters to rescue you? In the end, it became clear that the aviators who made it out of their planes safely were the ones who scrambled out as soon as they saw the fire; even a slight hesitation might have cost some pilots their lives. Those who survived wondered for years if the dead aviators might have been spared by a quick decision to eject, but they also understood why they decided against it.

For most of the sailors, however, there was no accounting for who survived and who didn't. Men tried to reason out the circumstances, certain that there must be a sensible explanation to something so important, but often the answer was nothing more than the capriciousness of a bomb fragment flying this way instead of that way. Over time, odd anecdotes appeared from the tragedy, some merely curious and some more poignant. The crew did not learn for a long time that a father and his own stepson had both died on the *Forrestal* that day. Two brothers were on board as well, one caught up in the blaze on the flight deck and the other fighting his way through the crowd belowdecks to get to him. They both survived. (Though the navy has avoided assigning family members to the same ship since World War II, exceptions were granted if the family requested it and the ship was not thought to be in danger of enemy attack.) They also learned of wives who had been coping with the absence of husbands while they were pregnant, only to receive the horrible news that their children would be fatherless. At least one wife miscarried when she was told her husband had died on the *Forrestal*.

In the days following the accident, while sitting around the table at chow time or in their quarters playing cards at night, the men of *Forrestal* swapped stories about the odd things they felt and saw during the fires. One aviator told his buddies about how he had lost his navy-issued survival knife while escaping the fire on the flight deck. The knife was a specialized piece of equipment for use if the aviator was shot down on a mission, and under most circumstances he could expect a serious reprimand for losing it. Even in the heat of the moment, he feared that reprimand so much that it momentarily outweighed his fear of the fire. He told the story to his buddies and they laughed at the absurdity of it all, but many of them understood because they, too, had seen the strange ways the human mind works in such a crisis.

Not everyone showed the stress. Even for those who managed to cope with what they had seen and experienced, their first weeks back home were rough. Young men tend not to acknowledge that they're hurting inside and they can be remarkably successful at hiding the pain even from their loved ones. But these men and their families found that sometimes the demons would reveal themselves at the most unexpected times.

Gary Pritchard, the sailor who was asleep in his bunk when the explosions started, and ran to the flight deck to help with the wounded, managed to shove aside most of what he had seen, repeatedly assuring his wife and family that he was okay, and offering little explanation of what happened to him. His wife sensed that he didn't want to tell her everything, at least not yet, so she didn't press him. Besides, he seemed to be dealing with it pretty well.

Soon after Pritchard returned to Norfolk, his family threw him a welcome-home party, more of a celebration than he expected, but he knew why. His family wasn't just glad he was home, they were relieved he was alive. Pritchard welcomed the party and had a good time seeing so many relatives and friends, especially because he had expected to be away from them for much longer. For most of the evening everyone enjoyed the food and drink, and no one bothered Pritchard with questions about what happened. But then as the evening wore on and many of the guests had left, the setting became a little more intimate with just Pritchard, his wife, and a handful of close relatives. As they sat and talked, there was a pause in the conversation, and Pritchard's sister-in-law finally asked what had been on everyone's mind all night long.

"Gary, what really happened out there?"

That was pretty much the last thing Pritchard remembered for a while. The next thing he knew, he felt like he was snapping out of a trance. A lot of time had passed and everyone around him was crying. He had no idea what he had been saying, nor could he ever remember.

On the drive home, Pritchard and his wife sat silently for the longest time. Her eyes were still red from crying and he felt bad about making everyone so sad. Finally, Pritchard couldn't resist asking.

"Honey, what did I say?" he asked quietly.

"You did all right, Gary," she replied, with a squeeze of his hand. "You're okay."

Pritchard didn't know exactly what that meant, but his wife wouldn't say anything more. He kept thinking about the tears and the look on everyone's faces, and before he arrived home, Pritchard decided that he should never answer that question again. It would be many, many years before he changed his mind. Like most others who survived the ordeal, he was always reluctant to share the worst memories with anyone, especially anyone he loved, because he preferred to carry that burden alone.

It didn't take long for some of the crew to get a feel for how the navy viewed the fire. The ship was out of commission for a while, so many of the crew were sent to various training programs, including firefighting. Ed Roberts had received no firefighting training before the Vietnam cruise, so he was sent soon after the carrier's return. He was sitting in a classroom one day, just one sailor among a couple dozen from various ships and divisions. The instructor started talking about how to fight fires and said, "Now this is what you're supposed to do, not like those idiots on the *Forrestal*."

Roberts's blood boiled and it was all he could do to sit quietly. *You motherfucker,* he thought.

Rear Admiral Forsyth Massey's investigation continued for months after the *Forrestal* was home. Massey and his team of investigators interviewed nearly every surviving crew member to determine just what happened that Saturday morning. The information they collected was voluminous, the final report eventually reaching seven thousand five hundred pages.

Even with a wealth of data and hard facts at their disposal, the investigators depended on the men on board to help them sort out just what happened. They interviewed anyone who might have even the smallest bit of information that might prove useful, and they meticulously dissected the procedures on the ship to determine how something as devastating as the mistaken firing of a rocket could have slipped through the navy's safety procedures. The big question for the investigators was whether the navy's safety procedures were somehow flawed or whether the crew had simply not followed the proper procedures. The answer was both, but in the big picture, the investigators may have been asking the wrong question.

As it became clear that the Zuni rocket had fired, the investigators focused on the many redundant safety procedures that should have prevented that accident. They interviewed dozens of people involved in the arming procedures for the planes that day, as well as others not working that day, in an effort to determine what was standard procedure on the *Forrestal.* Much of the questioning involved the TER intervalometer pins that should have been left in the rocket firing device as a safety measure until the very last minute before the plane was launched on the catapult. The crew had a habit of removing them early as a way to speed the launching process, but the practice had never been officially approved. When it came time for the crew to explain their actions on the flight deck, more than a few sailors squirmed when asked about removing the pins. They were being questioned under oath by lawyers from the Judge Advocate General's office and by some of the navy's highest-ranking officers. Their answers had to be truthful or they risked criminal penalties and the end of their navy careers. But they also knew that telling the truth might get them in trouble for failing to follow safety procedures to the letter.

Some of the crew who worked on the catapult teams reported that sometimes planes came to the catapults with the TER intervalometer pins already removed, but other planes had them still in place as required by the safety regulations. After many crew members were interviewed, the investigators could see that there had been no official change in the policy involving TER pins, but some of the crew had decided to take a shortcut. One crewman, nineteen-year-old Andrew Sappe, was especially helpful in explaining the circumstances of the TER pins. On the day of the fire, he was working on the forward catapults, responsible for the final arming of the rockets and missiles just before the plane was launched. Among other last-minute adjustments, Sappe was supposed to remove the TER pins to make the rockets fully armed.

Sappe spent an hour being deposed by a naval lawyer on the trip home to Norfolk, resulting in his official written statement to the board. In that statement, Sappe said he did not know what the policy was for removing TER pins.

In August he sat in front of a board of investigation and was advised of his rights not to incriminate himself. Then Sappe changed his story somewhat and said he now understood that the TER pins were supposed to be in place when the plane reached him. He told the investigators that he sometimes found the TER pins had already been removed, but he did not always report the missing pins to superiors because he had heard that some aviation crews preferred removing them early. The investigators insisted that Sappe be specific about who had said it was okay to remove the pins early.

"I don't think anyone said directly that we should take them out," he explained. "This was just a thought, just casual talk, and I didn't say anyone said we should actually take them out. This was just two sides of the story I've heard—why should we leave them in and why should you take them out."

Admiral Massey himself addressed the young sailor with a follow-up. "Why were you so impressed with the pins?" he asked Sappe.

"I think it's safer. It *is* safer. That's what it is for."

"Then it would seem to me that anyone that would advocate pulling it out would be unique. He would be unusual, wouldn't he?" Massey asked.

"Not actually," Sappe replied. "It depends on how your system was set up."

"There are a lot of people that feel that way, is that what you are trying to say?"

"There are some people."

"You can't remember anyone who was for outs?"

"No, sir. Not by name. No one actually said out."

"What did they want to do with them?" Massey asked.

"We were discussing both sides of the story. Nobody said they actually wanted them out."

Massey was losing patience with the sailor's equivocation. "Well, what *did* they want? Halfway in or what?"

Sappe felt the pressure and thought for a moment before answering.

"They wanted them in all the way like they were supposed to be."

Another investigator then asked Sappe who had recommended following the navy procedure and leaving the pins in.

"I guess all the senior petty officers wanted them in," Sappe said. "Anyone that knew anything about ordnance I think would want them in."

Sappe went on to explain that, in actual practice on the *Forrestal,* he saw differences between the way aviation groups armed their planes. The group known as VF-11, Sappe's own squadron, followed the safety procedure and left the pins in until the plane was on the catapult. But Sappe said that he often helped arm planes from the VF-74 squadron, and it was common for those pins to be missing.

"Are you saying, then, that you thought it was VF-74's practice, policy, to take them out?"

"Yes, sir. Well, I couldn't actually say, but that's what it seemed to me from the majority of planes that had no intervalometer pins."

Sappe then told the investigators he remembered one time in which a VF-74 plane had come to the catapult with the pin in place on one side of the aircraft and missing on the other side. When questioned on whether he had always reported the missing pins, Sappe said he hadn't, even though he was fully aware of the rule requiring them and even the purpose they served. He just assumed that VF-74 had their own system and he shouldn't interfere. The investigators noted that a key person in the arming of rockets was confused about what was allowed and what he should do when procedures were not followed.

Others in the system also testified to the same circumstances, and the board flatly accused some crew members of lying to the board when they tried to say there was no habit of removing pins early. In some cases, the safety officers who had been looking the other way when pins were removed early wanted to cover themselves. One safety officer, the last man responsible for ensuring the safety of the arming system, tried to explain away a subordinate's charge that he was ignored when he reported missing TER pins. The subordinate had reported missing pins by holding up the number of pins he had removed from a plane and using hand signals to indicate that some were missing. The safety officer responded by shrugging his shoulders as if to say he didn't care. When the board asked the safety officer for an explanation, he produced an elaborate explanation about how the shoulder shrug actually was a special signal he had developed with another member of the catapult crew and not a response to the missing pins. The board didn't buy it.

Having established that the *Forrestal* crew, or at least certain parts of its crew, were in the habit of removing TER pins back in the pack instead of waiting for the plane to reach the catapult, the board then turned its attention to the pigtail connectors. Even with the TER pins removed, the rocket still should have been safe from accidental firing if the pigtail cables were not plugged in. And navy regulations required that the pigtails be left unplugged until the plane was on the catapult.

This problem was a little easier for the board to figure out because the deviation from procedure actually had been documented. The board reviewed the records of the Weapons Coordination Board, made up of ordnance experts and other representatives from the aviation groups, which had met on June 29, 1967, just before the *Forrestal* reached Yankee Station. In that meeting, the ordnance experts reviewed some navy regulations that pertained to the safe handling of bombs, missiles, and rockets, with the intention of relating what they considered "ideal" handling to the real-world requirements of a combat situation. The weapons board determined that some requirements for handling weapons in a noncombat situation were impractical in the fast-paced demands of bombing runs on Yankee Station, so they decided to officially circumvent some specific navy requirements. Even so, the *Forrestal* crew was not running wild; as the first East Coast carrier to arrive in Vietnam, they had been advised by the West Coast carriers that some "normal" safety requirements had to be altered for combat. The other carrier crews suggested plugging in the rocket pigtails while the planes were still bunched up back in the pack, instead of waiting until they reached the catapult.

After considering the time demands when launching aircraft and the possible safety risks, the ship's Weapons Coordination Board officially determined that the crew should be allowed to deviate from navy regulations: "Allow ordnance personnel to connect pigtails 'in the pack,' prior to taxi, leaving only safety pin removal on the cat."

The weapons board clearly saw the TER safety pins as their backup, the other safety measure that would still ensure the rocket could not fire until it was on the catapult. To underscore the point, the weapons board stressed in its report that if the pigtails were to be plugged in early, "Safety pin *will not* be removed prior to aircraft being positioned on the catapult."

In hindsight, the conflict was clear. Admiral Massey and the rest of the investigations board could see that there was a terrible convergence. An official change in safety procedures collided with an unofficial change in safety procedures. In addition to that major conflict, the board's investigation determined that the *Forrestal* crew had violated several other safety procedures. Some, such as failing to have the pilot place his hands in view while crew performed certain tasks on the rockets, appeared not to be a cause of the fire but still were safety risks. Others, such as plugging in the pigtails and conducting stray voltage checks before the plane switched to internal power, were considered a direct cause of the rocket launch. The investigation revealed that the rocket had been *able* to fire because the pigtails had been plugged in and the TER pins had been removed. But it *did* fire because a freak surge of electricity jumped through the plane's system at the moment the pilot switched from the outside electrical generator to the plane's internal power system. The voltage surged through five sequential safety devices designed to prevent just such a stray charge from reaching the rockets.

The strange chain of events could not have happened without just one of the sequential causes. All of the causes had to come together at the same time, in the right order, on one plane, to make the Zuni rocket fire.

Now the board knew why the Zuni rocket fired and started the fire. But they still didn't know why that fire killed 134 men.

One of the last steps for the board investigating the *Forrestal* fire was to hear from Captain Beling. He had not been involved in the investigation by the board other than to make available his men and any information he might have at his disposal. He was, after all, one of the chief witnesses to the fire and potentially to blame for whatever failings the board might find. When Beling was finally called to testify, he knew that his career was on the line. He had no way of knowing what the board's findings ultimately would be, but he realized that this was his chance to address whatever problems may have occurred. Accordingly, he prepared a lengthy statement to read to the board before they questioned him.

The room was heavy with anticipation before Beling entered. The board already had some evidence that there had been problems in procedure, and the incident itself was one of the most dramatic that anyone in the navy could remember for many years. When Captain Beling walked briskly to the table in front of the board members, everyone knew that what he said might determine his future.

Beling never showed that he felt the pressure. He maintained his composure from the start and all the way through, addressing the board in a firm voice and never sounding defensive or angry. With the courtly manner that had become his trademark, Beling began his address to the board by reviewing some facts related to how he came to be in command of *Forrestal,* and then how the ship arrived at Yankee Station. The board members and others in attendance listened quietly, their ears perking up when they heard Beling approach the topics that most interested them.

"I have always had a deep respect for the destructive powers of modern ordnance—even in small quantities," Beling said. "Visualizing last summer the potential for disaster inherent in the pattern of operations in Southeast Asia with bomb assembly on the mess decks and bomb farms on the hangar and flight decks, I had extensive discussions with the weapons officer and others searching for safer operating patterns and procedures. The fire on *Oriskany* served as a concrete and shocking example that made it easy to create and maintain a climate of respect for ordnance and of willing adherence to safety regulations."

Beling went on to say that some standard procedures had been altered in anticipation of combat, and he pointed out that the navy had approved those changes in the ship's Operational Readiness Inspection (ORI) before she sailed for Vietnam. But he specifically denied that he had approved any significant changes thereafter.

"It was recognized that in Southeast Asia it would be necessary to vary somewhat from peacetime Atlantic Fleet training procedures. The policy was enunciated to the executive officer, air-wing commander, weapons officer, operations officer, air-wing ordnance officer, and to other key officers that safety was primary. These officers were instructed that variations from peacetime ordnance procedures were to be made only where essential on a case-by-case basis; that current WESTPAC [Western Pacific Fleet] procedures could be used as guides but that they must be upgraded for safety in every respect possible."

"These procedures were discussed with the ORI inspectors by opposite numbers whenever controversy or any question of safety arose. No subsequent relaxation of any aspect of safety ever was authorized by me, either specifically or by implication.

"With reference to the Zuni rocket, which surely has a special role in the matter under investigation, I am certain that the arming procedures validated on the ORI were more conservative, and safer, than those practiced generally on Yankee Station."

In other words, Beling was saying that the *Forrestal* had sailed for Vietnam with a safe policy on arming the Zuni rockets. He did not approve any change in that policy, even if others on board had.

Beling then turned his attention to how the crew had responded to the fire. "Fire prevention, firefighting, and damage control have received heavy emphasis during my tenure in *Forrestal*," he told the board. He pointed out that during the ship's forty weeks of overhaul before she went to Vietnam, there had been sixty-two fires on board, about one fire every five days. (Most of the fires were related to construction work on board.) With pride, he noted that every fire had been extinguished so quickly by the crew that the Norfolk Naval Shipyard's fire department never had a chance to respond. In the navy's major inspection of the ship just before she went to Vietnam, her crew was graded "outstanding" in fighting flight-deck fires. Beling made reference to previous testimony that 1,332 of the crew had undergone firefighting training in the year prior to the Vietnam journey, and then with a note of annoyance in his voice, he explained that he would have trained even more of his crew before going to Vietnam if the navy had let him. The firefighting schools were all booked up.

"Incidentally, my recent request for one hundred quotas on return to Norfolk and one hundred quotas per week thereafter had to be turned down because of present commitments of the firefighting schools," Beling said. He paused to let the board realize what that meant. Even after nearly losing his carrier to a major fire, he still couldn't get his men in the firefighting schools.

Beling was trying to show the board that he did not blindly sail the *Forrestal* into disaster. He knew the risks the ship would face from a high-tempo combat operation, and he had done everything he could to prepare. Beling knew that he had gone out of his way to prepare the *Forrestal* and her men, taking more steps than some captains would have. He hated to sit in front of the board and outline every little thing he did, because it felt too much like a blend of bragging and defensiveness. Neither came naturally to him.

But Beling also was a pragmatic man, a career naval officer who knew exactly why he was sitting there. He had been at the helm of a high-profile warship when disaster struck. If he didn't defend himself vigorously, the board could be expected to put the responsibility at Beling's feet. Without evidence to the contrary, that outcome would be almost obligatory.

Beling went on to describe a host of other precautions he had taken against fire and other accidents on board, noting in particular that he had used the *Oriskany* fire as a teaching opportunity for his crew. He explained that the *Forrestal* had changed some procedures relating to the storage of magnesium flares, for instance, and he showed the board the information on the *Oriskany* fire that he distributed to his crew. Beling also offered proof that he had spent $189,472 in discretionary funds on additional firefighting, medical, and damage-control gear that the ship was not required to have.

The reference to educating the crew about the *Oriskany* fire got Admiral Massey's attention. He soon asked Beling about it.

"You mentioned that you published to all hands a tract of some kind that came from the *Oriskany* fire. I would like to get on the record what that was, where you obtained it, and if it was part of the official board of investigation of the *Oriskany* fire."

Beling welcomed the question. He explained that, no, the article was not a product of the *Oriskany* investigation, and in fact, he had never been provided any official report on the *Oriskany* fire or informed of any lessons learned in that incident. He had sought some sort of report that outlined the seriousness of the fire for his crew and suggested improvements, but the navy had not provided any such materials.

"The document to which I refer, and which was only an isolated example of the efforts made on this ship to instill an awareness of the dangers of fire into the crew, was taken from *Reader's Digest*," Beling explained. "We wrote to *Reader's Digest* and requested reprints, some three thousand, and offered to pay for them. They said they couldn't provide them because it came from some other publication, and they had used a condensation. Accordingly, we reprinted it on our own and I believe informed them that we had done so. I made sure that every single man had a copy of it."

Admiral Massey was noticeably annoyed by what he was hearing. He took a deep breath and responded, speaking more to the other board members than to Beling.

"Well, it seems to me that for years we have been following this kind of routine where a board of this kind spends a number of weeks intensively looking at accidents of one kind or another, and somehow the system just never provides that the result of the board's work gets to the people that need to know it," he said. "And just for the record, I think this is one of our navy-wide weaknesses that must be corrected. For example, you had to go to the *Reader's Digest* to find out what's happening to carriers, carrier fires today! It just seems to me that is a pretty serious indictment of our system, that after six weeks possibly with a board of officers to determine all these facts, we have to go to a civilian writer to get it."

Beling agreed completely, but he was glad that he had led Massey into stating the absurdity of the situation instead of having to do it himself.

Continuing with his statement, Beling conceded to the board that, based on the evidence presented to it in the previous month, "a decision was made at a low level in VF-11 to shortcut approved procedures." Even though he repeatedly made clear that the Weapons Coordination Board had not sought his approval for the early plug-in of rocket pigtails, Beling told the board he didn't think that was the real cause of the rocket firing. The real cause, he said, was that the crew plugged in the rocket pigtails while the plane was still on external power.

"In my personal opinion, the rocket fired when the pilot of F4B number one-ten moved his generator switches from the external to the internal positions," Beling explained. "If this is in fact correct, it is tragic that squadron personnel were unable to apply enough common sense to conclude that stray voltage checks should be made and pigtails plugged in while on *internal power*. It is at least equally tragic that there does not seem be a recognition in any applicable publication of the wisdom of such an elementary precaution."

But Beling also made an important follow-up point. Though he was critical of how his own crew had made such a serious error, he insisted that the error could not have been overlooked for long. He pointed out that of the 486 aircraft the *Forrestal* launched on Yankee Station, only three were VF-11 planes carrying rockets. That gave the supervisory crew little opportunity to spot the problem.

"It is my carefully considered opinion that had normal Yankee Station operations continued, supervisory authority above the level of squadron commander would have detected these violations soon," Beling said. "I can assure positively that they would have been stopped as soon as detected."

Beling knew the board needed to hear that. It was one thing for the crew to make an error. It was quite another if Beling's command structure was so flawed that supervisors could not detect the problem quickly and take the appropriate action.

Not content to blame his own crew for failing to follow safe procedures in arming the rockets, Beling went on to tell the board that he had serious misgivings about the rocket-arming system itself. Drawing on his MIT education in physics and aeronautical engineering, he provided the board with his own analysis of the circuits and safety devices of the LAU 10 device that fires Zuni rockets, saying he had concluded that the system was fundamentally flawed and overly sensitive to human error. Even if proper procedures had been followed, Beling said, "similar discharge of a Zuni rocket would have been inevitable."

"It is evident that *Forrestal*'s ordnance personnel never had a safe system to work with and never had the technical information needed to design prudent, sailor-proof rocket-loading and -arming procedures. If *Forrestal* were still on Yankee Station, I would not permit any use of the LAU 10 with my present knowledge."

After the lengthy discussion of the rocket firing, Beling moved on to the question of how the sailors fought the fire. He cited information already presented to the board regarding how quickly the crew responded with fire hoses and fog foam, and he emphasized the extremely short interval between the start of the fire and the first bomb blast that killed so many firefighters and others on the flight deck. In his statement to the board, his answers to the follow-up questions, and indeed throughout the entire investigatory process, this was the only point where Beling ever officially addressed the issue of the old, decaying bombs that the navy had sent to his ship. And even then, he referred to them only in an indirect sense by citing the short cook-off time before the first thousand-pound bomb exploded. The explosion of the first bomb after an astonishingly fast one minute and thirty-four seconds in the fire turned a crisis into a catastrophe.

"The diagram shows that a massive effort to control the fire was under way and that hoses from the starboard catwalk and forward were surrounding it," Beling said. "About one additional minute would have been required to bring enough hoses into action to affect the fire and they would have been ideally placed to contain it. I feel, therefore, that had the bomb not exploded, significant headway could have been made against the fire by about three minutes after its inception. However, I consider it utterly beyond the bounds of possibility that the fire could have been suppressed in ninety-four seconds by *any* group of men with the equipment available."

Beling paused before moving on to his closing comments. He had said what he wanted to say, and he did so without directly accusing the navy of killing those 134 men by sending him faulty ordnance. But he wondered if the message had gotten across to the board.

We only needed three minutes. Just three goddamn minutes and we could have controlled that fire.

Beling took a moment for a sip of water and then proceeded to his closing. It was not just a perfunctory, polite end to his statement. He meant it, and it was the first time in his twenty-minute-long statement that he felt a bit of emotion welling into his voice. His own career was on the line, but at this moment, he was thinking about his men. While everyone was listening, he was going to make damn sure they got the credit they deserved.

"After an intense effort in the fields of material and training, *Forrestal* deployed to Southeast Asia well prepared to do her job. She had made a promising beginning on Yankee Station when a deeply tragic accident occurred. The cause was a combination of faulty rocket-safety devices and inadequate technical documentation of rocket-arming procedures. The quantity of high explosives detonated on board exceeded that in any marine disaster since World War Two."

Beling put down his prepared comments and finished from memory. He wanted to look the board members in the eyes.

"The crew responded with consummate skill and bravery. They saved their ship in a classic demonstration of damage control, so minimizing the injury that *Forrestal* can steam at more than thirty-two knots and retains her ability to launch and land aircraft.

"The men of *Forrestal* return to home port for a full repair looking to the future instead of the past. My pride in their behavior is so immense that I never will have the words to express it adequately."

Chapter 16

Iceland

After the board finished its investigation, Beling went back to his temporary assignment at the Pentagon to await the conclusion. Soon after the
Forrestal returned to the States, the navy had assigned Beling to work in
the office of Admiral Thomas Moorer, the chief of naval operations.
Moorer was the top man in the navy, and he knew Beling well from the
times their long navy careers had intersected. When Beling returned
home with a ship in need of long repairs and needing something to do in
the meantime, Moorer saw to it that Beling was given a desk job in the
Pentagon, working for him. At any other time, Beling would have hated
such an assignment. But right after returning unexpectedly from Vietnam and during the investigation, Beling knew that the assignment was
a vote of confidence from Moorer. So did everyone else.

Weeks after being interviewed for the investigation, Beling was working in his fifth-floor office at the Pentagon when he got word that the
board had found no individual at fault for the fire and the subsequent
deaths. An aide to the admiral visited Beling one day to let him know
that the report should be on the admiral's desk soon, and Beling could
expect to be exonerated. Beling was relieved, but he never showed it to

anyone. It just wouldn't be proper for the captain of a ship to rejoice at being let off the hook for such a disaster. Beling never thought he was at fault, but he nevertheless felt a terrible loss for the men under his command.

This is a good conclusion, Beling thought. *Maybe they figured out what the hell happened out there and can put a stop to that ever happening again.*

And Beling also felt a small sense of satisfaction that his testimony to the board had made a difference.

I guess my message did get through. And I didn't have to make a big fuss about it.

Though he would never forget the loss on the *Forrestal,* Beling was eager to put the investigation behind him and get on with his career. Just two days after the *Forrestal* sailed for Vietnam, Beling had received word that in the next year or so he would be promoted to rear admiral. That promotion was still on schedule. He had plenty more to do in the navy, and working at this desk was not in his plans for much longer.

The seventy-five-hundred-page report by the board of investigation found numerous faults that led to the accidental rocket firing and the subsequent fire on the *Forrestal,* but ultimately the board concluded that no individual could be held responsible. The report broke the incident down into tiny parts, meticulously describing what happened and critiquing the action of the crew.

The board concluded that the fire "was caused by the accidental firing of one Zuni rocket," which then struck John McCain's plane, "rupturing its fuel tank, igniting the fuel, and initiating the fire." The report went on to say that "poor and outdated doctrinal and technical documentation of ordnance and aircraft equipment and procedures, evident at all levels of command, was a contributing cause of the accidental rocket firing."

But most important for those whose careers were on the line, including Beling, the board concluded that "no improper acts of commission or omission by personnel embarked on *Forrestal* directly or indirectly contributed to the inadvertent firing of the Zuni rocket." In other words, the bottom line for the board was that no one should be held individually responsible for the disaster.

The board offered many other useful conclusions, addressing the question of rocket pigtails and TER pins at length. After closely studying how the use of rocket pigtails and TER pins affected the accident, the board concluded that the deviation from the rule for plugging in pigtails should have been forwarded to Captain Beling for his approval, but it was not. Even so, the board said such a deviation should have been approved by a navy official higher than Beling. The board went on to say that some of the ordnancemen responsible for arming planes on the flight were "generally competent as individuals but were poorly organized and instructed."

But also, the board gave the crew a break by saying that "at least part of the poor organization and procedures mentioned above, and the failure to uncover them, can be attributed to the short period during which the squadron had been operating on Yankee Station." The board also acknowledged that "the fire could not have been extinguished prior to the explosion of major ordnance (ninety-four seconds after initiation of the fire) regardless of the aggressiveness, readiness, response and expertise of personnel and readiness of equipment." The report went on to say that "the design and operating procedures of fire fighting equipment currently available in attack carriers is totally inadequate to the needs generated by modern combat operations and the concentrations of very large quantities of ordnance and fuel on jet aircraft."

The detailed investigation also led the board to recommend a great number of improvements in carrier operation, from minor procedural and equipment improvements to wholesale revisions. The investigators praised some actions taken by the *Forrestal* crew, such as the decision to cut holes in the flight deck so they could pour water into burning compartments, but they criticized the men for strategic errors in fighting the fire and a general sense of disorganization in some areas. Many of those faults were traced to a basic deficiency in training provided by the navy, plus the horrendous scope of the fire.

"Current fire fighting exercises do not provide adequate training for the type and scope of fire experienced by *Forrestal* 29 July," the board said.

There was very little mention of the faulty ammunition delivered the night before the fire, with the report detailing the ammunition taken on board but making no mention of it being old, faulty, or unstable. The report noted the quick cook-off time for the bombs, but did not point to that as the primary reason the *Forrestal* lost 134 men. Some navy officials familiar with the facts were realizing that the ship might have faced a much smaller crisis without the old bombs on board, but the official navy report glossed over that fact. The ship still would have suffered the accidental firing of the rocket and a bad fire, but some observers thought that fire could have been contained if not for the bombs blowing up so much sooner than expected. Beling knew that to be the case.

But the official navy report makes no mention of that alternative scenario and devotes scant space to the issue of short cook-off times, concluding only that "cook-off times of ordnance stores in use were not available to *Forrestal* and that considerable injury and loss of life can be attributed to the cook-off of installed ordnance stores at a time earlier than expected." So in that brief statement the board acknowledged that the short cook-off times were the real reason 134 men died, but took that conclusion no further.

There were no recommendations for preventing such a disaster in the future from old and faulty ordnance, and no indication that the navy should investigate the matter further. (The board did recommend that *normal* cook-off times for ordnance be posted at firefighting stations and on the ordnance itself, and it recommended that procedures be developed to rapidly cool ordnance in a fire.)

But even if the board didn't seem eager to hold the navy accountable for the old bombs, at least it did not make Beling a scapegoat for the disaster. The board noted that Beling had demonstrated a personal interest in the training of his crew and the ship's readiness for a fire disaster, concluding that "no blame attaches to Captain Beling in connection with the fire that occurred in *Forrestal* on 29 July 1967."

Instead, the board cited inadequate training for carrier crews and said "the deaths and injuries resulting from the fire aboard *Forrestal* on 29 July 1967 were caused by the negligence and inefficiency of the Headquarters, Naval Air Systems Command."

At the end of the report, the board listed its recommendations. After sixty-one recommendations covering a wide range of topics, recommendation number sixty-two appeared right over the signature of Admiral Massey: "That no disciplinary or administrative action be taken with regard to any persons attached to USS *Forrestal* (CVA-59) or Carrier Air Wing 17 as a result of the fire which occurred on board USS *Forrestal* on 29 July 1967."

Beling was itching to get on to his next assignment, probably the command of another prominent ship, since his experience and skills would be wasted if he remained with the *Forrestal* to oversee her repairs. But first, the Massey investigation had to make its way through the naval command structure and become the official word on the disaster. That would take some time, Beling knew, so he waited, impatient but at least content that he would be moving on to a real job soon.

The normal procedure was for the Massey report to be passed on from one high-ranking officer to the next for approval, until the top man signed off on it. The first officer to review the findings of the Massey investigation was three-star admiral Thomas Booth, commander of the naval air force for the Atlantic Fleet. Booth wrote a two-page response that disagreed with only one point, saying that a board recommendation for changing a test receptacle on the TER-7 rocket-arming device was not a good idea. He noted in his review that he had sent a copy of the board's findings and its "Lessons Learned" to all aircraft carriers in the Atlantic Fleet with instructions to require that it be read by all crew members now on board and all those assigned later.

Booth sent the report on to his superior, Admiral Ephraim Holmes, commander in chief of the Atlantic Fleet. A four-star admiral, Holmes was sort of the number-two man in the navy, one step below Moorer, who was the head of the entire U.S. Navy and Beling's current boss. At this step, Beling started to worry that there might be a problem.

Holmes was new to the job, having replaced Moorer when he moved up to become chief of naval operations. Moorer had been commander in chief of the Atlantic Fleet when the *Forrestal* sailed for Vietnam, but by the time she returned to the States, Moorer had moved up and Holmes was in that position. Beling did not know how Holmes would react to the report, but he did know one thing that gave him pause. Holmes was a black shoe.

In the highly stratified world of the navy, one of the distinctions among high-ranking officers was whether you were a "black shoe" or a "brown shoe." Deriving from the differences in their uniforms, black shoes were navy officers with no direct tie to flying, and brown shoes were aviators or former aviators like Beling. They all worked together on a carrier, of course, but their different backgrounds often led to good-natured rivalries, and sometimes more serious differences of opinion. Massey and Booth were brown shoes, so Beling wasn't surprised that they all saw the *Forrestal* fire from the same perspective. Holmes might be different. And he was brand-new to the job. Beling hoped that didn't mean he was eager to make a name for himself, but he wasn't worried much.

Unfortunately, Beling underestimated Holmes's reaction. Two months after Booth signed off on the report, Holmes issued his opinion on December 1, 1967. In an eight-page response, Holmes flatly refused some of the board's conclusions.

"The Commander in Chief, U.S. Atlantic Fleet, therefore, specifically does not concur in Opinion 115 of the Report of the Investigation wherein it is stated 'That the deaths and injuries resulting from the fire aboard the *Forrestal* on 29 July 1967 were not caused by the intent, fault, negligence, or inefficiency of any person or persons embarked in the *Forrestal*.' Further, the Commander in Chief, U.S. Atlantic Fleet, specifically does not concur in Opinion 4 of the Report which states 'That no improper acts of commission or omission by personnel embarked in *Forrestal* directly contributed to the inadvertent firing of the Zuni rocket from F-4 #110.' "

Specifically addressing Beling's role in the disaster, Holmes wrote that "the conduct of the Commanding Officer and the role played by him in connection with the tragic incident cannot be ignored." The admiral went on to criticize Beling for failing to properly supervise his crew, for failing to be aware of the procedural changes that led to the rocket firing, and for inadequately responding to the fire itself.

As for the Massey investigation's conclusion that the disaster should be blamed "solely on the negligence and inefficiency of the Headquarters, Naval Air Systems Command," Holmes refused to accept that criticism. There were deficiencies in training, he said, but the deaths on the *Forrestal* were caused by more than that. Individuals were responsible, Holmes said.

It didn't take long for word to reach Beling that Holmes had taken a hard-line approach to reviewing the Massey investigation. Beling was disappointed, but he had to let the scenario play out according to navy regulations. It wasn't long before Holmes sent a message to his superior, Moorer, requesting that Beling be transferred from the Pentagon to work under Holmes's command in Norfolk. Moorer's office approved the transfer as a routine matter, the admiral apparently unaware at that point why Holmes wanted Beling. But when he was told to catch a plane for a one-week assignment to Holmes's office in Norfolk, Beling understood. Holmes could not reprimand Beling unless Beling was serving under his command.

So, like a schoolboy being called to the principal's office, Beling had to go through the motions of transferring to Holmes's office in Norfolk, knowing that he had no duties to perform there. He was to go there and wait for his punishment. It came in the form of a three-page letter delivered to him one day as he sat alone in a temporary office.

Though he had braced himself for the moment, Beling's heart sank as he read the accusations. Holmes cited "loose procedures" and said "these facts clearly establish that your exercise of command was not effective." Regarding the rocket-arming changes and the fact that Beling was not aware of them, the letter said, "Your nonaction in this regard amounted to a dereliction in the performance of your duties, which dereliction materially contributed to the circumstances resulting in the tragic incident aboard the *Forrestal*."

The letter specified that Beling "showed poor judgment" by deviating from established safety procedures, failing to advise superiors of such changes, failing to "devote sufficient time and supervision to administrative and organizational procedures which resulted in a general squadron laxity." And finally, the letter stated, "Your dereliction of duty as pointed out above and your lack of supervision contributed materially to the inadvertent firing of the Zuni rocket and permitted a situation to exist which resulted in the fire of 29 July 1967.

"Pursuant to references (b), (c), and (d), you are hereby reprimanded."

Beling's heart was pounding as he finished the letter, but not loud enough to drown out the words still ringing in his ears: "Your nonaction." "Dereliction of duty." "Poor judgment." "Laxity." "Failure." "Reprimand." Nothing could have hurt him more at that moment.

Beling was right back on the bridge of the *Forrestal*, watching his ship burn. He should have known he would never escape with his career intact. Men died on his watch, and the navy was saying it was his fault.

When Beling returned to his office in the Pentagon after his week in Norfolk, he was still wondering what to do with the reprimand. After the initial shock of the harsh criticism, Beling got angry. The reprimand had hurt so much because it stirred his deep feelings of regret and sorrow at the waste of young lives he had seen on the *Forrestal*. But when he thought about the facts at issue, Beling couldn't sit still and just take the reprimand. To do so would be a sign that he agreed with Holmes's conclusions, a tacit acknowledgment that he was in fact to blame for the deaths of those men. Beling knew he wasn't. He knew the real reason those men died, and all the talk about why the rocket fired missed the point. Sure there were problems that caused that rocket to fire. But that rocket didn't kill 134 men. They died because one-thousand-pound bombs started blowing up only a minute and thirty-four seconds into the fire.

As angry as the reprimand made Beling, he still wasn't sure what to do about it. He didn't want to accept it, but he also was reluctant to make a big fuss about it. Even aside from the personal pain it caused him, and that was no small matter, the reprimand was a major blow to his career. The reprimand would be a red flag every time a superior considered an assignment for him, and it would sully his reputation among the entire navy community. Beling winced at the reception he knew he would receive from his next ship's crew if he showed up dragging that reprimand behind him.

Beling had the right to contest the reprimand, but to do so would require a full-fledged court-martial, the military equivalent of a trial. He would have to take his case before a panel of military judges and, with the help of legal counsel, show why the reprimand was not justified. It was up to Beling—just accept the reprimand or go through a complete court-martial. He struggled with the choice.

I could probably win that court-martial. I know this damn reprimand isn't right, and I could make a good case that I wasn't responsible for what happened out there. But a court-martial would be so public. What would that do to the navy? I'd have to air the navy's dirty linen. I'm not sure I want to do that.

After weeks of soul-searching, Beling decided that he couldn't do it. He couldn't demand a court-martial and accuse the navy, publicly, of killing those men on the *Forrestal*. The idea of just rolling over and accepting the reprimand made him crazy with anger and indignation, but in the end he decided that he'd rather suffer that defeat alone than force the navy to admit to its failings. After all, he thought, the investigations had turned up a great many problems that contributed to the *Forrestal* fire and it appeared the navy was going to correct them. Wasn't that really the more important question? And the country was right in the middle of so much dissension and protests over the Vietnam War. The military was taking a lot of hits already from people who had no respect for the institution or the people serving. John Beling didn't want to add fuel to that fire.

No, it was better that he accept the reprimand, as much as it hurt him. That's what a good officer would do, he told himself. He knew it meant his career might never recover, but he was beginning to think that might be the case even if the reprimand were rescinded. His initial thoughts after the fire were starting to sound more and more on target. A captain just can't recover from an incident like the *Forrestal* fire.

Just as Beling was resigning himself to the reprimand and whatever the future might not hold for him, the final report and reprimand reached Admiral Moorer's desk in the Pentagon. Beling knew that it would be typical for the admiral to sign off on his subordinate's assessment and leave it at that. That would be the final word, since Moorer was the navy's top man. It turned out that Moorer had other things in mind.

Moorer was none too pleased to see that Beling had received a reprimand. Moorer's reading of the investigation's findings, from a fellow brown shoe's perspective, suggested to him that everyone underneath Holmes had read it the right way. But still, Moorer wanted good reasons for concluding what he thought was the case from the investigation— that despite the size of the tragedy, neither Beling nor anyone else on board was personally responsible. To help him make a final decision, Moorer decided to launch yet another investigation.

Moorer called in an old friend and colleague, James Russell, who

had recently retired as vice chief of naval operations. Russell was familiar to Beling as well, a former carrier aviator whom Beling considered
superbly qualified to assess the situation. Beling still hadn't said a
word to Moorer to protest the reprimand, but he was thrilled to hear
that Russell had been asked to make a final assessment. Russell came
out of retirement, partly as a personal favor to Moorer, just for the
investigation.

Months passed as Russell went through the Massey investigation and
then went back with his own staff to investigate the incident further.
Finally, Beling's phone rang as he was doing paperwork in his office. It
was an aide to Moorer.

"Sir, Admiral Russell is going to brief the CNO on his investigation
in about ten minutes. Would you like to attend?"

"Yes, I certainly would like to attend," Beling replied. He put the
phone down and immediately left for Moorer's office.

When he reached Moorer's outer office, he found Russell and a group
of aides already waiting. Beling introduced himself and soon Moorer
stepped out. He and Russell greeted each other warmly, just as would be
expected of old friends, and everyone went into Moorer's office. Beling
sat quietly to the side, knowing that he was there only to observe. After
some chitchat to get things settled, Moorer got down to business.

"Okay, Jim, so tell me, what the hell happened out there?"

Russell didn't say anything right away. Instead, he got up and
walked closer to Moorer's desk, reaching in his jacket pocket. He pulled
a brass slide switch from the TER rocket-arming system, one of several
switches that were part of the redundant safety systems designed to
keep the rocket from firing. The switch wasn't much bigger than a key.

"That's the culprit," Russell said, handing it to Moorer.

"That switch failed, and so did four other safety devices. That's why
that rocket fired."

Moorer looked at the switch in his hand and thought for a minute.

"So you're saying this is the real cause? It was a device failure?"

Russell said yes, and that led him to begin discussing a wealth of
technical detail he and his staff had discovered in their investigation.
Much of it coincided with and supported the findings of the Massey
investigation. The failure of the electrical safety devices didn't negate
some of the other problems cited by Massey and Holmes, Russell said,

but they were all secondary to the failure of the safety devices. The rocket pigtails, the TER safety pins, and all the other factors still mattered, Russell said, but the rocket fired because the electrical surge made its way through safety switches like that one. They were supposed to stop just such an accidental voltage surge.

"Bottom line, if you want to know what caused the fire, you're holding it."

Beling left with everyone else when the meeting was over, knowing that Moorer would contact him when he was ready. He felt a great sense of relief walking back to his office, confident that he had been exonerated by the highest office in the navy. Within a few days, Beling received a copy of a letter that Moorer had sent to Holmes. It directed Holmes to withdraw the reprimand.

Soon, Beling received notice that he was once again being transferred back to Norfolk for a one-week assignment under Holmes. This time, he was glad to go. As before, he went to Norfolk and sat in a temporary office waiting for a delivery. When the delivery came, it was a much shorter letter. After the usual jargon referencing the investigation and the previous letter of reprimand, the final line was what mattered.

"Your reprimand is hereby rescinded."

Beling finally felt that the investigations were behind him and he could move on. He continued working under Moorer in the Pentagon into 1968 and was assigned to a prestigious task force of military officers and civilian scientists developing sophisticated tools for monitoring activity in Southeast Asia. It was satisfying work, but Beling was still eager to get back to commanding ships. He knew he was in line to be assigned as commander of a carrier battle group in the Pacific. Not only would he be back on a carrier, but as a rear admiral, he would be superior to the captain. The navy takes a while to process appointments like that, so Beling was trying to be patient, knowing that the desk job wouldn't last forever. He was encouraged when the Bureau of Naval Personnel sent word to Beling that the assignment was imminent and he should start preparing for the move to San Diego. Finally, he thought, July 29, 1967, was about to end.

And then, another twist. Before Beling's assignment to the carrier group in San Diego could be finalized, Admiral Moorer's term of office ran out. Beling's good friend, the admiral who had watched out for him in such a difficult time, was to be replaced as chief of naval operations by Admiral Elmo Zumwalt, Jr. This was not good news. Zumwalt was not a former carrier man, like Beling and Moorer and Russell. Zumwalt had earned his stripes on destroyers, and unfortunately, Beling had had a few run-ins with Zumwalt during his time at the Pentagon. Most of the problems came down to just fundamental differences in perspective because of their different backgrounds, but the end result was that Beling and his new boss didn't get along well.

But maybe it doesn't matter. I'll be out of here any day now for San Diego.

Beling kept plugging away at his desk job, waiting for the final orders to report to San Diego. He was ready to go as soon as the paperwork came through.

Beling waited and waited, and the orders never came. Zumwalt offered no explanation. Beling inquired with more friendly contacts in the navy about why he wasn't being sent to San Diego yet, and one admiral with an aviation background wrote to Zumwalt to ask why Beling was still being held in the Pentagon. Zumwalt did not reply to the letter, but Beling soon received transfer orders.

Beling opened the orders as soon as they arrived. But they did not say San Diego. Instead, Zumwalt was transferring Beling from the Pentagon to a desk job in Iceland.

Iceland. Not only was Beling denied the prestigious command of a carrier battle group as he had been promised, but he was being sent to Iceland, to a desk job that any black-shoe navy officer with none of Beling's experience could handle. The message was clear, and Beling believed it had little to do with his personal disagreements with Zumwalt. No matter how many investigations cleared him, the navy wasn't going to let Beling off the hook for what happened on the *Forrestal*. He was being exiled.

And once again, Beling found himself on the bridge of the *Forrestal,* staring in disbelief as a raging fire killed young men under his command. For John Beling and so many more of the men of *Forrestal,* the fires would never end.

EPILOGUE

Beling did transfer to Iceland and ended his career there, never again commanding a ship. He retired as a rear admiral and is greatly admired by the men who served under him. The other sailors went on with their lives, many of them leaving the navy after just a few years. The ship itself underwent a massive rehaul and then entered service again, but she did not return to Vietnam. She was still one of the country's mightiest warships even after bigger and more advanced aircraft carriers were introduced. The *Forrestal* was on active duty until 1993, when the navy decommissioned her after thirty-eight years. In that time, she saw only four and a half days of war.

The navy maintains the *Forrestal* in a Rhode Island shipyard, the gray hulk sitting quietly in the water with no visitors and no crew, waiting as her veterans continue efforts to turn the ship into a museum. The 134 men who died on the *Forrestal* on July 29, 1967, are memorialized on panel 24E of the Vietnam Veterans Memorial in Washington, D.C. Close by at Arlington National Cemetery, there is a monument to those never recovered or identified after the disaster, just behind the Tomb of the Unknowns. The monument marks the burial site of twelve to fourteen bodies that could not be identified, listing eighteen men whose families were denied the small comfort of taking their loved one home.

A number of sailors aboard the *Forrestal* received medals and other accolades for their actions on July 29, 1967, but none of the injured received a Purple Heart. The navy determined that the injuries were not incurred in combat.

The *Forrestal* tragedy produced a great many improvements in naval firefighting and overall safety. To the navy's credit, the lessons learned caused a major reassessment of firefighting training, techniques, equipment, and fundamental ship design. As a result, many of today's advanced safety precautions in place on aircraft carriers throughout the world can be traced directly to the *Forrestal*. The ship led the way in technological advances when she was launched, and she continued to do so even after suffering the worst disaster in the U.S. Navy since World War II. The *Forrestal* fire led the navy to strengthen firefighting training for sailors, improve the dissemination of pertinent information to both officers and crew, reduce the amount of crew turnover a ship can endure before sailing on a long voyage, and implement a wide range of procedural and policy changes that lessen the risk of accidental rocket firings. Some of the changes were small but significant: all flight-deck crew are now required to wear long sleeves while working, no matter how hot the weather, because long sleeves can make a difference when a sailor is close to a fire. Emergency breathing apparatus was redesigned to make it faster and easier to use. On the whole, safety and fire safety in particular are a higher priority for the navy now than they were in 1967. Some of that improvement is simply the normal evolution of a complex organization, but the navy also remembers the *Forrestal* fire as the singular moment when all its weaknesses in that area were highlighted. The navy's firefighting school in Norfolk, Virginia, is named after Gerald Farrier, the chief who charged into the fire scene and waved off other crew members just before the first bomb exploded.

But some of the most significant changes are purely mechanical. When the navy investigated the fire, its leaders realized that it was completely inadequate to rely on sailors rushing to a major jet-fuel fire with hoses. Instead, they said, carriers needed a way to automatically flood the deck with water or firefighting foam, similar to the way a building's fire-sprinkler system can instantly flood a burning room. At that time, the investigators saw such a system as an ideal solution but acknowledged that it would be difficult to design and implement. Nevertheless, all modern carriers now incorporate a "wash down" system consisting of hundreds of recessed sprinkler heads in the flight deck, and the *Forrestal* was even retrofitted with the system years after the fire. On the bridge and in flight control, a panel of switches can instantly activate the wash-down system on the entire flight deck or just on selected portions. The nozzles send water or firefighting foam arcing in every direction, deluging a fire far more quickly than even the fastest firefighting team could put a hose on it. With the wash-down system on board, it is almost unthinkable that a fire could spread as quickly and as far as it did on the *Forrestal*.

Other improvements also were incorporated into new carriers and retrofitted to existing ships. Carriers now have small fire trucks parked on the flight deck, loaded with equipment and manned during all flight operations by silver-suited firefighters ready to spring into action. The trucks are designed not only to get the firefighting gear to the scene quickly, but also to bulldoze wreckage out of the way. The oxygen-generating plant, which threatened to blow the *Forrestal* sky-high and had to be drained by a small hose for more than an hour, is now installed on rails so that the crew can push the entire thing overboard if it threatens the ship in any way.

Though the navy deserves credit for acting on many of the lessons learned in the *Forrestal* fire, the role of the faulty ordnance is a glaring omission in every official account of the disaster. The navy investigations and the official navy history of the fire point to a number of shortcomings, both in the navy bureaucracy and on the ship itself, but there is never any mention of the significance played by the decision to deliver old, unsafe bombs to the ship the night before the fire. Even if some criticism of the crew is justified, a full accounting of the incident would show that the overriding cause for the disaster was the navy's decision to deliver faulty ordnance, prompted in turn by the White House's unreasonable demands to escalate the bombing in Vietnam. Instead, the American government has been content to let the men of *Forrestal* shoulder an undue burden, to let them bear the brunt of the blame by pointing out their inadequacies while refusing to acknowledge the much larger danger that it thrust upon them.

The navy's focus on why the rocket fired was useful in preventing a repeat of that accident, but it missed the point in regards to the overall disaster. Though the entire incident began with the inadvertent firing of a Zuni rocket, it is clear that the rocket firing alone would not have led to such a terrible loss of life. Without the faulty ordnance, the rocket firing likely would have been a serious accident, still causing a fuel spill and a fire, but the crew would have been able to extinguish the fire before it spread too far. Men still may have died in that situation, but the facts clearly show that the *Forrestal* lost 134 men because of the bomb explosions, not the original fire. The explosions killed dozens on the flight deck and below, disabled the ship's firefighting response, and opened up decks below to a blaze that should have been contained where it started.

The navy's own analysis of the explosions on the flight deck shows the significance of the faulty ordnance. There were sixteen one-thousand-pound bombs loaded on planes that morning, all of them the older type that so concerned the crew when they arrived the night before, carried two apiece on eight planes. All of the other bombs on planes that morning were the newer type. Nine major explosions occurred on the flight deck during the fire, and all nine came from six of the planes loaded with the old bombs. (One major explosion occurred in between a plane with an old bomb and a plane with a new bomb. It is likely that the second old bomb on the plane is the one that exploded there, rather than the other plane's new bomb.) Of the eight planes loaded with the old bombs, six had their bombs blow up at full strength, and that happened far sooner than anyone would have expected of normal ordnance. The other two were far forward of the fire and never burned.

But perhaps the most telling fact is this: *None* of the newer bombs exploded at anything near full strength, even though some of the planes holding them burned completely.

Thirty-three years after the fire, Captain Beling was willing to speak freely about the role of the faulty ordnance. Referring to the first thousand-pound bomb that exploded only one minute and thirty-four seconds into the fire, Beling said, "It was a World War Two bomb we were required to carry for economic reasons. It was ancient. It was thin-skinned and susceptible to early cook-off."

The tragedy of the *Forrestal* fire continues for many. As the years tore at them, some would not be able to accept that some tragic turn of events was only that, only a coincidence or twist of fate. Some on the *Forrestal* could not escape the guilt that convinced them they were somehow responsible for the death of another crew member—a close friend or a complete stranger. Others took no comfort in the reassurance by their crewmates, superiors, and families back home that someone else's death was not their fault. No matter how tenuous the link seemed to others, they convinced themselves that they bore responsibility. They had survived, but they would suffer for a long time.

Much of Gary Shaver's year after the fire would be a blur of narcotics, surgeries, different hospitals, and nearly unbearable hours alone with his memories and his pain. He would remember terrible smells, the maddening isolation as he lay there for day after day, and the odd moments that his mind chose to save as he drifted in and out of reality. At one point, Shaver was visited by two naval officers with a tape recorder. They explained that his pain medication was being stopped so they could interview him about the fire. He pleaded with them not to stop the medicine, but they insisted. The interview lasted only about fifteen minutes, but Shaver was out of his mind with pain by the end. He wanted so much to jump out of the bed and kick the living shit out of those officers, but the days when that was even a possibility were long gone. He realized later that they had been so insistent because they thought he was going to die soon.

It would take more than a year for Shaver to recover physically, and much to everyone's surprise, he managed to keep his left arm. The extensive injuries to his internal organs were repaired, eventually leaving Shaver with a fully functioning body. He would learn later that, though his body could recover, his mind could not.

Many of the men suffered severe mental stress in the coming years, some bad enough to be diagnosed with "post-traumatic stress disorder," a problem more often associated with the infantry who fought in the jungles of Vietnam. Shaver tried hard to put the horror behind him and for many years, he thought he had succeeded. But as he grew older, he started wondering if some of the demons controlling his life had been spawned on July 29, 1967. He became a police officer after leaving the navy, but he lost two relationships because of his drinking, before seeking help. At that point, he didn't yet understand the underlying cause. He knew he still had terrible memories of the explosions, the pain, the descent to hell, and the loss of his friends, but it took him a long time with PTSD specialists to make the connection between that and his drinking. Even after acknowledging he had an emotional disorder related to the fire, he has found no easy cure. Intensive therapy has helped, but Shaver still is left completely disabled by PTSD. For him, dealing with the aftermath of the *Forrestal* fire may have been more difficult because his terror lasted so long. Instead of just a moment, or even a day, Shaver lived in terror and excruciating pain for a year. More than thirty years later, he can't stop reliving his year of hell, and he can't get rid of the guilt he feels for switching places with Lonnie Hudson. Shaver has come a long way in dealing with his PTSD, but the fire forever altered his life. He readily acknowledges that without the therapy provided by the Veterans Administration, he probably would have killed himself long ago. His daily struggle is a reminder of how a traumatic incident can linger long after the fires are out.

Robert Whelply, the nineteen-year-old left all alone in the corridor by himself, waiting for orders, never found out why the others had not shown up at his GQ station. He supposed they either were prevented from reaching it by fire damage, or became involved in firefighting efforts or rescues as they tried to get to the GQ station. The hours he spent at his GQ station without doing anything, and without knowing anything, left him shaken. It would take a long time to get over the fear of being left behind as the ship burned and sank.

But that fear is not what burdened Whelply for decades. He carried another burden, one that gnaws in a way that fear cannot match. Though he was following orders, Whelply wondered for years if he had done the right thing. He worried for many years that if only he had left his post sooner and looked for something useful to do, someone might not have died. Men died all around him as he followed orders and did nothing. *How could that be right?*

Most would agree that Whelply did nothing wrong, but he has a hard time believing it.

Robert Shelton, the crew member who was supposed to be working in the port-aft steering compartment instead of his buddy, had trouble living with the terrible guilt he felt for surviving the fire. Nothing was particularly unusual about trading work shifts, but Shelton knew that if he had not done so, he would have been one of the three men trapped in port-aft steering, horribly injured and dying slowly as Merv Rowland talked to them from damage control. Shelton felt that James Blaskis had died in his place, and not just another man, but *his friend.* The guilt weighed on him so heavily that within days of the fire he requested a transfer from the ship. Not surprisingly, he wasn't the first, and he was told that this was very unlikely unless he went directly to combat in Vietnam.

Shelton accepted the offer. He knew he was going from a relatively safe duty on a carrier, the next year or so tied to a pier in the United States, to being shot at in Vietnam. Within ten days, the navy transferred him to the most dangerous navy duty possible—a small gunboat that patrolled the riverways of Vietnam. This was known as "river rat" duty and it was extremely risky. He survived more than a year, even as his boat sank underneath him. Forever after he would think of it as a way of doing penance, taking some other young man's place the way another man had taken his.

Shelton still vividly remembers the two nightmares that preceded the fire, but thirty-five years later, the terrible images in the dreams are mixed with what he saw during the fire, so much that he can't be sure just how prophetic the nightmares actually were. He is inclined to think that the dreams were some sort of warning.

For years after the fire, Ed Roberts sometimes woke up at night consumed by a sense of doom, convinced that he was about to die. The feeling was so intense that he once got out of bed and wrote his will. Much of his lasting terror could be traced to an assignment he had on the trip back home after the fire. Roberts and his fellow blue shirts were brought to the flight deck one day and handed spoons. Then they were told that they had to clean out the "pad eyes," the little indentations all over the deck that held recessed metal crosses for attaching tie-down chains. The large debris had been cleared away by then, but the pad eyes had to be scooped out individually.

"If you find anything unusual, take it to the medical personnel," the petty officer said.

Roberts went to work with the other men, scooping out the fire debris from one pad eye and then moving on to the next. It was shrapnel, bits of melted plastic, glass, all sorts of things. And then Roberts scooped out something and held it in his hand for a moment. The realization hit him like a baseball bat. He was holding a piece of human flesh. It wasn't the first disturbing thing he'd seen the past few days, and it certainly wasn't the worst. But something about the moment got to him down deep. Ignoring his orders, he stood up and walked over to the deck edge and, with all his might, heaved the mass into the sea.

For the rest of his life, he thought of that moment as the eye of a needle. In his memories, he has to pass through that moment to get to any part of his life before that. July of 1967 seized many families in a similar way, forever changing them. The parents of Robert Zwerlein, who was caught up in the initial blaze and died on the hospital ship, never got over the loss of their Bobby. Years later, when Ruth Zwerlein thought she had learned to get through the day without sobbing, she would still find the sadness hidden in the most unlikely places. On an otherwise enjoyable trip to Disney World with her family, Ruth kept thinking she saw Bobby everywhere in the crowds. Every young man in the distance, every sailor, every face that had just a slight resemblance to her boy sent a jolt of recognition through her, a tiny second of joy followed by a deep sadness as she realized it was not her Bobby.

Merv Rowland, already a crusty old salt by the time of the fire, is still a much-beloved father figure to the *Forrestal* survivors. Eighty-three years old and a grandfather several times over, he regales anyone who will stand still with stories of his days on the sea, his gravelly voice bursting into laughter at regular intervals. But when the subject turns to July 29, 1967—and particularly the three men who died in the steering compartment while he talked to them—Rowland's eyes fill with tears and he sounds like a man who has lost his sons.

Many veterans still have difficulty talking about what they experienced and saw on the *Forrestal*. Some have only recently begun discussing their memories, and many of them report that it is therapeutic. The author noted that many of those interviewed for this book were willing to discuss their experiences more freely with a stranger than with their loved ones. On more than one occasion, veterans lowered their voices and checked to make sure that their wives or other loved ones were not listening.

Few people know the full story of what happened on the *Forrestal,* and why so many men died. Even those who were there that day often know the details only of their own experience. They and the relatives of those who died sometimes have heard only vague reports of "old bombs" but do not know how significant those bombs were. Some of those who know the real cause of the deaths are left uneasy, troubled by the idea that the *Forrestal* disaster was not just a terrible accident caused by an electrical glitch that no one could have foreseen. For Rocky Pratt, the aviator who witnessed the delivery of the bombs and the crew's concern over their safety, the conclusion was so troubling that it led him to leave the navy despite a family tradition of service. The ensuing years without a full accounting from the Pentagon have only compounded his disappointment.

Nevertheless, the men of *Forrestal* are unlikely to ever complain about the navy or the country in any meaningful way. If they know the full story, if they feel mistreated by the navy's compliance in allowing the crew to take more of the blame than they deserved, they aren't likely to say so except when they're having a beer with a trusted buddy. They're too proud to ask for recognition, and they love their country too much to stir up trouble. The 134 men who didn't have the opportunity to grow old probably would have felt the same way.

KILLED ON BOARD
USS *FORRESTAL*
JULY 29, 1967

Marvin J. Adkins
Everett A. Allen
Gary J. Ardeneaux
Tony A. Barnett
Dennis M. Barton
Robert L. Bennett
Mark R. Bishop
James L. Blaskis
William V. Brindle
Bobby J. Brown
Jerry D. Byars
Marvin F. Campeau
Jack M. Carlan
Daniel G. Cavazos
Ray A. Chatelain
Richard D. Clendenen
William D. Collins
Robert B. Cotton
James L. Crenshaw
Mario C. Crugnola, Jr.
Robert J. Davies

Thomas J. Dawson, Jr.
Jerold V. Despard
Edward R. Dorsey
Joseph G. Dugas
Paul A. Dupere
John S. Duplaga
Walter T. Eads
James A. Earick
John T. Edwards
Gerald W. Farrier
Kenneth L. Fasth
John J. Fiedler
Russell L. Fike
Harold Fontenot
Johnnie L. Frazier
Gerald G. Fredrickson
Herbert A. Frye
Ramon Garza
Robert E. Geller
Richard H. Gibson
Laurence J. Gilbert

William T. Gilroy
Larry E. Grace
Russell A. Grazier
Charles C. Gregory
William C. Hartgen
Robert L. Hasz
Richard A. Hatcher
William K. Hinckley, Jr.
Stephen L. Hock
Larry D. Holley
Calvin D. Howison
Philip L. Hudson
Julius B. Hughes
Donald N. Hugo
Ralph W. Jacobs
Donald W. Jedlicka
William B. Justin
Thomas M. Kane
Charles D. Kieser
Joseph Kosik III
Edward L. La Barr
Wade A. Lannom, Jr.
William Lee
Robert C. Leonberg
John T. Lilla
Arnold E. H. Lohse
Charles E. Long
William E. Lowe
Kenneth W. Lozier, Jr.
James S. MacVickar, Jr.
Ralph E. Manning, Jr.
Earle E. McAuliffe, Jr.
Brian D. McConahay
George C. McDonald
Frank C. McNelis, Jr.
William V. McQuaide
Allan R. Metz
George D. Miller
Edward A. Mindyas
Hubert H. Morgan, Jr.
Leroy Moser
James E. Neumeyer
Gary E. Newby
James E. Newkirk
Ronald R. Ogring
Thomas D. Ott II

Wayne H. Ott
Richard L. Owens
Richard T. Pinta
Raymond N. Plesh
John C. Pody
Ernest E. Polston
Douglas A. Post
Robert M. Priviech
John M. Pruner
Robert A. Rhuda
Charles R. Rich
Jerry P. Rodgers
Dale R. Ross
James M. Runnels
Harvey D. Scofield
Joseph C. Shartzer
William J. Shields
Richard M. Sietz
David W. Smith
Richard T. Smith
John F. Snow
John C. Spiess
Nelson E. Spitler
Johnny W. Spivey
Gerry L. Stark
Walter E. Steele
Wendell W. Stewart
Robert A. Stickler
Kenneth D. Strain
Robert H. Swain
Delton E. Terry
Norman A. Thomas
William F. Thompson
Richard J. Vallone
Robert J. Velasquez
Juan A. Velez
George E. Wall
Harold D. Watkins
Gregory L. Webb
Gerald A. Wehde
Judson A. Wells, Jr.
Richard L. Wescott
Edward J. Wessells
Fred D. White
Kerry D. Wisdom
Robert L. Zwerlein

USS *Forrestal* Flight Deck

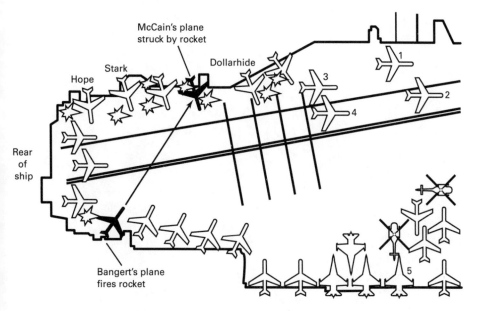

McCain's plane struck by rocket

Stark

Dollarhide

Hope

Rear of ship

1

3

2

4

Bangert's plane fires rocket

5

Explosion marks indicate where bombs exploded during the fire.

Planes 1–4 were about to take off. The rest were being armed and preparing to taxi forward to the catapult. Plane 5 was a tanker loaded with 28,000 lbs. of jet fuel.

Area of flight deck shown in detailed diagram (overhead view)

NOTES

Chapter 1

Page 5   "Four hundred thousand ground troops." Robert McNamara, *In Retrospect* (New York: Vintage Books, 1995), p. 221.

Page 5   "targeting North Vietnamese supply lines." George C. Herring, ed., *The Pentagon Papers* (New York: McGraw-Hill, 1993), p. 132.

Chapter 2

Page 15   "ground targets within distance of her planes." The navy has a strict policy of neither confirming nor denying that nuclear weapons are on board certain vessels, but retired officers confirm that nuclear bombs were on board when the *Forrestal* went to Vietnam in 1967. The navy's subsequent investigation makes reference to the handling of "conventional (and nuclear) weapons aboard *Forrestal*."

Page 16   "calculated to be 2.5 million pounds." The design of the chain proved sound, and after the *Forrestal* was decommissioned in 1993, the chain was transferred to the *Harry S. Truman,* currently the newest and most sophisticated nuclear-powered aircraft carrier in the world.

Page 17   "$188.9 million." The price of a modern Nimitz-class nuclear aircraft carrier is about four billion dollars.

Page 17   "five-hundred-ton air-conditioning units." R. F. Dempewolff, "Our Navy's Mightiest Carrier: USS *Forrestal,*" *Popular Mechanics,* November 1954, p. 84.

Page 18   "make the *Forrestal* a 'happy ship.' " Ibid., p. 264.

Page 18   "to hold that record." In her thirty-eight-year career, the *Forrestal* continued to undergo design changes to keep her at the head of the pack in terms of usefulness and efficiency. In 1961, she entered the Norfolk Naval Shipyard to have the forward five-inch gun mounts removed when the navy decided that changing trends in warfare made them unnecessary on a carrier. The accompanying ships and the *Forrestal*'s own aircraft would provide much more defense than the five-inch guns, and besides, the heavy concussions from the guns caused too much disruption to flight operations. The five-inch guns to the rear remained on the ship as an extra measure of safety, but no one really expected to use them. The arresting gear, including the huge wires that are used to snag planes as they land, also was modified at that time. Originally designed with six wires, the configuration was changed to just four wires. An updated signal-light system to guide pilots was also installed at that point, replacing the earlier version.

Page 25   "follow in their footsteps." John McCain and Mark Salter, *Faith of My Fathers* (New York: Random House, 1999), pp. 118–152.

Chapter 4

Page 51   "beaten his flashlight." Dempewolff, p. 270.

Page 51   "falling overboard into the sea." On a modern carrier, everyone on the flight deck must wear a "float coat," a color-coded garment that looks like a long vest but actually is an important piece of survival equipment. The float coat is comfortable to wear even while working. It normally is flat and thin like a typical vest, but it can be inflated to act as a life preserver in the water, and it also carries some important gear to help in your retrieval if you go overboard: a dye pack to mark your location in the water, a whistle to signal for help, a flashlight that can be stuck to your helmet with Velcro, and reflective tape on the shoulders and back to make you more visible.

Page 52   "lose consciousness in thirty minutes." *Think Safe* (Washington, DC: United States Coast Guard, 1999), p. 14.

Page 53   "he was never recovered." William Jordan, "USS *Washington* BB56: Man Overboard!" http://home.flash.net/~hfwright/moverbrd.htm.

Chapter 5

Page 66   "hundreds of smaller incidents." Kit Bonner and Carolyn Bonner, *Great Naval Disasters: U.S. Naval Accidents in the 20th Century* (Osceola, WI: MBI Publishing, 1998), p. 5.

Page 67   "fire was at the top of the list." Largely as a result of what happened in 1967, the navy now takes fire safety aboard ships very seriously. Visitors to a carrier, whether civilian or military, are greeted by a safety officer who provides an immediate lesson on fire safety. Before their feet have been on the carrier for sixty seconds, they receive detailed instructions on how to use an emergency breathing apparatus during a fire, where to find one, and how to call for help in an emergency from anywhere on the ship.

Page 67   "Skyhawks on an attack just after midnight." Ibid., pp. 85–91.

Page 74   "They say it's the only way to get all the planes launched fast enough." Ironically, the navy had just produced a training film on board the *Forrestal* earlier in 1967 that specifically addressed flight-deck hazards, including the arming of planes. The film shows *Forrestal* sailors arming planes with rockets and bombs, noting that "most of these weapons have considerable firepower packed into a small space, and need only a tiny electric current to fire them." The film warns that "careful handling alone will not protect you from two prime hazards of arming: the presence of stray voltage and the unintended actuation of the weapons-system firing circuits. Avoid these dangers by professional adherence to ship and squadron safety rules when arming aircraft."

Chapter 6

Page 77   "2,475 railroad cars, and 11,425 water craft." Ibid., p. 212.

Page 77   "assessed the war effort." United States Department of State, *Foreign Relations of the United States 1964–1968* (Washington, DC: United States Government Printing Office, 1998), vol. IV, p. 11.

Page 78   "send the execute order." Ibid.

Page 78   "sorties have been canceled." McNamara, p. 242.

Page 78   "knew the truth was different." http://www.pbs.org/wgbh/pages/frontline/shows/military/guys/smith.html.

Page 80   "provided ammunition." The description of the *Diamond Head* and its mission to deliver bombs to the *Forrestal* is based on an interview with Greg Strain, a sailor aboard the *Diamond Head* in 1967.

Page 85   "been manufactured in 1935." The navy's official report on the incident says those bombs were made in 1953, not 1935 as Rocky Pratt recalls. Pratt allows that he may be mistaken about the exact date he saw on the bomb shipment, but he says it was prior to his birth in 1940. He also suggests that a bomb made in 1953 and stored in the Philippine jungle still would have been dangerous by 1967.

Chapter 7

Page 94   "back to work that day." Official records from the *Forrestal* indicate that the man run over by the plane most likely survived the incident, although he suffered extensive injuries, including the loss of a foot. However, Gary Shaver was certain for the next thirty-four years that the man had died, and his guilt over the incident figured prominently in his post-traumatic stress disorder. Research for this book revealed the discrepancy between Shaver's memory and the records.

Page 117   "put this plane ACOP." *Situation Critical: The USS Forrestal* [videotape] (Arlington, VA: Henninger Media Development, 1997).

Chapter 8

Page 122   "One minute and thirty-four seconds." There is some discrepancy among sources as to the exact length of time before the first bomb exploded, usually one minute and twenty-eight seconds versus one minute and thirty-four seconds. The official navy investigation determined that the bomb exploded after one minute and thirty-four seconds.

Page 122   "high pressure and temperature." http://wseweb.ew.usna.edu/wse/academic/courses/es300/book/chapte13.htm.

Page 124   "a headless body." Robert Timberg, *The Nightingale's Song* (New York: Touchstone, 1996), p. 98.

Page 128   "felt particularly helpless." Associated Press, "Forrestal Crewmen Become Fireballs." *New York Times,* August 12, 1967, p. 1.

Page 132   "as the first bomb blast hit." *Manual of the Judge Advocate General: Basic Final Investigative Report Concerning the Fire on Board the USS Forrestal (CVA-59)* (Washington, DC: Department of the Navy, 1967). The navy's report concludes that the Zuni rocket fired at 10:51:21, then the first bomb exploded one minute and thirty-four seconds later, at 10:52:55, then general quarters was sounded five seconds later, at 10:53. It is likely that the time for general quarters was not recorded precisely because of the emergency. Most of the veterans remember that general quarters was sounded immediately before the first explosion, but some recall it sounding just after. All agree that the general-quarters alarm was sounded at almost the same time as the first blast.

Page 145   "fireballs hopping and tumbling." Ibid.

Chapter 9

Page 145   "One of the most sensitive spots." *USS Forrestal* (Newport News, VA: Newport News Shipbuilding and Dry Dock Company, 1954). The oxygen-generating plant was another of the *Forrestal*'s technical innovations. Previously, it was typical for carriers to keep individual oxygen cylinders for use on board the planes. But enough cylinders to supply the planes for five days would weigh seventy thousand pounds, whereas the oxygen-generating plant itself weighed only twenty thousand pounds. In addition to the weight reduction, the plant made the *Forrestal* self-sufficient for liquid oxygen instead of relying on deliveries at sea.

Chapter 10

Page 164   "doing a pretty good job." *Situation Critical: The USS Forrestal.*

Page 169   "explosion aboard the carrier *Bennington*." Scott Vanier, "A Survivor's Story," *The Flagship*, July 29, 1999, p. A4.

Page 170   "certainly would have survived." "Tragedy's Start: A Blast Is Heard," *New York Times* July 31, 1967, p. 1.

Page 176   "disappeared as quickly as it had arrived." "Chicago Sailor sees 'Great Lady' Burn." *New York Times,* July 31, 1967. There is no official report of a U.S. ship engaging one of the local boats, but Ed Roberts and others on the *Forrestal* witnessed the boat being destroyed. In addition, a newspaper account quotes twenty-five-year old Tony DeBella of Chicago, a tower-control leader aboard the carrier *Oriskany,* describing the same scene.

Chapter 12

Page 185   "That list was dangerous." Associated Press, "Forrestal Fire Took 29 Lives," *Norfolk (VA) Ledger-Star,* July 31, 1967, p. 1. Though Beling and Rowland maintain that they never feared losing the ship, Beling was quoted soon after the fire as saying that it was "absolutely possible" the ship could be lost. He apparently meant the ship could be lost without a proper response from the crew, but he was confident the crew would perform well.

Chapter 13

Page 206   "McCain quickly left the sick bay." McCain and Salter, p. 179; Timberg, pp. 98–99.

Page 206   "more than three hundred." The official count is 161 injured from the *Forrestal* fire, but Kirchner says the sick bay saw far more than that. Not all were serious injuries, especially toward the end of the day, and many may not have been officially recorded if they needed only superficial care.

Page 212   "a dark ammunition elevator." Lenny Julius confirms that the *Oriskany* used the ammunition elevator to transport the wounded. Normally, crew were forbidden to ride on the ammunition elevator because it was designed only for cargo and not considered safe for people. When the volume of patients forced the use of the ammunition elevator, Julius feared the doors at the top of the elevator would not open in time and the patients would be crushed as they were raised to the flight deck.

Chapter 14

Page 229   "photo of flames and smoke." William Mason, a photographer's mate on the *Forrestal,* rushed topside to take photos during the fire, many of which were used in *Life.*

Page 229   "occurs about once a week." R. W. Apple, Jr., "Heroism on Big Carrier," *New York Times,* July 31, 1967, p. 1.

Page 237   "yet another fire." Associated Press, "12 Sailors Still Listed as Missing," *New York Times,* August 12, 1967, p. 1.

Chapter 16

Page 264   "you are hereby reprimanded." The wording of the reprimand is taken from a draft of the letter provided to the author by the navy, which refused to release it until Beling personally intervened. The navy states that the final version of the reprimand letter is not in its files and may have been different from this draft version. Beling did not retain a copy of the letter and does not remember the exact wording, but he confirms that the gist of the letter is correct.

Epilogue

Page 271   "worst disaster in the U.S. Navy." Bonner and Bonner, p. 5. The loss of life on the *Forrestal* was superseded by an incident in 1952 when the carrier *Wasp* ran over the destroyer *Hobson* during nighttime flight operations. The accident killed 176 men, including the captain of the destroyer. Sixty-one men were recovered from the *Hobson*, some without serious injuries. There were no injuries on the carrier. Since 134 men died on the *Forrestal* and 161 were seriously injured, the combined death and injury toll was slightly higher for the *Forrestal* incident.

Page 274   "It was thin-skinned." *Situation Critical: The USS Forrestal; Symposium 2000—Valor Under Fire: Forrestal, 29 July 1967* [videotape] (Pensacola, FL: Naval Aviation Museum Foundation, 2000). Vice Admiral Thomas Kilcline stated at a naval symposium in 2000, in reference to the bombs that exploded in the *Forrestal* fire, that the military was compromising by using old bombs. A pilot aboard the *Forrestal* in 1967, Kilcline stated that he overheard the conversation between Captain Beling and the skipper of the *Diamond Head* while the ammunition was transferred to the ship the night before the fire. He said Beling "was not very happy with what he was going to get in the thousand-pounders," but the other skipper replied that the old bombs were all they had to provide. Kilcline said, "We were making a lot of compromises in those days and this was one of them. This was a World War Two bomb. It was not something new. We were buying a lot of new things, but much of our attention was being paid to nuclear weapons and modernization of that type."

BIBLIOGRAPHY

"46 killed, 56 hurt in *'Forrestal'* fire." *Norfolk Virginian-Pilot,* July 30, 1967, p. 1. *1967 Fire Chronology.* Sterling, VA: Records of the USS *Forrestal* CVA/CV/AVT-59 Association, Inc., 1967

1MC Recording, USS Forrestal, July 29, 1967. Sterling, VA: Records of the USS *Forrestal* CVA/CV/AVT-59 Association, Inc., 1967.

Anderson, Terry. *The Sixties.* New York: Longman, 1999.

Apple, R. W., Jr. "At least 70 dead in *Forrestal* fire; 89 others missing." *New York Times,* July 30, 1967, p. 1.

Apple, R. W., Jr. "Death count on *Forrestal* rises as flooded compartments are searched." *New York Times,* July 31, 1967, p. 1.

Apple, R. W., Jr. "Heroism on big carrier." *New York Times,* July 31, 1967, p. 1.

Arnett, Peter. "Eyewitnesses relate stories of disaster aboard *Forrestal.*" *Lake Charles American Press,* July 31, 1967, p. 8.

Associated Press. "12 sailors still listed as missing." *New York Times,* August 12, 1967, p. 1.

Associated Press. "*Forrestal* crewmen become fireballs." *New York Times,* August 12, 1967, p. 1.

Associated Press. "*Forrestal* fire took 129 lives." *Norfolk (VA) Ledger-Star,* July 31, 1967, p. 1.

At Sea [videotape]. Washington, DC. United States Navy Memorial, 1992.

Beling, Eve. Personal interview with author.

Beling, John K. Personal interviews and correspondence with author.

Bennett, Christopher. *Supercarrier: USS George Washington.* Osceola, WI: Motorbooks International, 1996.

Bonner, Kit, and Carolyn Bonner. *Great Naval Disasters: U.S. Naval Accidents in the 20th Century.* Osceola, WI: MBI Publishing, 1998.

Buckley, Tom. "The *Forrestal* set afire by blast, 29 planes burn; some aboard feared dead." *New York Times,* July 29, 1967, p. 1.

Burner, David. *Making Peace with the 60s.* Princeton, NJ: Princeton University Press, 1996.

Carlin, Michael Joe. *Trial: Ordeal of the USS Enterprise.* West Grove, PA: Tuscarora Press, 1993.

Chesneau, Roger. *Aircraft Carriers of the World, 1914 to the Present: An Illustrated Encyclopedia.* London: Arms and Armour Press, 1984.

"Chicago sailor sees 'great lady' burn." *New York Times,* July 31, 1967.

Clancy, Tom. *Carrier: A Guided Tour of an Aircraft Carrier.* New York: Berkley Books, 1999.

Costello, Joe. *The Pacific War 1941–1945.* New York: Quill, 1982.

Crutchley, Milt. Personal interview and correspondence with author.

Dale, Edwin L. "Johnson asks for 10% surcharge on personal and business taxes; 45,000 more men to go to Vietnam." *New York Times,* August 4, 1967.

Davison, Dog, ed. *USS Forrestal 1967* [cruise book]. Norfolk, VA: Walsorth, 1967. Courtesy of Ed Roberts.

DeBella, Tony. Correspondence with author.

Dempewolff, R. F. "Our navy's mightiest carrier: USS *Forrestal.*" *Popular Mechanics,* November 1954, pp. 81–85, 262, 264, 266, 268, 270.

Department of the Navy. *Manual of the Judge Advocate General: Basic Final Investigative Report Concerning the Fire on Board the USS Forrestal (CVA-59).* Washington, DC: United States Navy, 1967.

Federation of American Scientists. "Military Analysis Network: Zuni 5.0-Inch [130mm] Rocket." http://www.fas.org/man/dod-101/sys/missile/zuni.htm.

Eurice, Frank. Personal interview and correspondence with author.

Fasoldt, Al. "*Forrestal* ablaze." *Stars & Stripes,* July 31, 1967, p. 1.

"Fighting Flare Fires." *All Hands: The Bureau of Naval Personnel Career Publication,* September 1967, pp. 4–6.

Flight Deck Safety: Hazards of the Flight Deck [training film MN-10131]. Washington, DC: United States Navy, 1967.

Friedman, Paul. Personal interview and correspondence with author.

Garrison, Peter. *Carrier Aviation.* Novato, CA: Presidio Press, 1987.

Goshorn, Howard. "New jet fuel, tank may bar fire disasters on carriers." *Pittsburgh Press,* August 10, 1967, p. 17.

"Heroes of *Forrestal.*" *All Hands: The Bureau of Naval Personnel Career Publication,* September 1967, pp. 2–3.

Herring, George C., ed. *The Pentagon Papers: Abridged Edition.* New York: McGraw-Hill, 1993.

Julius, Lenny. Personal interview and correspondence with author.

Killmeyer, Ken. Personal interview and correspondence with author.

Kirchner, G. Gary. Personal interview and correspondence with author.

Kohler, Robert. Personal interview and correspondence with author.

Marwick, Arthur. *The Sixties.* Oxford: Oxford University Press, 1998.

McCain, John, and Mark Salter. *Faith of My Fathers: A Family Memoir.* New York: Random House, 1999.

McMillen, Ken. Personal interview and correspondence with author.

McNamara, Robert S., and Brian VanDeMark. *In Retrospect: The Tragedy and Lessons of Vietnam.* New York: Vintage Books, 1995.

"Navy shipboard disaster." *Fire Engineering,* June 1968, pp. 42–43.

Newport News Shipbuilding and Dry Dock Company. *USS Forrestal.* Newport News, VA: Newport News Shipbuilding and Dry Dock Company, 1954.

No Easy Day: The Incredible Drama of Naval Aviation [videotape]. Louisville, KY: Avion Park, 1998.

Noel, John V., and Edward L. Beach, eds. *Naval Terms Dictionary*, 5th ed. Annapolis, MD: Naval Institute Press, 1996.

Pailthorpe, Robert L., ed. *USS Forrestal (AVT-59)* [1993, final cruise book]. Norfolk, VA: Taylor Publishing, 1993.

Plat coverage, USS Forrestal CVA-59, 29 July 1967 [Film 428 NPC 38757, raw flight-deck film footage]. Washington, DC: United States Navy, 1967.

Pool, Robert. *Beyond Engineering: How Society Shapes Technology.* Oxford: Oxford University Press, 1997.

Pratt, Rocky. Personal interviews and correspondence with author.

Pritchard, Gary. Personal interview and correspondence with author.

Public Broadcasting System. *Frontline: Give War a Chance,* May 11, 1999. http://-www.pbs.org/frontline/programs/.about/1715.html.

Roberts, Ed. Personal interviews and correspondence with author.

Rogue Rocket [videotape]. London: ITN, 1997.

Rowland, Merv. Personal interview with author.

Shaver, Gary. Personal interview and correspondence with author.

Shelton, Bob. Personal interview and correspondence with author.

Situation Critical: The USS Forrestal [videotape]. Arlington, VA: Henninger Media Development, 1997.

"Start of tragedy: Pilot hears a blast as he checks plane." *New York Times,* July 31, 1967.

Strain, Greg. Personal interview and correspondence with author.

Symposium 2000—Valor Under Fire: Forrestal, 29 July 1967 [videotape]. Pensacola, FL: Naval Aviation Museum Foundation, 2000.

"The responsibility: White and black." *New York Times,* July 30, 1967.

Think Safe. Washington, DC: United States Coast Guard, 1999.

Timberg, Robert. *The Nightingale's Song.* New York: Touchstone, 1996.

"Transcript of the president's news conference on domestic and foreign affairs." *New York Times,* August 1, 1967, p. 16.

Trial by Fire: A Carrier Fights for Life [training film MN 11204]. Washington, DC: United States Navy, 1973.

USS Forrestal [training film MN 8087]. Washington, DC: United States Navy, 1956.

Vanier, Scott. "A survivor's story." *The Flagship,* July 29, 1999, p. A4.

Whelply, Robert. Personal interview and correspondence with author.

Wingo, Hal. "Hell aboard CVA-59." *Life,* August 11, 1967, pp. 21—27.

Zwerlein, Bill. Personal interview and correspondence with author.

Zwerlein, Ruth. Personal interview and correspondence with author.

ACKNOWLEDGMENTS

I must thank a number of people who contributed to this book and supported my effort to shed light on the story of the *Forrestal*. First, I thank my dear wife, Caroline, for all the love and support she provided. The productivity kits were greatly appreciated.

I owe a huge debt of gratitude to the veterans of the USS *Forrestal* for sharing their stories with me, many of them intensely personal and painful to remember. Among the *Forrestal* veterans, I extend a special note of thanks to Kenneth Killmeyer, who served on the *Forrestal* during the 1967 fire and has since become historian of the *Forrestal*'s veterans association. Ken was tremendously helpful in explaining the details of the incident, providing original records, and establishing contact with other veterans. Ken's dedication to the *Forrestal* is evident in the way he carefully guards her honor, and I am grateful that he saw fit to aid me as thoroughly as he did. It is no exaggeration to say that this book project would not have progressed without Ken's help.

The USS *Forrestal* CVA/CV/AVT-59 Association itself, made up of those who served on the ship, deserves recognition. This group of veterans welcomed me to their inner circle and provided all manner of assistance, not to mention encouragement. In addition, I must specifically thank a number of individuals who personally shared their stories with me: John and Eve Beling, James Bloedorn, Milt Crutchley, Frank Eurice, Paul Friedman, G. Gary Kirchner, Bob Kohler, Lenny Julius, Ken McMillen, Rocky Pratt, Gary Pritchard, Ed Roberts, Merv Rowland, Gary Shaver, Bob Shelton, Greg Strain, Robert Whelply, and Bill and Ruth Zwerlein.

I also wish to thank Christine Burton, Marge Buschman, and Shelly Taylor for their research assistance. A special thanks is due Maureen Hardegree for her invaluable critiques and for commiserating with me as only a fellow writer can.

Mel Berger, my agent, and Henry Ferris, my editor, are trusted colleagues and I am glad to have them on my side. I thank you both for making this book happen. Thank you, Henry, for seeing what I can't.

The staff at the Fire Fighting School in Norfolk was helpful in showing me the state of the art in firefighting education. Bill Natter, a former navy pilot, is due a hearty thank-you for his assistance in getting me aboard an active-duty U.S. aircraft carrier during my research. Some things become clear only when you experience them yourself. Likewise, I thank the U.S. Navy and the men and women of the aircraft carrier USS *Harry S. Truman* for their gracious welcome.

In particular, I'd like to thank one sailor aboard the *Truman*. In my brief time at sea, I encountered hundreds of young men and women on board who gave me a strong sense of confidence about our navy and the generation of young people who serve in it. I was thoroughly impressed when watching them perform some of the most dangerous and demanding jobs in the world. As I prepared to leave the carrier, however, I came upon one young sailor who seemed to embody the essence of the crew.

I never spoke directly with him, and I'm certain he has no memory whatsoever of me, but I had the opportunity to sit and watch him for a long time as I waited for the catapult launch that would send me off the deck and back to Norfolk, Virginia. He was one of the crew in charge of organizing flights off the carrier for visitors like myself, as well as crew who were being flown to the mainland for some reason. It was a big job, as many on a carrier are.

This young man looked to be about eighteen, so youthful and fresh-faced, energetic and eager, exactly like everyone's brother, or son, or boyfriend. A handsome kid with a big smile, he captivated me as I sat there in my float coat and helmet, listening to the noise of the flight deck just outside and waiting for my ride home. As I watched him work, switching effortlessly between a stern demeanor for getting the job done and a wide grin for cracking jokes with his buddies, I realized that so many of the *Forrestal* crew in 1967 would have been just like him. They weren't just names and faces that no one remembers. They weren't just old men with a story to tell. They were young men like this.

I am grateful to that young man and the others who reminded me what this book is really about.

GAF

Index

Eurice, Frank (*continued*)
  firefighting activities of, 157—59,
    186—87, 195—96, 197—98
  smoke seen by, 110, 195

F4H-1 Phantom II, 18, 100, 101, 169
Fair, John, 224
Family, Friends, and Dependents Cruise,
  56—57
Farrier, Gerald, 119—21, 123, 124, 127, 147,
  271
Fasth, Kenneth, 180, 182
fat boys, 85, 167
fire-deluge system, 188—89
fire-main pressure, 137
fires, shipboard:
  on ammunition supply ship, 81
  navy history of, 66, 67—70
  newer bombs designed to withstand
    conditions of, 85, 126
  on *Oriskany*, 67—70, 71, 159, 208—9, 251,
    253, 254
  training programs in response to,
    245—26, 252—53, 271
  see also Forrestal, USS, fire on
fish pole, 172
flares, magnesium, 62—63, 67—69, 70, 159,
  253
flight deck:
  aircraft positioned on, 23, 98—99, 101—2
  ammunition stored on, 88
  angle design for landings on, 17
  armor plate of, 197
  camera transmission of activities on, 105,
    106, 170
  color coding by job on, 42—43
  dangers of work on, 27, 44, 46—48,
    49—50, 53—54, 62—63, 93—94, 282*n*
  escalator to, 17—18
  fire and explosion damage to, 197, 199
  fire-safety regulations for apparel on,
    271, 282*n*
  Forrestal-class and, 15
  heat conditions on, 46—47
  island structure on, 127, 128—29
  length of, 15
  man overboard from, 53—55
  planes chained on, 23
  safety net on, 24, 117—18
  sleeping berths beneath, 131—35, 154

flight operations:
  catapult system of takeoff in, 20—21,
    43—44, 53, 99
  in high tempo, 72, 83
  in landing procedures, 21—24, 26—27
  launch activities of, 42—44, 62—63, 72,
    92—95, 98—100
  primary control center of, 130
  wind direction accommodated in, 20
flight quarters, 90
flight surgeons, 201
float coats, 282*n*
FOD walkdown, 47—48
fog-foam firefighting equipment, 70,
  118—19, 155, 156, 160, 216
foreign object damage (FOD), 47
forklifts, 168—69
Forrestal, James V., 9
Forrestal, USS:
  air-conditioning system on, 17, 18, 197
  aircraft capacity of, 16, 19
  air strikes launched from, 2, 5, 83—84,
    92
  anchor chains of, 16, 281*n*
  in battle group, 79—80
  building costs of, 17
  charity work performed by touring crews
    of, 9
  command of, 129; *see also* Beling, John
  complexity of inner structure of, 19,
    50—51
  crew size of, 16, 241
  daily work schedules on, 1, 5, 88—89,
    90—91, 96, 131—32
  decommissioning of, 270
  design innovations of, 15—18, 281*n*-82*n*,
    284*n*
  duty assignments on, 2—3, 5, 27—28, 44,
    48, 60, 63—64, 140, 187
  emergency preparedness on, 65—66,
    70—71
  equatorial crossing of, 57—58
  firefighting equipment of, 40, 118—19,
    156, 260
  firefighting training of crew on, 252—54,
    257, 260
  first combat operations launched from,
    83—84
  five-inch gun mounts on, 186, 187,
    281*n*—82*n*